Professional Risk and Working with People

of related interest

Competence in Social Work Practice
A Practical Guide for Students and Professionals
2nd edition
Edited by Kieran O'Hagan
ISBN 978 1 84310 485 8

Handbook for Practice Learning in Social Work and Social Care
Knowledge and Theory
2nd edition
Edited by Joyce Lishman
ISBN 978 1 84310 186 4

The Post-Qualifying Handbook for Social Workers
Edited by Wade Tovey
ISBN 978 1 84310 428 5

Good Practice in Risk Assessment and Risk Management
2 volume set
Edited by Hazel Kemshall and Jacki Pritchard
ISBN 978 1 85302 552 5
Good Practice in Health, Social Care and Criminal Justice series

Risk and Risk Taking in Health and Social Welfare
Michael Titterton
ISBN 978 1 85302 482 5

Working with Adult Abuse
A Training Manual for People Working With Vulnerable Adults
Jacki Pritchard
ISBN 978 1 84310 509 1

Morals, Rights and Practice in the Human Services
Marie Connolly and Tony Ward
ISBN 978 1 843104 865 1

Risk Assessment in Social Care and Social Work
Edited by Phyllida Parsloe
ISBN 978 1 85302 689 8
Research Highlights in Social Work series

Professional Risk and Working with People

Decision-Making in Health, Social Care and Criminal Justice

David Carson and Andy Bain

Jessica Kingsley Publishers
London and Philadelphia

First published in 2008
by Jessica Kingsley Publishers
116 Pentonville Road
London N1 9JB, UK
and
400 Market Street, Suite 400
Philadelphia, PA 19106, USA

www.jkp.com

Library of Congress Cataloging in Publication Data
Carson, David, 1950-
    Professional risk and working with people : decision-making in health, social care and
criminal justice / David Carson and Andy Bain.
        p. cm.
    Includes bibliographical references.
    ISBN 978-1-84310-389-9 (pb : alk. paper) 1. Risk management. 2. Risk managers. 3.
Decision making. 4. Social service--Decision making. I. Bain, Andy, 1971- II. Title.
    HD61.C373 2008
    361.0068'4--dc22
                                                                2007032751

British Library Cataloguing in Publication Data
A CIP catalogue record for this book is available from the British Library

ISBN 978 1 84310 389 9

Printed and bound in Great Britain by
Athenaeum Press, Gateshead, Tyne and Wear

Contents

Preface

Yes, yet another book on risk!

How can we justify it? How will it be different from the many other books available about risk? Why should you consider reading it?

Goals

After you have read this book you should be able, or better able, to do the following.

- You will be more competent when analysing, assessing, managing and taking risk decisions in your professional capacity.

- You will find it easier to justify to others, including employers, judges and official inquiries, the risk decisions and judgements that you make.

- You will be better informed of ways to take risk decisions which reduce the likelihood that you, or your employers, will be sued, prosecuted or criticised for your professional risk-taking.

- You will know about a number of practical steps that you and your organisation can take to improve your professional risk-taking.

- You will be able to make better risk decisions.

Our goals are predominantly practical. We want to make a difference to how risk decisions are taken and to reduce (where proper) risk-takers' fears of being blamed.

What is distinctive about this book?

This is not just another book that notes how many issues can be analysed in terms of risk, or that describes the development of a risk society. It tries to find, and walk, a line between philosophical, theoretical and sociological discussions of risk-taking and a discussion of applied professional practice distinctive of different disciplines and professions. Thus the aim is to be practical (offering a number of devices which individual decision-makers and organisations might adopt), but never to speak for, or tell, any professional about his or her distinctive knowledge base or practices on risk-taking. The intention is that this book should be of value to several professions: medicine, social care, offender management, education and, it is hoped, to others, such as policing.

A distinctive approach is taken to risk and risk-taking, always demonstrating how this can benefit the reader. In particular the following are emphasised.

- Risk-taking is an inevitable feature of professional work. Thus, it must be promoted. Indeed, risk-taking, with or for clients or patients, regularly involves the specialist knowledge and skills that characterise professionalism.

- The 'blame culture' culture is real, counterproductive and needs to be challenged. Legal liability for risk-taking should not be feared. It cannot be guaranteed that people who are adversely affected by risk-taking or that ignorant (process-driven) managers or employers will not complain or begin legal proceedings. Nobody can, or should, make that promise because it is very easy to threaten proceedings. However, this book will show you how you can make it much less likely to occur whilst still doing what is professionally proper.

- Risk-taking is often exciting. The book will demonstrate how and why you can and should identify potential benefits and opportunities as well as possible harms. The reader is encouraged to be positive about risk-taking.

- Risk-taking can be difficult. It is often complicated, with lots of information to examine and issues to consider. For these, and many other reasons, it is easy to make mistakes. However, many causes of poor decision-making have been identified. We can, and should, use this knowledge to improve the ways in which we make risk decisions.

- Pathologies – things going wrong – take up an inordinate amount of time particularly in comparison with prevention. Prevention is advocated, but not in the sense of avoiding risk-taking. Avoidance will often involve unprofessional conduct. But the book will identify ways in which harmful outcomes, and other possible problems, may be minimised.

If the quality of risk-taking in professional contexts is to improve, we need to focus on making improvements at a number of different levels, and not just concentrate on the individual decision-maker. A number of practical suggestions for organisational improvements are made.

Risk is everywhere. It is involved in every aspect of our lives – professional, domestic and leisure. It is a source of excitement as well as a cause for concern. Is this book equally relevant to every sphere of life and form of risk?

Whom is this book for?

Although we believe we have several important things to say about risk in general, the focus and target audience of this book is those who are involved in taking decisions that concern other people. This is referred to as 'professional risk-taking'. So, although it is hoped there is much of value here for those taking risks in their private lives the book is written primarily for professionals who are employed to take risks that affect other people. Among the wide range of people who are contemplated (using alphabetical order to avoid any suggestions of priority) are the following.

- *Doctors*, who are employed to diagnose our ills (taking a risk, for they might be wrong), decide on treatments (e.g. particular pills and dosages) and make many other decisions (e.g. decide when it is appropriate to discharge patients).

- *Nurses*, irrespective of their specialty, level or experience, who have to make judgements, also known as 'risk decisions'. These include deciding what information to communicate to others, and when.

- *Police officers*, who take risks when they arrest and charge individuals with offences, decide whether to undertake further enquiries, decide whether to caution an offender only and take risks in many other ways.

- *Prison officers, governors* and *others*, who take risks such as when to recommend prisoners' early release from prison, when to transfer them to less secure conditions and when deciding on staffing requirements.

- *Probation officers*, who take risks when they make recommendations to the courts with regards to sentencing, during inter-agency planning, when considering the risk of harm (not only to others but also to themselves).

- *Social workers*, who take risks with regard to a wide range of vulnerable clients and others. Some have to decide whether, how and when to act when there is suspected abuse of children. If they act they may be criticised; if they fail to act they may be criticised as well.

- *Teachers*, who take risks when taking children on outings. Some of the very few outings which have led to harm (which we will always be quick to insist does not demonstrate that going on the outing was a bad decision) have received extensive publicity.

The above is not an exhaustive list. However, it is not intended to include pilots and other related professionals. Pilots, for example, are employed to take risks that affect other people, such as deciding whether an aircraft is safe for take-off. This book is concerned with professionals who need to assess and manage risks associated with individual clients. All of these people have specialist knowledge. A pilot makes risk decisions in relation to all the passengers and, reassuringly, his or her own life. This book focuses upon those who need to consider the risk potentially posed by or affecting particular individuals, although they will often have to include the risks that affect other people, including themselves.

The book is aimed at all levels of practitioners, from student to manager, and is designed to be of value to all. It is *not* trying simply to describe current professional practice. The book is more normative – about what people *ought* to do – rather than descriptive – what people *currently* do. It disagrees with many current practices and is particularly concerned about the lack of leadership and support provided by managers.

The most difficult risk decisions

The risks that this book focuses upon involve the most difficult decisions anyone has to take. Imagine that you are employed to buy coffee beans on a futures market. If so you are employed (and are likely to be well paid) to take risks; you might pay too much for your beans. You need to gain specialist knowledge of how markets operate, how coffee plantations are expanding or contracting, of changes in consumers' preferences, of likely changes in different countries' climates and more. There are risks: you might miss a bargain. But, do you appreciate how lucky you are? You are concerned with relatively stable factors. Climate changes can be tracked over time and thereby predicted with relative ease. And you are using money. Certainly there are the complications of different exchange rates and fluctuations in values (although you can minimise these in a variety of ways, such as by only using stable currencies), but your task is nowhere near as difficult as those of professional risk-takers.

Professional risk-takers are involved with people who have considerable free will – and rights – to be awkward and very difficult to predict. The knowledge base needed for coffee futures, and many other areas of risk-taking, is much more predictable. The relevant factors are much easier to control. Risks are compared in terms of how much, or how little, things cost. Professional risk-takers have to – somehow – compare risks such as the damage to a child from neglectful parents with the different, but very real, harm that will occur if they take the child into local authority care. You can think about the likelihood of losing, or gaining, xxx amounts of money from one transaction versus another option. You can use money as your comparator. But, how do you compare the risk of a lost life with the risk of unnecessarily detaining someone for many years?

Is there anything in the suggestion that the more difficult the risk decision, the less well paid you are to take it? There is not the time or space to investigate that theory here, but it is offered, free of charge and copyright, to anyone who is looking for a doctoral thesis to pursue.

Two distinctive features of the types of risk decision-making this book is concerned with are problems surrounding whose decision it is to take a risk. Competent adults are usually entitled to make their own risk decisions. Doctors and other professionals concerned may recommend treatment, but a patient may refuse it. An individual may wish to take a risk but it may have a considerable impact upon others: physical injury, emotional distress or financial loss. When can an individual's right to take a risk be interfered with? What should the professionals who are concerned with a client who proposes taking a risk, which they believe to be unwise, advise and do? Risk-taking is a key means by which we represent our individuality – what we do, where we go, how we do it – so professionals may feel torn between how to advise and, if necessary, act to prevent a risk taking place. These and similar issues are addressed in this book.

Making the most of this book

A number of examples have been provided to help to explain the ideas. Space limitations preclude the provision of appropriate examples for many lines of work; unfortunately this is inevitable when writing an interdisciplinary book, and it is hoped that the points made will be clear and easily transferred to other professions. The text has been kept informal and unburdened by the detritus of academic writing.

You may wish to read the chapters in a non-chronological order. However, it is strongly recommended that you read Chapters 1 and 2 first. The ideas developed there serve as a foundation for the rest of the book. Initially, you might prefer to skip Chapter 3, at least until later. However, you should find it very useful in appreciating how the law can be used pro-actively.

Go on; take a risk. Having read this book, and adopted at least some of the advice, you should find it much easier to justify – and improve – your decisions.

CHAPTER 1

Risk: Making It Work For and Not Against You

Introduction

'Risk'. It is such a short, abrupt, single-syllable, matter-of-fact, word. Everyone uses it, and regularly. Everyone takes risks, considered and unconsidered. So it must have a clear, agreed and easily understood meaning. Unfortunately not!

Many of the problems we have with risk-taking arise because we do not have an agreed, settled definition of 'risk', let alone for related concepts such as 'risk assessment', 'risk management' and 'risk factors'. Meanings and practices vary within and between the human, health and social services. Indeed, some professional risk-takers effectively 'shoot themselves in the foot' when they adopt certain existing definitions of risk. They make it much more difficult to justify their decisions. So the key objectives of this chapter are to:

- identify problems with existing definitions of 'risk' and related concepts
- provide definitions which will work for you
- make the case for a 'shared vocabulary of risk'.

This 'risk vocabulary' will be added to as we progress through the book. It is easier, and more appropriate, to explain some concepts later. It is recommended that professionals formally adopt this vocabulary. Not only will it improve their communication about risk, but it will make it easier to explain and to justify individual risk decisions. If you wish to criticise and find fault with professionals' risk-taking then one of the easiest and most productive places to look at is risk communication.

This chapter offers a number of definitions of 'risk' and related expressions. It is not argued that these are the correct definitions. They are not prescribed by law. They differ, significantly, from some dictionary definitions. But they can, as will be explained, be justified. And, unlike some definitions, they work for, rather than against, professional risk-takers. A number of key working definitions have been grouped together at the end of the book.

'Risk'

Risks are everywhere: at work, at home, at play, in both activity and inactivity. We take many risks each day, usually without thinking about them, even without realising that they could be analysed as such. For a bit of fun, next time you visit a supermarket, watch people choosing their wine and consider your own decision-making. There is a risk that the bottle chosen will prove to be a mistake, a waste of money. How long do they, and you, take to make your choice? How do you cope with the amount of information available: price, nationality, colour, grape varieties, alcoholic strength, year, label, name and so on? Are there any features which distinguish quick risk-takers from the more contemplative?

We take risks for ourselves and we impose them on others, such as when we drive our vehicles. Often, we perceive the risks as choices; should we travel by train or by car? Should we change our plans because there was a train crash last week? We give each other advice about which products to buy and what action to take. It could prove wrong; we might be blamed. We do not need special training or aids to help us to make these decisions, or most of them. (There is a considerable industry giving advice on minimising the risks of buying wine.) We get anxious about some risks, for example agreeing to surgery, flying or before buying something expensive. We rely upon other risks, in sports and entertainment, to provide us with excitement. We build amusement parks, with ever more dramatic rides to frighten ourselves, simultaneously insisting that they are very safe. We risk our money in gambling or investments. Indeed, we cannot live without risk-taking and yet, sometimes, it kills or injures us. We embrace risk and reject it, simultaneously. We condemn dangerous and reckless conduct, and yet we also condemn, as paternalism, attempts to restrict our 'right' to take risks. Risk-taking is commonplace. Everyone does it. Surely it is a simple concept to understand?

We may be experienced in risk-taking. We may be able to take most of the risks which confront us in our daily lives without detailed analysis and thought. But, whilst that provides our lives with excitement and vitality, it is also a major part of the problem. We are so used to taking risks that we do not seem to feel a need to examine the concept, and the practice, of risk-taking more closely. And when we do examine what different people mean by a 'risk', we discover considerable differences. This is important. Imagine, for example, that you are in court, in the witness box. If you mean one thing by 'risk', and the cross-examining lawyer and judge assumes another meaning, then you will have problems. You might, for example, be describing something which would be better analysed as a 'dilemma'. If it is a 'dilemma', or emergency, then that should entitle you to extra consideration from the court. If you present the decision as merely a risk then you will have lost that potential benefit.

Towards a working definition of 'risk'
Here are a few questions for you to reflect on your understanding of the term 'risk'.

- What are the essential ingredients without which it would not be a 'risk'?

- Which words and phrases are synonymous with 'risk'?

- How does 'risk' differ, if it does, from 'fate', 'gamble', 'chance', 'dilemma', 'choice', 'decision'?

- Do you take 'risks', or do you 'gamble', with your patients or clients?

- Why did Shakespeare use 'fate' (frequently) but not 'risk'? (For an entertaining history of 'risk' see Bernstein (1999). He maintains that serious study of risk only began during the Renaissance (p.3).)

- Do you use 'risk' in the same way in both your professional and your private lives?

- Does your employer or professional association have an official or agreed definition of 'risk' or 'risk-taking'?

- Are your assumptions about the nature of 'risk' consistent with the law?

- Does your definition of 'risk' help or hinder you when you come to make and to justify your decision?

When we have problems understanding the meaning of a word we can consult a dictionary. These tell us how different words are, or were, used at the time the compilers completed that edition. Dictionary definitions can, and do, change over time to reflect changes in usage. They are helpful but they are not binding. There is no legal requirement that we adopt, or limit ourselves to, dictionary definitions. The issue is *communication*. If we do not use words in consistent ways, which others understand, we will not communicate efficiently, if at all. The working definitions of 'risk' which we develop are similar but not identical to those articulated in several dictionaries. So this book has to convince you that it is both possible and proper to communicate using our slightly but significantly different meanings.

Consult a dictionary on the meaning of 'risk' and you are likely to be given a definition that highlights three other concepts. These are:

- harm
- likelihood
- uncertainty.

Of course, different dictionaries will use different words; 'uncertainty' may not be included but it will be implicit. There are lots of synonyms for, and different ways of describing, each of the three concepts listed above. 'Harm' or damage might be described as the consequences, or the outcome, of risk-taking. 'Likelihood' may alternatively be described as chance or possibility. But those are the three key ideas: outcome, likelihood and uncertainty.

Blackburn (2000), an eminent British forensic psychologist, says:

> Risk generally refers to the possibility of loss or costs when an outcome is uncertain, but in clinical and criminal justice settings, it means *the chance of an adverse outcome*. (Blackburn 2000, p.177, emphasis in original)

The first key argument of this book is that such dictionary definitions are inadequate, and are thus wrong to use in this context. They make risk-taking with people more difficult. Clearly, some people do use 'risk' in the way that the dictionary suggests. Blackburn (2000) clearly does. And, as will be seen in later chapters, legal definitions of risk are very similar to these dictionary definitions. Perhaps the dictionaries are correct in terms of what they set out to do, that is, to describe how the terms are commonly used. There is no doubt that Blackburn was reflecting normal usage in the settings to which he referred. However, a change in the usage of 'risk' is discernible, and it is towards the ways in which we use the terms. Ideally, these new usages should find their way into new editions of dictionaries. Words and definitions should be tools rather than obstacles.

Several organisations, as well as individuals, have developed definitions of risk and associated concepts. The Royal Society is arguably the premier group of leading academics in the UK. The Society examined the issues in a 1992 report. For the Royal Society 'risk' is 'the probability that a particular adverse event occurs during a stated period of time, or results from a particular challenge' (Royal Society 1992, p.2). The Health and Safety Commission, and its Executive (HSE), has statutory responsibilities for health and safety at workplaces in the UK. Arguably, the HSE is the premier practical authority on risk-taking in the UK. Encouraging good, and discouraging poor, risk-taking is central to its work. Therefore the HSE definition of 'risk' should be of considerable practical significance. The HSE has defined 'hazard' and 'risk' as:

- A *hazard* is anything that may cause harm, such as chemicals, electricity, working with ladders, an open drawer, etc.

- The *risk* is the chance, high or low, that somebody could be harmed by these and other hazards, together with an indication of how serious the harm could be. (HSE 2006, p.2, emphasis in original)

This definition identifies two factors. First, there are the outcomes or consequences – these are the references to people being harmed and the seriousness of the outcome. Second, there is the likelihood – the references to chance and its level being high or low. The hazards are the causes of the harm. There is no reference to uncertainty but it is implicit.

'Risk' has variable 'elements' and 'dimensions'

These definitions of 'risk' are very similar. They may use different words, and some may treat uncertainty as implicit, but they agree on the two core features of risk-taking: the potential outcomes and their possibility. Clearly, there is much more to it but these are the two key features, which are referred to here as the two elements of risk-taking.

'Risk' may be divided into its 'elements' (the features inherent in a risk proposal) and its 'dimensions' (features that may be influenced by the decision-maker). Both are important. Both must be considered when taking a risk decision. Both are relative; they involve matters of degree. The *elements*, the core ingredients or requirements of a risk, are particularly relevant to risk assessment. The *dimensions* are particularly important for risk management. As will be further discussed in Chapter 4, risk assessment is the stage in risk decision-making when information is collated. It is concerned with predicting the consequences of taking the risk decision and their likelihood. It focuses on the key *elements* of a risk. Risk management involves implementing, monitoring, influencing, controlling and reviewing the risk decision. This is discussed in more detail in Chapter 5. Risk assessment precedes the risk decision. Risk management follows it, for it is concerned with its implementation. A risk management plan, which deals with the risk dimensions, needs to be considered within the risk decision. The *dimensions* of a risk in particular relate to this controlling, implementation, stage (see Table 1.1).

The three concepts of the meaning of risk identified by many dictionaries and other sources – harm, likelihood and uncertainty – are variable. There can be many different degrees of harm, or loss, from the trivial to the catastrophic; from that which is not worth bothering about to that which could lead a court to award thousands of pounds in compensation. Likelihood is also variable. It can range from the nearly certain to the nearly impossible. Note that if something is bound to occur, or it could not possibly occur, then we would not describe it as involving a risk. There is no risk involved in a one horse race (assuming the horse does not fall or meander off the course). No bookmaker would be prepared to accept a gamble on that race.

The outcomes, and their likelihood, are the two elements involved in risk-taking. When a risk is taken with an offender, for example, we are concerned with (a) the possible consequences and (b) their likelihood. The possible *consequences* will vary from case to case and be of varying levels of seriousness. Similarly, the *likelihood* of those outcomes will vary from case to case and in degrees of probability. These two elements, the outcomes or consequences and their likelihood, relate to the references to harm and likelihood that are commonplace in dictionary and other definitions of 'risk'.

Table 1.1 An overview of 'risk'

Risk assessment	Risk management
Collating and assessing information about the risk elements	Discovering and manipulating the dimensions of the proposed risk into a plan to control the risks when implemented
Risk elements	**Risk dimensions**
Features inherent in the risk proposed:	Features of the risk that may be influenced by the decision-makers:
a) The outcomes, e.g. the harm possible b) Their likelihood (See Chapter 4, Risk Assessment, for a fuller discussion)	The resources available to manage the proposed risk, including uncertainty (i.e. the quantity and quality of knowledge about those resources and the risk elements) (see Chapter 5, Risk Management, for a fuller discussion)

What about 'uncertainty', the third concept in many dictionary and other definitions? Transferring a prisoner to an open prison involves risks. He or she might, among many other things, escape from that prison and offend again. Leaving a child with potentially abusive parents may lead to child abuse. We will never know for certain how likely or how serious that would be. (If abuse happens that does not – see the following arguments – prove that it was inevitable.) Uncertainty is certainly a feature of risk.

Uncertainty is a dimension, not an element, of risk-taking. It is relevant, it is something which we can and should take into account in relation to risk management. For example, we will often be able to delay taking a risk decision (travel during the spring rather than the winter) in order to reduce our uncertainty. Uncertainty is within our control – to an extent. We may be more ignorant, or more uncertain, about the risks with offender A than with offender B. (Perhaps we have more experience of offender B.) But, and this is a key point, that does not make the consequences of taking a risk with offender A any more serious or more likely. Offender A is not more likely to abscond or to remain unlawfully at large for longer, or both, just because we are more uncertain of the risks in relation to him than offender B. Something is not more (or less) likely to happen just because we know less about it. We need to be aware of our uncertainty when we make a decision. We could, for example, decide to adopt a wider 'margin of error'.

Uncertainty is not directly linked to the likelihood or the seriousness of outcomes. Imagine that you are more ignorant of the safety record of Xanadone Airlines than Yillybilly Airlines. Does it follow that Yillybilly Airlines is the better risk, the safer airline? No, we do not know that, and cannot know that, until we become less ignorant. It could be that Xanadone Airlines has a much better safety record, we just do not know about it. If we get some information, for example that we are ignorant about Xanadone Airlines because it used to be called Zilly Airlines but changed its name because of a disastrous safety record, we can now make a better risk assessment. That new knowledge was directly relevant to one of the elements of risk-taking, likelihood. We might decide to devote some of our resources, for example time, to investigating the safety of both airlines. That would be an example of risk management.

MacCrimmon and Wehrung (1988) developed other expressions:

> [We] have developed the concepts of the *components of risk*, namely the magnitude, chance, and exposure to loss, as well as the *determinants of risk*, namely the lack of control, lack of information, and lack of time. (MacCrimmon and Wehrung 1988, p.18, emphasis in original)

Their approach is the same as ours. 'Magnitude' and 'exposure to loss' relates to the seriousness of the outcomes. 'Chance' and 'exposure' are other ways of saying 'likelihood'. So their 'components of risk' relate to our 'elements' of risk. 'Lack of information' relates to 'uncertainty' in our approach. Their 'lack of control' and 'lack of time' are further 'dimensions' of risk within our system which are relevant to risk management. This discussion of the dimensions of risk, which includes references to control and time, and some other ideas, is extended in the discussion of risk management in Chapter 5.

The two 'elements' of risk

So, a risk is made up of two variable elements: outcomes and likelihood. To assess a risk we must consider both. That may appear obvious. But it is the source of many problems in practice. For example, a case may arise in which a person is detained in a hospital for treatment of mental disorders because he or she is considered to be a risk to others if discharged. When asked about 'the risk', in such cases people have replied that it is 'very high', 'very serious', 'dangerous'. (The media regularly makes this error when reporting risk decision-making cases.) When asked why the risk is assessed as so high, it is explained that the individual could kill someone if released. That outcome would certainly be serious, but it does *not* justify assessing the overall risk as 'high', 'serious' or 'dangerous'. The outcome may be very serious but the *likelihood* of it happening may be very low. *Both the seriousness of outcomes, and the likelihood of them happening must be considered.* It is not justifiable in law or morally, even in these days of extreme anxiety about terrorism, only to consider possible consequences. There is a risk of being killed every time we cross a road. But that risk is well worth taking in most cases because the likelihood of it happening is low. It is even more justifiable when we manage the risk, such as by waiting until there are no vehicles approaching, crossing at regulated junctions, or both.

Equally, just because something is extremely *unlikely* to occur (such as an accident in a nuclear reactor), we are not entitled to conclude that it is a low risk. We need to consider the potential seriousness of what might occur, as well as the likelihood of it happening. However, this works both ways. Something is not a serious risk just because it is virtually certain to happen. The outcome must have a degree of seriousness. For example, it is almost certain that I will jump if someone shouts 'Boo!' when I am not expecting it. That is not serious in any realistic assessment of what is harmful and serious in this life. But it would be different if we were undertaking an assessment of the risk of my having a heart attack or dropping some precious vase I was handling.

Any professional risk-taker who assesses risk only in terms of the seriousness of outcomes or only of their likelihood is not just negligent but incompetent. But some human service professionals who are employed to take or advise on risk decisions are reluctant to contemplate taking a risk just because someone has noted that death is a possible consequence. They think that they are acting safely, that they are protecting people by not countenancing taking the risk. They are wrong, and they are only looking at half of the job. They need to examine both outcomes and likelihood.

Some politicians and journalists also demonstrate sloppy reasoning. They demand that 'the risk' should be eliminated, should never recur. They seek the impossible in a rage of ignorant indignation. The only way, for example, to stop murderers from committing further murders (i.e. to make it a zero likelihood) is never to release them. If that is to occur, and the politicians and journalists are to be consistent, they will have to promote increased taxation and accept responsibility for increasing the risk inside the prisons.

Justifying risk-taking

Unfortunately, there has been a critical 'error' in the discussion up to this point. It is not any less serious just because it is basic, is encouraged by all the definitions discussed above and by most legal assumptions about the nature of risk. The source of this problem can quickly and easily be identified by asking 'Can risk-taking ever be justified?'

The answer has to be 'Yes'. Our decision, invariably made without a second thought, to take the risk of using a bridge to cross over a river is justified. And yet that bridge might have collapsed under us. Some do. Having an operation to remove an appendix is easily and readily justified. Cosmetic surgery can also be justified. The drive to work, even though we know that we may have an accident (some 3500 people die on the roads of England and Wales each year according to the Department of Transport (DoT) (DoT 2004)) is regularly justified. Your boss would not excuse failure to come to work just because you feared you might injure others or yourself on the trip in. Most decisions to discharge patients from hospital (or to detain them), to grant parole to prisoners, to remove children from possibly abusive parents, can be justified.

Why take a risk?

What is the justification for taking a risk? It cannot be that the feared harm has not yet occurred. The issue is the justifiability of *the decision to take a risk*; we cannot, properly, take into account anything that happened after *the decision was taken*. A risk decision can be justified even if harm results; the surgery could have been justified even thought the patient suffered harm. A risk decision could have been unjustified even if, because of good luck, harm is avoided. 'Risk' is not synonymous with 'harm avoidance'. When we take risks we certainly hope to avoid harm occurring but, because it is a risk, we have to accept that there can be no guarantee that it will not occur. For example, we take risks when we play some sports – but that involves embracing the controlled chance of harm. We know that the chance of harm cannot be entirely removed. We do not justify surgery merely on the basis that harm might not occur. We want, and expect, more than that. Justification involves much more than just excusing, or not noticing, a possibility of harm. We want surgery to remove the nasty symptoms we are experiencing; we want sport to give us pleasure, as participants or observers.

We can, and we need to be able to, justify taking a risk *before* we learn whether harm actually results. The risk involved in flying abroad for a holiday (ignoring for these purposes the environmental issues) can be justified before we get to the airport. This point is particularly important for the principal audience for this book. Social workers, doctors, nurses, teachers and so on all need to be able to justify taking a risk with other people, such as taking some children on a school outing even though they know that harm may occur. If 'risk' was synonymous with 'harm avoidance' those jobs would be exclusively preventive and protective. But we know that they are not. Indeed, we pay such people, in part, to take risks with those in their care. Risk-taking is a characteristic feature of those jobs.

The benefits of risk

Risks can be, and from time immemorial have been, justified because their likely benefits are judged to be more important than the possible harms. In every area of life, and every part of the day, such decisions are made. Most of us decide, for example, that the advantages of someone else cooking a meal for us are well worth the chance that we may suffer food poisoning. The vast majority of us prefer to take prescribed medication, despite the chance of nasty side-effects, than continue to suffer symptoms. In our professional and private lives we can justify risk decisions that affect other people on the same basis. Official bodies, such as the Parole Board, decide that the likelihood of achieving the benefits that could follow from the early release of a particular offender outweigh the likelihood of the possible harms, such as further offending. Individual professionals, such as teachers, know that the likely benefits of taking a class on an outing will regularly outweigh the possible harms that might occur – although they will be worried about being pilloried in the press if harm should result.

If the value of the likely benefits of taking a risk outweighs the value of the likely harms, that decision can be justified. Certainly, it is not as simple, in practice or theory, as that straightforward proposition suggests. There are major problems of principle, policy and practice, which are discussed in the following chapters. For example, we can justify detaining a mentally disordered person, against his or her will, if the value of the likely benefits of doing so outweigh the seriousness of the likely harms. But how do we know, let alone value, what the benefits and harms might be? How do we know how likely the benefits or harms are? How much faith can we place in those estimates? Risk-taking, especially when it affects other people, is a very value-laden activity. How do we discover and justify these values, which often compete? And, when we find them, how do we undertake the weighing process? It is also quite, but not entirely, subjective. Then there are all the issues surrounding managing the implementation of the risk decision. But the two key, elemental variables in 'risk' are the consequences or outcomes and their likelihood. The key point here is that consequences can be beneficial or harmful. They can range from exceptionally valuable through the neutral or unimportant to the disastrous and fatal.

Blame and balance

Some people will still wish to argue. Perhaps relying upon a dictionary definition, or that of the Royal Society (1992) or the HSE (2006) discussed above, they will insist that 'risk' means, and only means, the chance of harm. And it is certainly true that many people do think of 'risk' exclusively in terms of possible loss and harm avoidance. Try an experiment, particularly with colleagues who work in the human services. Outline a basic risk scenario, such as whether someone should be discharged or released from institutional care or custody. Then, ask the colleague to identify the risks. You will find, at least among those who have not been exposed to this or similar discussions about the nature of 'risk', that they will emphasise the possibilities of harm rather than the chances of benefit. Many professions, especially those involved in taking risks that affect other people, naturally perceive risk as potential loss. It is how they have been taught. Risks, they assume, are for avoiding rather than for embracing. Unfortunately, this has become part of our culture. Risks, with their attendant fear of legal action, are feared rather than embraced as opportunities.

But this is the product of socialisation. There is no law – of the land, of logic or of morality – which requires us to define or to use words in particular ways, particularly 'risk'. If we wish to interpret 'risk' as concerned with potential benefits as well as with potential harm then we can. Certainly, it is important that others understand us so that we are effective when communicating. But it is critically important that definitions work for us, not against us.

Some people will accept that 'risk' involves potential advantages as well as disadvantages. But they go on to argue that the potential benefits are only relevant in a balancing operation, after the 'real' risks of harm have been identified and assessed. This is the implicit position of the House of Lords, the most senior court in the UK. This position is discussed in greater detail in Chapter 3. In summary, it was said in *Bolitho* v. *City & Hackney Health Authority* [1998] AC 232 that, although risks are concerned with the chances of harm, it is perfectly permissible to take into account the benefits of a particular risk in order to balance them against the possible harms.

In cold theory it may not matter whether the benefits which might accrue from taking a risk are identified and assessed after or at the same time as the harms are assessed. But, in practice, there is a considerable difference. First, there is the culture of risk-taking to be considered. If risk-taking continues primarily to be associated with the chances of harm then it will continue to be associated with damage, loss and blame. People will naturally wish to avoid risk-taking because it is about possibly harming others. Second, if the primary focus is on possible harms, their seriousness and their likelihood, then decision-makers will be in a much poorer position when it comes to having to justify their decisions and action. Imagine a risk decision must be made whether to return a child to his or to her previously neglectful parents. It is assessed in terms of whether the potential harms are too serious, too likely or both. When the professionals who made that assessment come to justify it they will be able to tell the court why they thought the possible harms and/or their likelihood were not too serious. But they will not be in a good position to explain why they thought that the potential benefits of taking the risk, and/or their likelihood, were significant and valuable. If they try to develop arguments about possible benefits during the trial then they may appear, desperately, to be trying to find excuses for their decision after the event.

Third, only looking for possible benefits to balance out possible harms may involve a 'cancelling-out' exercise. It will be about finding enough possible benefits to cancel out the possible harms. But a 'tit for tat' approach is profoundly wrong. The magnitude of the possible benefits and the possible harms may be entirely different. They do not just cancel each other out. And only identifying sufficient possible benefits to cancel out the possible harms could seriously understate the case for taking the risk. Indeed, if that is the case then the decision-maker may wish to consider whether he or she should be taking a greater risk. Risks are justifiable, not just excusable. That is very important for the culture of risk-taking.

Some might declare that, in order to be as careful as is possible, they only take risks after an assessment of whether the potential losses are 'too' great. But that position is full of problems. How can that risk-taker know whether the possible losses are 'too' high? That assessment begs a comparison; but what are they comparing? For example, some teachers may consider taking a class on a cross-country expedition. They may decide to go when discovering that the risks of harm, the warnings, do not seem to be too serious. But that is not actually a risk assessment by measuring harms only. They are simply not being explicit about how important the cross-country expedition is to the children and their work as their teachers. They have – implicitly – weighted the importance (the benefits to them) of going on the expedition but they have not been explicit in their assessment, to others or themselves.

If you know that there is a risk of the plane taking you on holiday crashing, or that there are possible complications from undergoing surgery, you may, pessimistically, concentrate your thoughts on what might go wrong – but you may still decide to take that trip or to have that operation. You have not failed to consider the possible benefits, you have just not been explicit about them. If you had not thought about the benefits of that flight, or that surgery, you would not be considering the options. Fear of harm can dominate our thoughts but that does not make the potential for benefits irrelevant, either in theory or in practice.

Some people might argue that by only considering the potential harms from a risk they are being especially careful and that they deserve praise for that, but this is misguided thinking. They are only looking at one side of the equation, or balance, and are therefore deliberately calculating, weighing or making the decision poorly. There is, most certainly, a place for being careful. But being careful should take place when assessing, implementing, or so on the decision, not by wrongly analysing the issues from the start. For example, more time or other resources could be spent on getting extra or better information, or both. Risk management explicitly concerns controlling and/or manipulating the 'safety' of a risk decision. Also, when making the risk judgement, the decision-maker may decide that the particular risk is only justifiable if the likely benefits outweigh the likely harms by a considerable margin. That could be considered a safety margin. Such strategies are appropriate for maximising safety. But ignoring the value and likelihood of possible benefits is not. Equally it would be wrong to value the possible harms as being more serious than they are just because they are harms. A broken arm or a fatality is serious enough as it is. It does not become more serious just because it is harmful.

Kindler (1990) writes from a management science background. He wants to encourage better decisions. His definition is:

> Risk is a course of action or inaction, taken under conditions of uncertainty, which exposes one to possible loss in order to reach a desired outcome. (Kindler 1990, p.12)

Arguably, his emphasis is still upon the harms, rather than the benefits, of risk-taking. But Kindler (1990) critically recognises the purposive context of risk-taking, which is the pursuit of benefits despite feared harms. His definition is broadly acceptable within the context of this book. However, it will be argued throughout that being more explicit about the potential benefits as well as harms will make it much easier to justify a risk decision taken as well as to improve it.

A study by Norman (1980) commented:

> If people are entrusted to take difficult decisions regarding risk taking, it must be accepted that they cannot later be blamed if the outcome leads to tragedy. (Norman 1980, p.27)

The sentiments may be endorsed by many practitioners, particularly if and when they feel that whatever they do carries risk of harm. But such a statement cannot be accepted, as its author seem to have appreciated:

> As a society we need to clarify our attitudes and support those to whom we have delegated authority to take such decisions despite the consequences, provided they are based on proper consideration of the circumstances. (Norman 1980, pp.27–28)

The risk decisions confronting professionals may be very difficult, sometimes exceptionally so. But they can still be taken well or badly, even with those difficulties taken into account. That is what the law requires. However, it will be much easier to demonstrate that, despite all the difficulties, a reasonable decision was taken if the potential benefits were explicitly identified and taken into account when the decision was taken.

Identifying justifications
Those who take risks as part of their jobs invariably find it very easy to think of possible harms that may befall their clients, their colleagues or members of the public. They find it much more difficult to think of

possible benefits, and thereby possible justifications, for taking the risks. That type of risk decision-making might have been acceptable in the past. It is unlikely to satisfy many people, especially judges, for much longer.

Some would argue that the potential benefits of taking a risk can always be identified *after* the event. They argue that there is no point in spending time, and other resources, to discover and to assess possible benefits until any harm has occurred. It only needs to be justified now that an inquiry, litigation or disciplinary proceedings are being considered. But consider this argument, particularly as a potential 'victim' of it. Imagine that someone took a risk, knowing that it might damage *you*, and it has. That person now says, 'Although I did not think about them, before or at the time, there were several justifications for what I did.'

If you are being sued (more on this in Chapter 3) that answer may be sufficient to protect the risk-taker because of the rules of causation. (If the same decision would have been taken, if the potential benefits had been considered, then the same harm would have been suffered. If that decision, with the justifications taken into account, would have been professionally acceptable, there would be no liability in the law of negligence.) But this decision-maker is acknowledging that he or she did not make a good, informed decision at the relevant time. Perhaps, in this case, there were justifications for the decision. But there might not have been. Even if the risk decision can be justified after the event, and there is no liability in negligence, any employer of the decision-maker, and any professional association or regulatory body to which he or she belongs, will be entitled to take disciplinary action. (This is explained in more detail in Chapter 3.)

Risk-takers in human services sometimes identify the potential harms of risk-taking much more quickly and with greater ease than they identify potential benefits. This is part of a culture of blame and fear that has developed and been fed by litigation and inquiries. But it is remarkably easy to find potential justifications. Take, as an example, the risk of not detaining John, a person with a mental disorder who is threatening to commit suicide. The potential harms are obvious. But what are the benefits? Well, why are the professionals involved in John's case contemplating that he should not be detained? Likely reasons include the concern that intervening and hospitalising John will just make him less motivated to confront his problems and to change. By not detaining John there may be opportunities to maintain and develop relationships in the community which would be lost if he was detained in hospital. If not detained John may be more willing to work with community staff. By not detaining John in a hospital more money will be saved since institutional care is much more expensive than community care. So there are considerations, reasons, in support of a decision not to detain. Whether they are as important, or as likely to occur, as the harms of self-injury are separate issues. But they are reasons for taking the risk not to detain. These are all potential justifications.

When seeking to justify a proposed risk professionals should ask themselves what they are hoping to achieve. What are their goals, their objectives, whether long, medium or short term? What do they hope to see happen to, or with, the patient, client, offender or whoever? Perhaps they are working towards discharging a patient, providing rehabilitation. They should have short-, medium- and long-term goals in mind. These are all potential benefits of risk-taking and, therefore, are all potential justifications for taking the risk. You would not be contemplating working towards these ends and those objectives if they were not, in some way, potentially beneficial and possible. So the best technique for developing lists of potential justifications for taking a risk is to ask 'Why are we proposing to take this risk; what are we seeking?'

Note the purposive context
Why do you go to your doctor when you feel ill or in pain? Because you hope he or she will be able to relieve your symptoms. Why do you, if you do, buy lottery tickets? Because you hope to win lots of money, or enjoy dreaming that you will. Why do you, if you do, engage in sporting activities that might lead to your injury? Because you enjoy them, or the celebrations afterwards. Each of these risks has a purposive context. And the kind of 'professional' risk-taking focused upon in this book is even more purposive. Decisions are taken about, with or for other people, with a view to moving them on to another stage or, at least, to try and prevent them going in a more harmful direction. A risk is taken when removing a child from possibly abusive parents because it may lead to better outcomes. A patient is discharged from hospital, an offender from a prison. These decisions are, or should be, part of a plan. That plan represents a list of possible benefits, and therefore justifications, for risk-taking.

Risk-taking is purposive. Risk-takers should identify their purposes, goals and objectives. They should identify what they are trying to achieve. Those purposes represent potential justifications. Without them it will be very difficult to justify taking, let alone imposing, a risk on another person. Professionals should not be taking risks, at least with other people, just because they are 'there' or 'for fun'.

Risks, gambles and dilemmas

Writing of 'fun': what is the difference between a 'gamble' and a 'risk'? Gambles are a kind of risk. All gambling involves risk-taking but not all risk-taking involves gambling. They both involve the same two key elements, outcomes and likelihood. They also involve uncertainty, even though some experienced people, for example horse-racing tipsters, will offer assessments of likelihood (the odds) which we take seriously. Do you and your colleagues in human services gamble with your clients, your patients, the children in your care?

Social workers took a child from its parents who had been abusive. Time has passed, the family circumstances have changed and there has been some progress. The social workers are now considering whether they should return the child to the parents. They are considering whether to take a risk. Are they also about to gamble with that child's future or life? If the child were abused again, would it be appropriate and fair for the media to describe those social workers as having gambled with the child's life and safety? If not, why not? A key answer is to be found when asking *why* the decision was taken.

Risk-taking is purposive. So is gambling. But we should look more closely. We take gambles because we want to gain something (often money) and for the pleasure involved in making the decision and anticipating success. Gambling involves and encourages anticipation. Gamblers study 'form' and other guides; they contemplate what they will do with their winnings. So when we gamble we buy some pleasure as well as a chance of success. Gambling involves excitement. (Note that we describe some people as being addicted to gambling, not as being addicted to risk-taking, although we do refer to some people as 'risk-seekers'.) It is the pleasure, excitement, vitality that gambling induces that makes it potentially addictive.

Is the experience of sitting in a case conference, say, to decide whether a child should be returned to formerly abusive parents, exciting in the same sense as gambling? There may be pride in participation and contribution to a process of risk decision-making that is well analysed, investigated, assessed, taken and managed. But that is hardly the same experience as waiting to see if your horse will win the race, whether your hand of cards will trump those of your partners, whether your drip of water will reach the bottom of the window pane first. Both gambling and professional risk-taking are undertaken for the potential benefits involved. That is part of the purpose. But with gambling we also seek our pleasure, diversion or whatever, in the decision-making process. Professional risk-taking is undertaken for the benefit of others from a duty (moral, legal or employment-based) to assist them. The social workers may return the child to the formerly abusive parents because they assess and believe that this is the best thing to do in the child's interests. They are employed and trained to do their best for that child. They may be proud of their decision but they are risk-taking rather than gambling with that child. If that risk decision was well taken and managed then they ought, logically, to remain proud of their decision even if harm actually results to the child. However, as human beings, they are likely to feel sad, rather than proud, if harm results. The fact that harm results, as it must with some risks, does not turn a risk into a gamble. The determining factor is the reason for, the purpose for, taking the risk beyond the hope for benefits. Both gambling and risk-taking involve possible benefits and harms, but we engage in them for different reasons, purposes.

A dilemma involves a particular kind of decision. So does a risk. Are they different? Do they overlap? All decisions arising from dilemmas involve taking a risk. But all risk decisions do not constitute dilemmas. A useful working definition of a 'dilemma' is a situation, requiring a decision to be taken, where every option bodes ill. Whatever is done, when there is a dilemma, harm will or may result. There is no option for action that would be harm-free. Indeed, when and where a dilemma is involved you cannot even delay or avoid making a decision, for that would also entail danger.

Time is needed if a risk is to be carefully analysed and assessed. Delays may be unavoidable if necessary information is to be collected and people consulted and involved. But if the risk is also a dilemma then that time can only be obtained by imposing, by causing, extra harm. Dilemmas involve more pressurised decision-making than risks. The fact that harm or loss may occur if additional time is taken over making the decision is a defining characteristic of a dilemma. It is a feature of the kind of decision involved rather than the decision-makers. Thus, when we judge those who make risk decisions which are also dilemmas, we should apply a lower standard. We should have fewer expectations of the quality of the decision-making process where dilemmas are involved. We should not stop being critical and questioning, but it would be improper of us to expect the same standards from a dilemma as we would of those who had the time, the absence of pressure and the availability of harm-free options, when making their risk decision. The law acknowledges this situation, although it calls them 'emergencies' rather than dilemmas (Rogers 2006). (All dilemmas involve emergencies; not all emergencies involve dilemmas.) As will be explained in Chapter 3, the law of negligence applies a lower standard of care when an 'emergency' is involved. The surgeon who has to amputate a leg at the scene of a motorway accident will not be judged by the same standards as the surgeon who performs the same operation in a planned admission to a fully equipped and staffed operating theatre.

Does this distinction between a risk and a dilemma justify or give succour to *delayed* decision-making about risk? No. A risk might be proposed, say, in relation to treating a patient's symptoms. The clinician's decision is to do nothing, to delay any action, perhaps to get more information or to see what happens. Further decisions to defer any action might be made several times. But then a stage is reached when action must take place because any further delay will be harmful. The risk has become a dilemma. The eventual decision may be judged by a lower standard because it is a dilemma. But we ought to consider the total process. Were those decisions to delay or to defer action well made? Did delaying action create problems? Perhaps if the patient's symptoms had been treated earlier then less invasive and/or more successful treatment than that eventually offered might have been provided. Decisions to delay taking a risk are themselves risk decisions. They, too, may be justified by comparing the likely benefits of delay over the likely harms. So it would be wise to keep records of the positive reasons for delaying a decision.

Imagine that you are a judge. With which of the following two witnesses do you have more sympathy?

- 'I am dreadfully sorry about the harm that resulted, but I had to take a risk.'

- 'I am dreadfully sorry about the harm that resulted, but I had to face up to a dilemma.'

Most people have more sympathy with the second witness. They will have even more sympathy if the circumstances which made the event a dilemma rather than a risk are explained.

Courts and other tribunals should be told if the decision was a dilemma rather than a risk. If the court analyses an event as risk-taking then the judge, deciding a claim of negligence, will apply the ordinary requirements of the standard of care. The judge cannot know whether it was a risk or dilemma unless the witness explains the circumstances. If they are going to be witnesses then professional risk-takers should be prepared to argue that they faced up to a dilemma rather than just took a risk.

Whether a risk involves a dilemma is not given; it is not pre-ordained. Analysing a case as a dilemma or a risk involves interpretation and the application of certain values. For example, Daphne is an elderly person who has been treated, and is recuperating in hospital, after having fallen and broken a hip while she was at home. Should she be discharged from hospital? Clearly, this is an example of a risk because the staff do not have to discharge her. She could remain in hospital a little longer. Daphne will be safe in hospital and, anyway, the delay in discharge harms nobody. Well that is what one person thinks. Another could argue that this is a dilemma. The longer that Daphne remains in hospital the more she will lose the necessary skills for coping at home. She is also likely to be missing her home and community. Hospital care is also expensive. So delay in discharge is harmful. Whether she is kept in hospital or discharged harm may occur. Neither decision is necessarily correct. It depends upon how the hospital staff and others value the different items involved. For some this example is a dilemma, for others just an ordinary risk. If you prefer to analyse it as a dilemma you can. You just need to develop your arguments and organise your supporting evidence using the ideas discussed above. Whether a judge or other relevant decision-maker agrees with you will depend upon the quality of your analysis and evidence. Note that no special laws giving powers and duties to detain certain people, such as the Mental Health Act 1983, were involved in the making of this example.

Judging risks

How do we, and how should we, judge risk decisions? Many people do it by examining the outcome. Has the risk decision led to success or failure, to benefits or to harm? If it led to harm then it was a bad risk decision.

Quite simply, those people are wrong. Worse still, with their bad reasoning, they contribute to the culture of fear about risk-taking in human services. They encourage unnecessary defensive practices and overlook many examples of genuinely poor risk-taking.

Judging by outcomes or processes

We cannot, properly, judge a risk by its outcome. When we take a risk of something harmful occurring, justified by likely benefits, we know that harm may occur. The aircraft may crash, a pupil may drown on a school trip, the treatment may produce side-effects and the prisoner might re-offend. We know that because that is what risk-taking involves. If that harm could not have occurred then it would not have been a risk. Say there was a one in ten chance that harm might occur, and it did. Without more information we cannot know whether our case, where harm occurred, was that one in ten case or another instance. If harm results from a risk decision then that might be the consequence of poor risk-taking. It might be. We would need to investigate. We would need to examine the total process of decision-making and risk management that went into the making of that decision. Risk-taking can, and should, be judged by the quality of the decision-making and its management.

Imagine that the best current knowledge indicates that there is a one in 1000 chance of quadriplegia arising from the proposed surgery. In the circumstances, which must include the nature and degree of the current symptoms that the surgery is designed to treat, that risk may be justifiable. Achieving the benefits from that surgery may outweigh the 1:1000 chance of very serious, permanent disability. (How that judgement might be reached will be considered in later chapters.) The surgery takes place, but quadriplegia results. The feared outcome has occurred. But that is not enough to demonstrate poor risk-taking. *If* that risk was properly assessed and was justified before the operation then it has to remain justifiable after the event. To decide whether the surgery was actually justified we need to consider whether the risk, in that particular case, was and remained 1:1000 (or the level considered acceptable before the risk was implemented). We need to investigate to discover whether the way in which the surgery and other treatment (e.g. anaesthetics) were undertaken increased the risk, in terms of its likelihood, the seriousness of the outcomes or both. If, for example, the surgeon was not as careful as he or she should have been then the likelihood of serious disability might have increased. If there was carelessness then that is what must be identified and challenged, not the risk decision. We cannot, properly, judge a risk as bad just because the feared or similar harm occurs. We must look at the processes and actions involved in implementing the decision.

Equally, we cannot judge a risk by its 'non-outcome', in the sense of harm not occurring. The aircraft may have landed safely, the patient may have survived the surgery, the offender may not have transgressed again and the school trip proceeded without mishap. But the pilot may have flown the plane badly; those bumps may not have been caused by air turbulence. Perhaps we are very lucky to still be alive. The surgeon may have made mistakes, but rectified them in time. That the offender does not offend again may have little or nothing to do with the quality of the risk decision to release him or her. The school children may have remained safe because they were more sensible than their teachers. A risk decision may be poorly made, or managed, but still not lead to loss or harm. That lack of harm cannot excuse poor risk practice. Poorly performing pilots, surgeons and teachers should be made responsible for their poor practices – even if no harm resulted. To judge a risk we need to examine the processes and procedures involved, not just the outcomes.

But we all do it to some extent. The media thrives on it and the legal system is particularly bad at it. We all focus upon risk-taking that is associated with harm. We tend to overlook poor practices that do not lead to loss. But if we are truly concerned with the quality of risk-taking then we ought to be concerned with poor decision-making and poor practice, whether it is associated with outcomes that are harmful or beneficial. Of course, a major problem is that we do not 'see' many of the examples of poor risk-taking practice when there is no loss. If harm occurs we have an excuse for an investigation. That may reveal poor practice. But if harm does not occur why bother with an inquiry? For the very good reasons that we may discover that, actually, there was poor practice and, if not, we might be able to learn from the good practice.

A blame culture has developed and is particularly associated with risk-taking by human services professionals (Power 2004). It associates the occurrence of loss or harm from risk-taking with poor decision-making. But it simply does not follow. The nature of risk-taking requires that harm can, and sometimes does, occur from good decision-making. Note that the blame culture does not focus on poor risk-taking which, because of good fortune, does not lead to loss. Nor does it consider all the risk decisions that ought to have been taken, but which were not. Some of those failures to take a risk will be a consequence of the fear of being blamed. The blame culture can be blamed for making risk-taking more difficult.

Karl has a mental disorder. He has a history of being violent and is detained in hospital. Being closely supervised and actively treated in hospital Karl is not violent and harm does not befall anyone. Keeping Karl in hospital looks like good risk-taking. But we cannot know that. Perhaps a risk should have been taken. The likely benefits of moving Karl on to the next stage of rehabilitation, perhaps supervised discharge, might greatly outweigh the likely harms. If that is the case then the failure to take a risk was not good practice. But as the risk was not taken, and no loss was noted, few people would have thought to wonder about whether that individual, his or her carers and the public were being properly treated.

An easy way to stop harm occurring from risk-taking, some foolish people think, is not to take risks. If we do not want to risk prisoners not returning late to prison after day release then we should not give them day release. If we do not want to hear in the news about children being injured while on a school outing then they should not be allowed to go on outings. But just a little thought should reveal that this position is untenable. We allow some prisoners some day release because the likely benefits, in terms of reduced likelihood of re-offending (because the prisoner has re-established himself or herself in the community with accommodation, job and so on), are adjudged to be more important than the possible harms. If we do not take risks of that nature we make things worse. Quite simply, risk-taking is sometimes a duty. Not taking a risk can be bad professional practice. Often, the real problem is that too few, not too many, risks are taken (HSE 2006). And there can, and should, be legal liability for that. To judge a risk fairly it is necessary to look at the total process.

The risk process

As argued above, time is not an element of risk. However, as a dimension of risk, it is a core ingredient of risk management, which concerns the appropriate implementation of a risk decision, based upon risk assessment. This may be perplexing. Much of the confusion arises from some of the risk concepts being 'static' while others are 'dynamic'. The analysis and assessment of a risk are static. They examine a particular risk, or set of risks, at a particular time, in a particular context. Risk assessment may be likened, just for illustrative purposes, to an X-ray image. It provides a picture of a state of affairs at one point in time. If it is a useful risk assessment then it will have revealed, like the X-ray, information that would not otherwise have been available, or readily comprehensible, to 'the naked eye'. But it is a picture, a snapshot, at one point in time. It may take time to collect the information together, to organise a case conference or similar. The discussions may be protracted before the risk assessment is concluded and the risk decision is made. But that does not invalidate the argument that the risk decision is basically made at and about a particular time.

But circumstances change. Things move on. A decision is made, even if only to postpone the risk proposal under discussion. Another risk may be proposed. Alternative objectives may become achievable; different problems may raise fresh fears. The different circumstances, or greater knowledge obtained with the passage of time, may lead to a reassessment of the likelihood of the original, different, possible consequences. Even if the same risk decision is proposed the exercise, on another date, is liable to produce a different assessment, even if the risk judgement does not change.

Risk-taking, in particular with regard to other people, involves a process. An occupational therapist, for example, may be asked to assess a potential client. She or he may report that the individual does not need a service. It is a risk decision because there is a chance of harm arising from it. But, presuming that decision was made in a proper manner, then that will be the end of that issue. The individual may come to the attention of that service again at a later date, perhaps with a different result. In this example only one risk decision has been made: to deny services. In such cases it is appropriate to think of risk as a 'one-off decision' or as justifying a 'snapshot' assessment. There is to be no continuing relationship with that individual, at least until a fresh assessment is made which leads to a different conclusion. But it will be very different if the occupational therapist recommends that the individual is provided with a service and that is accepted. That assessment will just be the first of many risk decisions. Each risk decision will be taken, or avoided, at a particular time. Each of those decisions may be regarded as a 'snapshot' of the risks as then assessed. Indeed, those 'snapshots' may be placed in an album, otherwise known as a case file. They may be looked back upon, fondly or with embarrassment.

If placed in a sequential order they will tell a tale, record a history. Now they begin to resemble a 'film' more than a series of snapshots.

In order to analyse a risk, to make a risk assessment or to make a decision about it, we have to look at the particular proposal. That involves what is being described here as a 'snapshot'. A problem when taking risks with other people is that this snapshot quality can provide a false impression. It is much more appropriate to examine and to judge the quality of risk judgement and risk management by the sequence of risk assessments made and the risk decisions taken (or not taken). This is where experience becomes relevant and valuable. Risk-takers will learn from the experience of taking a sequence of risk decisions. They will learn, for example, which sources of data may be trusted and which risk management plans work well. Although every risk decision is necessarily different the presence of processes permits opportunities to learn.

But it is not just the processes that are important when judging risks and risk-takers. We should also consider systems and structures. These are examined further in Chapter 9, which includes how risk-takers use the opportunities for learning that they gain. Risk-taking involves potential harms as well as benefits and uncertainty. There should be a constant drive to reduce the degrees of uncertainty involved in risk-taking and to increase the potential for successful risk management. That can be achieved by using risk-taking as an opportunity to learn and to develop more information to assist in the future. Risk-taking should be associated primarily with learning, and not with blame or liability.

Shared vocabulary of risk and risk-taking

Below is an initial list of definitions of risk terms. These definitions are justified by current usage; they will work for risk-taking professionals more than many current alternatives and, if they are adopted by all the staff in a service, they will make an important contribution to improving the quality of risk communication within the organisation. These, and further suggested special terms for a shared vocabulary, are also to be found in the Appendix at the end of this book.

- *Risk*: An occasion when one or more consequences (events, outcomes and so on), could occur. Critically (a) those consequences may be harmful and/or beneficial and (b) either the number and/or the extent of those consequences, and/or their likelihood, is uncertain and/or unknown.

- *Risk assessment:* Collecting information (a) about a risk, both the possible consequences and their likelihood, and (b) about the sufficiency and reliability of that information.

- *Risk management:* Identifying, in advance of a decision to risk, and thereafter utilising the resources available to make it more likely that a risk decision will succeed, in the sense that the benefits and/or the likelihoods will be maximised, and that the harmful consequences, and/or their likelihood, will be reduced.

- *Risk judgement:* Comparing the value and likelihood of the possible benefits with the seriousness, and the likelihood, of the possible harms, but always in light of the plans for managing the implementation of that risk decision.

- *Dilemma:* A situation where every option available bodes ill, although there may be less harmful options and some potential benefits. Action needs to be taken because even delay is harmful.

CHAPTER 2

Map and Model

Introduction

Chapter 1, Risk: Making It Work For and Not Against You, introduced the concept of 'risk'. It demonstrated how, despite being a commonplace term and a regular activity, risk is understood in different ways. It offered definitions slightly different from those in common use, and explained why professional risk-takers would be wise to adopt this approach. In particular, it was stressed that risk-taking should be understood as involving balancing the likely benefits against the likely harms. From that consistent definitions for such terms as 'risk assessment' and 'risk management' were developed.

In this chapter those and other terms are taken and it is explained how they relate to each other. In doing this a 'map' of how the parts (of risk-taking) relate to the whole is offered. This is an explanatory device; it should help readers to obtain an overview of the total process, to see how their contribution fits in and to understand others' contributions. Professional risk-takers – those who are employed to take or advise on risks affecting patients, clients, and so on – are advised to adopt these terms. Subsequent chapters focus on parts of this 'map'.

This approach emphasises the importance of decision-making, and ways in which it might be improved. So the second key objective of this chapter is to offer a five-level model of risk and risk-taking. This model, particularly understood alongside the 'map', is designed to demonstrate the interdependence of the different parts of risk-taking and of those involved in making the decisions. In particular, it emphasises that those who design, manage and review risk-taking also have an important responsibility. It argues that if risk-taking is to be improved then action on all five levels is necessary. It encourages a systemic analysis of risk-taking.

It is designed to be a contribution towards reducing the 'blame culture' that has developed around risk-taking, in particular by those who are employed to take risks with, or for, clients.

It is emphasised that the 'map' and model are heuristic devices, and are methods of explaining points. You may find more detail to insert for your own purposes. You are welcome to do so. We have tried to keep the detail to a manageable level, for our explanatory purposes.

The 'risk map'

Clearly, the law is very relevant to risk-taking, but where does it fit in? What about the research on risk factors, risk protocols, decision aids? How should we review risk-taking as a process, and not just examine individual decisions? Most discussions of risk and risk-taking do not make the relationship of the parts to the whole explicit. We believe that this is essential. One theory is summarised in Figure 2.1, which takes the form of a map. The parts have been positioned to facilitate explanation. Each part, and how it relates to the other parts, is explained in more detail here in the text. Then, Figure 2.2 re-presents this 'map' with added details and arrows indicating beliefs as to the direction of the relationships between the parts.

The 'map' is both descriptive and normative. It describes what is believed to be the correct relationship between the parts. It also suggests how the parts should relate to each other. This may appear an unimportant point, but, in practice, many people and organisations often implicitly ignore or misrepresent the relationship between these parts. For example,

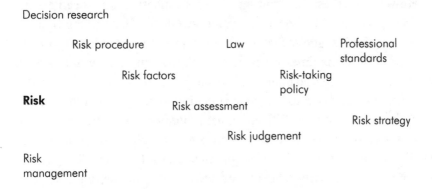

Figure 2.1 A 'map' of risk taking: But how do the parts relate to the whole?

it often appears to be forgotten that a risk is one type of decision. Thus, research on decision-making may inform risk-taking. It is emphasised here that risk assessment and risk management are separate, equally critical, processes. However, it is quite common to see and hear about risk assessments being required or undertaken without any reference to risk management.

Decision research

Taking a risk involves making a decision. Risk-taking is a subset of decision-making. There are other kinds of decision-making, for example choosing, calculating, guessing and confronting dilemmas. There are overlaps, similarities and differences between these kinds of decisions. So research on decision-making, of which there has been a considerable quantity and quality (e.g. Fischoff 1975; Gigerenzer and Goldstein 1996; Kahneman, Slovic and Tversky 1982; Tversky and Kahneman 1974), may inform risk-taking. Professional risk-takers need to know about this research, even if their professional training has not provided them with the information, which has primarily been generated by psychologists and economists. Not knowing about or not acting on, or both, the clear conclusions of this research could easily be the basis for a claim of negligence against a professional risk-taker. When the five-level model of risk-taking is described in the second half of this chapter, it is argued that employers, managers and supervisors all have a role and a responsibility in improving the quality of risk-taking in their organisations. The implications of this research are more fully discussed in Chapter 7.

However, one research finding deserves a mention at this early stage. This refers to 'cognitive' or 'information' overload. This finding by Janis and Mann (1977) suggests that we cannot cope with a lot of information in our head at the same time. We cannot 'think straight', we cannot 'take on board' or 'work with' too many pieces of information at the same time. It is not just that when given too much information we fail to remember it all. It is also that when tasks get difficult we use a number of aids and devices – in research referred to as 'heuristics' – in order to help us to cope (Kassin 2004). Heuristics may help us to complete a task (e.g. describing someone), but they regularly lead us into error. For example, we may have noticed that someone was old and assume, fill in or jump to the conclusion that he or she had grey hair. We may recall accidents involving trains, reported extensively in the media, but be incapable of accurately estimating the numbers of train trips or passengers who are safely carried by train.

In Chapter 1, Risk: Making It Work For and Not Against You, we suggested that you consider why it takes some people so long to decide which bottle of wine to purchase in a shop. After all, there is a limited amount of information for them to take into account: colour, country of origin, grape varieties, age, label, any quality control scheme, alcoholic content, cork or screw cap, price. That is only nine variables. When comparing two or more bottles some people take an inordinate amount of time to make a choice. They are experiencing 'information overload'; they have 'bounded rationality' (Simon 1956). They are trying to work on, compare and evaluate a lot of information at the same time. Perhaps you have experienced the problems yourself. Perhaps you have devised an heuristic, a decision aid such as recalling the bottle label, in order to help you make your decisions.

That was a trite example to make an important point. Compare the risks involved in purchasing the wrong bottle of wine with the risks that may be involved when taking a decision with, or for, other people. Is choosing the right bottle of wine easier? Do we always take longer to make risk decisions that affect other people? If buying wine is a complex decision – and notice the number of wine correspondents who make a living by seeking to help us – how much more difficult is deciding whether a prisoner with a reputation for violence should be granted parole or whether a child at risk should be returned to previously abusive parents, for example? There is no comparable industry of experts offering their advice – at least until harm occurs – in the public gaze.

The research on decision-making demonstrates that we can all be poor decision-makers, particularly when the decision is complex. Research has identified a number of reasons why we make mistakes (see Rachlin 1989; Slovic, Kunreuther and White 2000 as well as the sources cited earlier). This research is as applicable to risk decision-making as to other forms of decision-making. We should draw upon it to improve our risk decision-making. That is the principal purpose of Chapter 7. The key point of this chapter is to locate risk-taking within decision-making.

All risk-taking involves decision-making, but all decision-making does not involve risk-taking. This relationship could be represented in Figure 2.1 by a double-headed arrow drawn between 'Risk' and 'Decision research'. It is double-headed because they inform each other.

Decision-making research can, and should, be used to inform a risk-taking procedure. So, in Figure 2.1, another arrow may be drawn from 'Decision research' to 'Risk procedure'. The research should inform the procedure, not the converse, thus it should be a single-headed arrow from 'Decision research' to 'Risk procedure'. What 'Risk procedure' could, and should, contain will be discussed in greater detail in Chapter 7. It should, for example, confront the problems that risk-takers have with cognitive overload. A risk procedure could ensure that complicated decisions, with lots of information, are broken down into smaller parts. In that way less information would have to be recalled and worked on simultaneously in the decision-maker's head. A sequence of 'small-step' decisions could be taken, rather than one that is so complex that no individual ought to claim competence with it. But, of course, those 'smaller' decisions will have to be organised into an appropriate, logical sequence.

Risk factors

A key feature of professional risk decision-making is the use of risk factors whenever they are available. For example, there has been extensive interest and research into the prediction of violence. The Macarthur study of mental disorder and violence undertook a carefully controlled research project to discover the predictors of violence by mentally disordered people. This was a paradigm study (Monahan *et al.* 2001) which was able to go beyond a simple listing of factors to take into account by including an assessment of their relative importance. The researchers were able to produce an iterative decision tree where the answer to a query about one factor determined which questions and factors should be considered next, and how they should be weighted. It has also led to the production of some software based on the methodology (Monahan *et al.* 2005).

Risk factors should be based upon quality empirical research, wherever that has been undertaken. But where that is not available, risk factors may be based upon practitioners' experience. The nature of such experience deserves examination. This raises the perennial debate between 'actuarial' and 'clinical' factors (see Hare (2002) and Maden (2002)). Actuarial factors involve the sort of information which insurers and actuaries prefer. For example, car insurers want information such as your age, the make of car you drive, the number of accidents you have had, where your car is parked overnight and your annual mileage: concrete information. They are not interested in anyone's opinion about how good or bad a driver you are. The car insurers have found that this 'background' (actuarial) information best enables them to predict how good a risk you are for car insurance purposes. Actuarial factors in relation to predicting the extent to which a client poses a danger to others would include similar factors, such as gender, age and number of prior convictions. This information requires good record-keeping rather than professional opinions, although it does include some judgements because prior convictions are far from the same as prior offences. 'Clinical' factors, by contrast, are more concerned with opinions and interpretations, for example attitudes and motivations. Which factors, clinical or actuarial, should be used when, or which factors should predominate, is a continuing and important debate for professional risk-takers. But this is only one of several problems with risk factors. These problems are addressed in Chapter 7. It is argued that actuarial risk factors should be used, where available, for risk assessment. 'Clinical' risk factors should be used for risk management. This may be an unusual recommendation, but the analysis will demonstrate its value.

The core problem is that although risk factors are an exceptionally important part of risk decision-making they are also ripe for misuse. For example, as will be seen, they can lead to 'double-counting' and other forms of bias. As lawyers and other professional critics become aware of these problems, they must be expected to ask ever more penetrating questions in inquiries and at trials. Research on decision-making needs to inform a decision procedure and that procedure needs to ensure that risk factors are used properly. So, on the map in Figure 2.1, there should be an arrow from 'Risk procedure' to 'Risk factors'.

Risk assessment

A single-headed arrow should be drawn from 'Risk' to 'Risk assessment'. The meaning of 'risk' must, obviously, partially determine the meaning of 'risk assessment'. Chapter 1 proposed that 'risk' referred to occasions when uncertain outcomes, good or bad, or both, could occur to an unknown degree of likelihood. 'Risk assessment' was then interpreted as the collation and evaluation of information about those outcomes and their likelihood. Thus, as 'risk' is about possible benefits as well as harms, 'risk assessment' must involve collecting information about potential successes as much as about potential failures.

A single-headed arrow should be drawn from 'Risk factors' to 'Risk assessment'. Existing research and other forms of knowledge should be used to inform the collection of information about the possible benefits and harms. Risk factors may identify relevant information and be particularly valuable when they identify the comparative importance of the different forms of information available. However, as we shall see in Chapter 7 this sort of information is often missing. For example, the research may tell us that the number of prior offences and the age of first offending are predictive of future offending. But which of these two pieces of information is the more important; indeed, is one twice as valuable as a predictor as the other? Researchers are often good at listing relevant risk factors but are reluctant to suggest their relative value, or weighting. They are concerned that the research is insufficiently robust to permit them to be sure and this may be an appropriate concern. But if the researchers' knowledge is better than that of a lay person then it should be given. Uncertainty may be an essential (because definitional) feature of risk-taking, but it should be reduced wherever reasonably possible.

The law

In an important sense the law applies to every part of risk-taking. For example, a good case can be made for drawing a line in the 'map' shown in Figure 2.1 from 'Law' to 'Risk procedure' on the basis that if a procedure is so poorly designed, managed or implemented that it produces bad decisions it could give rise to liability. That possibility will be discussed in Chapter 9. But, unfortunately, current legal practice is to focus on the quality of decisions made by individuals, rather than on the processes whereby they are made and managed. For present purposes the traditional focus has been adopted.

The law affects risk-taking in three main ways. First, a single-headed arrow should be drawn from 'Law' to 'Risk assessment'. This reflects the fact that the law sometimes directly determines the tests to be applied in risk assessment. Take, for example, risk-taking in relation to child care. Section 1(1) of the Children Act 1989 prescribes, for England and Wales, that when a court makes a decision about the upbringing of a child then 'the child's welfare shall be the court's paramount consideration'. Then, in respect of residence, contact and certain other orders that a court can make, the Act specifies criteria that are to be taken into account. In this way the law is determining the criteria that are to be involved in such risk assessments.

Another example is the Mental Health Act 1983. (Since submission of the manuscript this act has been amended by the Mental Health Act 2007) Its sections provide different orders that authorise the detention of people with a mental disorder who are perceived to be a risk to themselves or others. The orders prescribe different standards, or criteria, for detention. But, despite their critical importance for civil liberties, these criteria are very vague and imprecise. For example, the difference between a 'hospital order' and a 'restriction order' in relation to a patient is that the latter requires the risk posed to be of 'serious harm' (see Section 41(1)). What does that mean? For example, which element does 'serious' relate to: the *outcomes* or their *likelihood*?

These examples are, however, exceptional. It is rare for the law to specify the criteria that must be taken into account in a risk assessment. And when it does, as in these examples, it does not prevent other factors being taken into account. Nor does it specify the relative importance of the factors.

The second role for the law is much more important in practice. It concerns whose values are to be taken into account. Again, fuller details will be provided in the next chapter, but the key issue of 'Whose risk?' needs to be confronted at an early stage. Imagine that you have consulted your doctor. He or she recommends and prescribes some tablets, but advises that there could be some nasty side-effects. Can the doctor insist that you take those tablets? No, presuming that you are a competent adult. It is your right and responsibility to decide. It is your life, your body. Similarly, if you are in the doctor's position, you may be employed to make risk decisions, but you may not be entitled, in law, to impose them upon others. You may work in adult social care. You may believe that a client is at risk, perhaps because he or she wishes to live alone or declines certain services. If the client is competent to make that decision, it does not involve committing a crime and it does not endanger other clients for whom you are responsible, you may not impose your decision (see the Mental Capacity Act 2005, discussed in Chapter 3). You may think that there is a serious risk. You may be right. But you cannot impose your values, your risk decision. You can – indeed, morally, professionally and legally you should – advise the client of it, and why you believe the risk is unjustified, dangerous even. And you should inform and advise the client about ways in which, if he or she decides to go ahead,

the risk can be managed. But you cannot impose your values. The law pro-
hibits it.

But, then again, you may work with certain clients, or in certain contexts, where you are entitled, indeed obliged, to make decisions for clients,
even against their wishes. Some clients are not entitled to make risk decisions for themselves. The main groups are *some* children and *very few* adults
with a mental illness or a learning disability or both. It is particularly difficult to decide clearly who does and who does not have capacity because it
also depends upon the risk proposed and the complexity of the decisions
involved. This makes risk-taking professionally exciting because it permits
dynamic decision-making. Someone may appear to be incapable, for
example because of a learning disability, of making a particular risk decision for him or herself. But if the individual is provided with some
additional skills, and the information necessary for making a competent
decision is explained well, that person may be made competent (enabled)
to make the decision and apply his or her own values and standards. And
there is another group which cannot make certain risk decisions; those
who have been detained (primarily prisoners and patients detained under
the Mental Health Act 1983) because they are considered a danger to
themselves or others are not entitled to decide (in any sense that others
must act upon it) that they do not actually pose a risk.

But the third way in which the law is relevant is the most important,
even though its effect is indirect. To summarise this go back to the 'map' in
Figure 2.1 and draw a single-headed arrow from 'Law' to 'Professional
standards'. Then draw single-headed arrows from 'Professional standards'
to 'Risk-taking policy' and from 'Risk-taking policy' to 'Risk assessment'.
As Chapter 3 explains in much more detail, the law of negligence is pervasive with regard to risk-taking. But it is widely misunderstood and
wrongly regarded as an enemy of good-quality professional risk-taking. In
essence, the law of negligence provides that professionals taking risks with
clients and others will not be liable if their decisions, and other acts, are
consistent with what a responsible body of their colleagues would do. The
law supports and reinforces professional standards. And when those standards are clearly articulated in a risk-taking policy or similar document,
they may be used as the criteria and values needed when making a risk
decision.

For example, take the case of *Porterfield* v. *Home Office* ([1988] *The Times*, March 9) A prison governor received information which suggested that a named prisoner was liable to be attacked by another prisoner to punish him for helping the police with their enquiries. The governor considered the information. He had to make a risk decision. He considered how likely it was that the attack would be carried out. He often received such reports, but found that the attacks rarely took place. He considered his options. He could have the prisoner placed in a segregated wing of the prison. That would protect him from attack but considerably reduce his freedom. It would also make it likely that other prisoners would think he had been placed there because he was a child sex offender. That would make it more likely that other prisoners would assault him if and when he returned to the main prison wings. Or the governor could, as he did, ask the prison officers to pay special attention to him in light of the warning. Guess what happened, remembering that this is a case that went to trial? The prisoner was attacked and injured. He sued the Home Office as the employer of the governor. The crucial evidence indicated that other responsible prison governors would have made exactly the same decision. Thus this governor was not negligent.

Risk assessment, risk management and risk judgement

Now, in the 'risk map' shown in Figure 2.1, draw a double-headed arrow between 'Risk assessment' and 'Risk management'. And somewhere along that arrow, draw a single-headed arrow towards 'Risk judgement'.

Risk assessment involves collecting and assessing the quality and significance of information about a perceived risk. It does *not* include making a decision on that information. It is true that we often run the two together in our daily life. You approach a road. You look both ways, you do not see or hear any traffic approaching so you walk straight across the road and carry on without ever thinking of having made a risk decision, let alone having undertaken a risk assessment. Where the assessment is so clear, that is, both the nature of the information (about what could happen and its likelihood) and its quality are clear, you make quick decisions. There is little point in forcing definitional points for such daily occurrences. But, when you are concerned with taking or advising on risks affecting other people, these semantic niceties are much more important.

Imagine you have collated information about a risk, be it granting parole to an offender, detaining someone considered suicidal or surgically removing someone's appendix. You need to consider whether you have enough information of sufficient quality. (There is more about this in Chapter 3.) Because this is risk-taking you, by definition, have incomplete information. If it were complete, if you knew exactly what was going to happen, it would not be a risk. So this requires a judgement. You need to consider, for example, what more or better information, or both, it is possible to obtain, at what cost and to what advantage. In the last resort you have to take a risk about whether to seek more and better information.

You also need to think about how you are going to implement the risk decision. How senior and experienced a surgeon should be involved in the operation to remove the appendix? How often should the released offender be required to report to a police station or probation officer, and for how long? Who might give you timely, accurate information about any further deterioration in the patient's mental state, if you decide against detention? In other words, you need to think about how you are going to manage the risk. There is much more about this in Chapter 4.

Risk assessment and risk management are interactive and iterative. Risk *assessment* provides information for a possible decision. Risk *management* suggests ways in which that decision may best be implemented. Different levels of resources, for example, may be applied. The child who is perceived possibly to be at risk may be visited with greater frequency by social workers. Further information may be sought and, perfectly properly, an entirely different risk decision may be proposed. That may mean that the initial information collected is inadequate to judge fairly the new proposal. So another risk assessment may be required. Quality risk-taking, particularly when it concerns other people, should not simply involve judging initial proposals. It should include being prepared to reconsider, entirely, those proposals in light of information generated in the processes of risk assessment and risk management. Frequently, it will be perfectly appropriate to assess and manage the original proposal because it was a wise hypothesis to propose. But, equally, there will be many occasions when it would be inappropriate, possibly negligent, to continue with the initial proposal rather than to generate a fresh suggestion. Quality risk-taking is a creative process. It calls for imaginative consideration of alternative strategies, as well as more reactive competencies in assessment and comparison. Quality risk-taking (at least when dilemmas, which demand immediate action, are not involved) is about finding an appropriate decision and the strategy for implementing it. It is about seeking to ensure success, not just about deciding 'yea' or 'nay'.

At some stage, depending on the risk involved, during the discussion about the risk, its assessment and management it will become appropriate to make a decision, even if that is only to conclude what to advise a competent patient or client to do about the risk. This is risk judgement. It involves a comparison of the value of the likely benefits with the seriousness of the possible harms, but always in light of the plans for managing the implementation of that decision. The issues must not be abstracted from their context, even if consideration must always be given to the degree of uncertainty that necessarily will remain about whether the management plan will succeed. For example, a risk management plan may require a patient to report certain information at regular stages. But he or she may not do that.

Risk strategy
There is just one phrase in the 'risk map' shown in Figure. 2.1 that has not been explained or linked to the others. It is of a different character to the other topics, which makes it a little more difficult to explain. There are two linked ideas. So far, at least implicitly and in all the examples, we have been thinking of single risk decisions. The focus has been on the risk assessment and management of a particular case. But that focus would be atypical in the context of risk decisions affecting other people. Risk-taking guides should not be based upon the unusual.

Consider risk-taking with clients and patients. How often is only a single risk decision involved? It does happen, for example, if someone has to decide whether a patient or client needs to receive a service. Perhaps a social worker may be sent to assess whether Emily needs assistance with her domestic chores. Without that assistance, because of her age and physical incapacities, Emily might injure herself when doing her chores. The social worker may decide that Emily does not require support or does not match the current standards of need. That is an end to that issue; there is no continuing relationship between the social worker and Emily, at least on that issue. There is no question of a continuing review of need. Or is there? In such cases it is likely that another assessment and decision will have to be made in due course, particularly if Emily's independence continues to deteriorate. It is a one-off decision if there is no need to review it some time later. Because another decision is taken, on the same issue and in the same case, does not prevent the first decision from having been a one-off. But if provision is made for a review or follow-up of a risk decision then it implies a continuing relationship. Most of the risk decisions that this book is concerned with will be part of a continuing relationship. Your general practitioner (GP) refers you to a hospital specialist, who decides you need surgery. Even though different people are involved, making overlapping risk decisions, you have a continuing relationship from first consultation with your GP through hospitalisation and discharge, back to follow-up by the specialist or GP, or both.

Take an example of Fred, who is considered to be at risk of self-harming. Fred comes to the attention of services. An initial risk decision is taken. It might be to detain Fred in a hospital because of the level of risk judged to exist and the inability to manage it elsewhere. That would be a difficult decision. The individual may disagree and the law may have had to be relied on in order to impose the decision. But that is the start, not the end of it. A major goal will be to discharge Fred just as soon as it is wise to do so. But that risk decision is some time away. Before then a whole sequence of risk decisions will have to be taken. For example, on admission the likelihood of serious self-harm may be assessed as so high that the appropriate risk management plan requires that Fred is kept under constant supervision and has to use plastic cutlery. However, over time, that requirement may be relaxed. Access to metal cutlery will be allowed and time off the ward will be negotiated.

A useful analogy is the 'risk path'. In the previous example the path begins somewhere upon detention in hospital. Some goals, or places to be visited, may be identified right at the start; for example, in the medium term, discharge from hospital and, it is hoped, in the longer term, discharge from community support services. But the route to those places cannot be mapped with any great precision. There will often be opportunities that are unique to the case (e.g. specialist services) and which permit routes not always available to others. A series of steps – risk decisions – will be taken towards the goals. Some will involve large steps: significant risks taken. Some will be small. Sometimes the steps will be very direct, towards the goals. Sometimes they will be more indirect, perhaps towards an ancillary, supportive goal, such as increased self-confidence and self-care rather than discharge. The risk path may zig-zag towards the goals. Indeed, it may sometimes go backwards when circumstances show that it would be wise to return to a previous position and either delay repeating the risk or approach it using smaller steps.

The analogy is appropriate and useful. But perhaps you feel it is only that – a way of describing reality. Actually, it is very important. If it is recognised that this is an accurate way of describing professional risk-taking then it should be proclaimed. It should be emphasised that, in this context of taking risks with or affecting other people, taking a *series* of related decisions is anticipated. This is the context. Useful information will be obtained from each decision taken, which may be used to support succeeding decisions. Each successful decision should give a measure of confidence about those that follow, although as Chapter 7 will emphasise, knowledge and experience must not be abused. Each decision is different.

Courts, complaints and criticism can follow when harm results from risk-taking, not from success. Imagine that harm has resulted from a particular risk decision that you took, or advised a client to take. It is appropriate to consider whether you made a bad decision, in particular so that you can learn from it. Perhaps that was the tenth risk decision you had taken with that client, but the first to lead to harm. And you may have been contemplating assessing some further risk proposals, if only the tenth had not led to harm. It is appropriate for people to consider whether your tenth decision was wrongly taken. But is it inappropriate to examine the tenth risk decision in isolation from its context of the preceding nine decisions? To an extent, yes, it is fair because it was a unique decision, differing from all the others, as all risk decisions do. But it is also very unfair to take the final decision out of the context of those that preceded it. The context of the first nine risk decisions formed part of the reasoning for the tenth. Your experience of the previous risk decisions, for example, could have given you confidence about certain aspects of the tenth decision, for example the extent to which it was appropriate to rely upon the client's motivation to co-operate. You should be entitled to rely upon that experience. But a court, a complaint or a criticism might seek only to examine the last decision, and to ignore any further decisions which were being contemplated if the last succeeded. This practice should be condemned. Provided it does not become an excuse for tardiness, it is more appropriate to take a sequence of small steps, which can be learnt from, than to take a few large-step risks. Courts, complainants and critics should be encouraged to

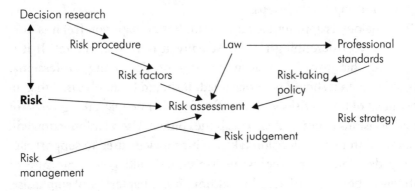

Figure 2.2 The risk-taking 'map': How the parts relate to the whole

appreciate the broader picture of professional risk-taking as a process, as a sequence of decisions.

That is one reason why 'Risk strategy' is located on the 'risk map'. It is there to emphasise that individual risk decisions are likely to be part of a broader risk strategy. But it also has a second meaning.

Risk-taking is a science as well as an art and skill. There will always be more that we could know about it. By its very nature it requires us to act without perfect knowledge. And it requires that decision-makers learn and practise a process demanding considerable mental agility and critical imagination. Values are involved. There are plenty of opportunities for error; these are emphasised in Chapters 6 and 7. We all need to learn more about, and from, risk-taking so the second reason for including 'Risk strategy' on the 'risk map' in Figure 2.2 above is to emphasise this interrelation. The parts of the risk 'map' fit together; they interrelate. To improve risk-taking we need to learn more both about the parts and their interrelating. Risk decision-makers should have a strategy, in the sense of ensuring that they seize opportunities to learn from individual decisions and review their practices and processes. Colleagues, professional associations, managers and employers should support them in this. The 'systemic' nature of risk-taking should be recognised, particularly by professionals acting for, or affecting, others. More will be written about this in Chapter 8, but the point is reinforced below in a five-level model of risk that emphasises the critical responsibility of managers and employers, among others, to help to improve risk-taking as a system. This is the second sense in which a 'Risk strategy' is considered a core element of the risk landscape. Perhaps it might be best represented on the 'map' as a coil of circles denoting the interrelationship of the parts but also moving forwards to better decisions.

Responsibility for risk-taking: a five-level model

The description of the 'risk map' concluded by stressing the importance of a system perspective on risk. This emphasises the interrelationship of the parts to the whole. It should also emphasise the interdependence of the many people involved in professional risk decisions. Even if one person insists – rather incompatibly in multidisciplinary teams – on making the final risk judgement, he or she will be supported, informed and, it is hoped, advised by many others. With so many people being involved responsibility may become diffuse and confused so it is important to address the question of who is responsible for the risk decisions. This is best examined by developing a five-level model of risk-taking. The first level is well known; it is the traditional understanding of risk and dangerousness. The second is sometimes included in discussions. But, currently, the other three are given scant attention.

Level 1: Risky or dangerous people, circumstances, events or articles

The first level of the model argues that there are some risky or dangerous people, things (such as weapons) or circumstances. The focus of attention, and the research effort of those who consciously or unconsciously adopt this approach, is on increasing knowledge of these people, events and so on in order to regulate the risk. They wish to understand why this person does, or these people (such as incompetent parents) do, dangerous or risky things. Is George dangerous as well as being an offender? What is it about George that makes him such? What are the key risk factors affecting him? Are delusions a relevant variable affecting the likelihood or degree of his future violence? What, if anything, is the risk attached to this medicine or procedure?

Note that, with this approach, the focus of attention is George or the equivalent patient or client. The focus is away from the risk-takers or advisers. The risk or danger is reified into something 'in' or 'over there'. The problem or risk is in other people or is in external events or substances. It is amenable to traditional forms of scientific research; it permits comparing and contrasting. It is also moral, or normative; it ought to be avoided or prevented. 'Blame', 'danger', 'risk' and other loaded labels may be attached to the people and the activities.

But the focus is not political. It does not, on its own, challenge social structures or relationships. It does not require us to think radically about our assumptions or practices. More money for research will always be considered desirable, but the availability or distribution of resources is not part of the problem. With research into this form of 'danger' or 'risk' we get a 'handle' on the problem. We begin to describe it, to understand it better and, thus, begin to proscribe it. This approach is consistent with a 'medical' model. The problem or 'disease' is in a person, article or circumstances, and it needs to be isolated and treated.

Level 2: Dangerous contexts and social settings

The second approach to, or 'level' for, understanding risk emphasises not the people or things considered to be risky, but the context within which they live and interact. It involves a social work, rather than a medical model. It stresses that we always live, and risk or danger always exists, in a social context. We interact with our surroundings and those people we meet. These are critical factors in the degree of risk or danger that exists. Some living arrangements are more risky than others. Risk is not evenly distributed between places, people and so on, and some settings, such as prisons and secure hospitals, exist because they reduce danger for those living outside but increase it for those inside. Other settings and circumstances, for example living near a school or being unemployed, increase the risk from paedophiles or for those liable to stress. Social settings make it both more and less likely that certain outcomes, positive and negative, will happen to people. The key point is that the danger or risk is not just 'in' individuals but also 'in' where and how they live. Poverty and powerlessness, for example, can be part of the problem.

Opportunities are critical to an appreciation of risk. If they are unemployed then parents will have more time at home and thereby more opportunities to abuse their children. The ready availability of illegal substances will increase the likelihood of their use. Getting someone a job, or more appropriate accommodation, will often be the most useful method, even if apparently indirect, of reducing an individual's dangerousness. It reduces opportunities. Providing social support could reduce feelings of isolation and stress, thereby reducing the likelihood of self or other injury.

This second level for understanding risk is political, but not in a party political sense. It acknowledges that social circumstances, and the quality and quantity of support structures, can increase or reduce danger. Thus, the degree to which appropriate resources are available is a risk factor. A very dangerous person can be rendered of little danger by the investment of resources – physical, human and intellectual. This is readily recognised by building institutions, such as prisons and secure hospitals, to contain dangerous people. But resources can also be expended in other ways, such as in intensive skilled community supervision. This second 'level' or approach to analysing risk acknowledges that money, in its myriad forms, can reduce or increase the degree of danger and risk. This contextual approach is also morally equivocal. Blame and distaste can still be attached to dangerous people, particularly if they are offenders, but we can begin to understand why they behave in this way, and why they may be maintained in it by circumstances outside of their control or influence.

But it is much more difficult to undertake traditional forms of controlled scientific research into this second approach to risk. It is much more difficult to control social circumstances than it is to control which patient receives a drug and which the placebo. It would often be immoral, if not unlawful, to undertake research where the presence or absence of social supports was a variable to be tested. But, as Monahan, the doyen of research into risk posed by people with mental disorders (Monahan *et al.* 2001), has commented, although these situational or contextual factors are among the most powerfully predictive, they are among the least researched. They are particularly important for risk management decisions.

Level 3: Dangerous decisions

The first level or approach to risk-taking focuses upon the person, incident or circumstances thought liable to harm or be harmed, to be 'at risk'. The second focuses upon the context, the social setting, within which the risk is to be taken. But the third level focuses upon those people who make and take the risk decisions. We have moved from perceiving the risk or danger as being in other people, events, machinery and so on, who may be affected by the risk decision, to now also seeing it as within us, or the decision-makers. The simple point is: those who take risk decisions can make things better or worse, depending upon how well they make their decisions. Of course, there would be no problem, no risk, if there was not a dangerous or risky person, circumstance or article to create the initial risk problem. But the risk decision-maker can make things better or worse. Making a poor-quality decision can (not necessarily will) make the risk or danger much greater.

These perspectives on, or levels of, risk are not alternatives. They are cumulative. They are all relevant. Each one needs to be appreciated and acted upon if decision-making is to be improved.

Risk-taking is a skill. It can be improved upon. Being qualified as a psychiatrist, a social worker, a judge or whatever does not, by itself, make anyone a good risk decision-maker. It is not an art or skill that can be completely and exhaustively described or analysed. Equally, 'professional judgement' is insufficient on its own. Detailed knowledge of the discipline involved, and sincere empathy with the patient or client concerned is helpful, but insufficient. The risk-taker needs also to know how to take competent risk decisions. He or she needs to know about the findings of decision-making research as sources of common errors have been identified by extensive research. Have decision-makers been informed about these potential pit-falls and advised how to avoid them? How many people, who currently take risks with other people as an integral part of their jobs, have received training in risk analysis, assessment and management? The study and knowledge of relevant risk factors, which is often part of professional training, is not the same thing. That is but a small part of it all.

How many people know how good they are at taking risks, whether for themselves or for others? Do you know how good or bad you are? For example, what is the ratio of your 'successful' to your 'unsuccessful' risk decisions? Of course, there are problems in determining both what 'success' and 'failure' mean in this context. But if you do not have an idea about the proportion of 'good' to 'bad' risk decisions that you take how can you know whether you are getting better over time? What constitutes a 'good' and what a 'bad' decision may be controversial, but only on the margins. A working definition, for these purposes, could treat it as a success when the benefits sought by the risk decision, or at least some of them, are achieved and the harms feared are avoided. Although the absence of harm is not a guarantee that it was a 'good' decision (it may have more to do with good luck than a good decision), the presence of 'harm' also cannot, by itself, demonstrate that it was a poor risk decision.

Some people argue that the best technique for avoiding both blame and poor decision-making is to avoid making a decision. But they are – very – wrong. A decision to do nothing is as much a decision as one in favour of action. Just as decisions to take a risk can be criticised, so can decisions not to act, not to risk. The patient who is refused discharge because he or she is considered to be at too much risk will experience loss and a sense of harm. Actions have consequences. Inaction also has consequences. It can be negligent, as the next chapter will explain, not to act.

This third level of risk-taking focuses on questions such as whether decision-makers use appropriate risk factors:

- Do they have procedures for coping with too much information?
- Do they assess the likelihoods well enough?
- Do they value the degree of benefit and harm possible in an appropriate manner?
- Do they use appropriate risk factors in a proper manner?

If not they are liable to contribute to a poor decision and thereby make things more risky or even dangerous. Decision-makers can be part of the problem. But it may be said that they rely upon colleagues and employers to help them. Cue another 'level' of risk.

Level 4: Dangerous management

Wherever people are employed to take risks there are managers and employers who should be supporting, supervising and managing them. The fourth level or approach to risk-taking emphasises the contribution of managers and supervisors to making things better or worse, less or more dangerous and risky. They, too, can be part of the problem. People may be promoted out of front-line services. They may not be directly involved in making decisions about clients or patients. But they have not been promoted out of risk-taking – just to a different role or level within it. They are now responsible for promoting, facilitating and ensuring quality decision-making by others as well as by themselves. For example, consider managers of a community service where, at nights and weekends, computerised information about clients is switched off. How can staff make quality decisions if they need that information out of office hours? There may be justifications for that working method but the key point is the responsibility for that working method lies with the managers and employers, not with the people trying to access the information out of hours. It is not something that their staff can control; they have to work with the system.

Employers know that they must provide a safe system of *work*. This understanding needs to be extended to a duty to provide a safe system for *working*. Managers are in a strategic position to supervise processes, for example ensuring the quality and collation and dissemination of information and experience around their organisation and others with overlapping remits. They are responsible for auditing processes and intervening where and when necessary. This can and should include auditing risk-taking processes.

One inquiry into risk decision-making by mental health professionals (Woodley *et al.* 1995) concerned a homicide committed by a mentally ill man (SL in the following extract). It criticised some of the professionals involved and concluded that:

> Our main criticism over the period of SL's care and treatment in the community is that attempts to provide him with good social care were undermined by inadequate health care. (Woodley *et al.*, p.99)

But then, after 47 words of further criticism of the healthcare provided, the report continued:

> We have identified the following contributory factors which militated against high quality care in the community by both health and social services:
>
> - organisational change
> - pressures on human resources
> - poor communications
> - poor administrative systems
> - lack of effective risk management
> - lack of effective multi-disciplinary working
> - inexperience. (Woodley *et al.*, pp.99–100)

How were good services to be provided, good risk decisions to be made, in the midst of such a poorly managed system? The inquiry team concentrated upon the responsibility and accountability of individual decision-makers, and was quite explicit about blaming individuals. It appears to have been a case crying out for an analysis of how poor management can make a risk more dangerous. That different agencies, not just healthcare, were involved is not an excuse. Basically the inquiry team only considered 'risk' in terms of the first two levels described in this book.

This is not to deny the importance of the contributions of individual professionals. Some would argue that risk-taking is their responsibility; indeed, that it is the acme of their professionalism, and that their employers have no positive contribution to make. Administrators cannot, and certainly should not, tell surgeons how to take the risk decisions that arise during surgery. And some professional groups are statutorily required to act independently. For example, under the Mental Health Act 1983, which applies in England and Wales, approved social workers have statutory responsibilities with regard to the detention of mentally disordered patients. Social work departments have to appoint such staff. They employ, monitor and can discipline those workers. But they cannot tell them what their decisions must be under that Act.

Individual professionals remain responsible for their decisions. The point about managers' responsibility for risk-taking relates to the support and training they provide for decision-making by their staff, and not the actual decisions made. Employers are in an excellent position to ensure that a positive learning culture exists to support professional risk-taking. For example, consider how best we learnt at school, and subsequently. How do we continue to learn new skills and improve old ones? Do we learn best by having our errors, failings and inadequacies pointed out to us? To an extent, but surely the best, and most, learning comes from being shown what works, how and why it is correct, and what is good practice. Highlighting errors can be illustrative and illuminating, but it only shows what should not be done, and sometimes also why. Instruction, guidance and support in what ought to be done is also needed. Consider what actually happens in practice within the disciplines that are targeted by this book. Consider the roles of government and the legal system. Many inquiries are held into poor risk-taking, at considerable expense. Their messages are relatively similar (Johnson and Petrie 2004; Laming 2003). Where is the investment in examples of good practice? Might not more be learnt by an inquiry into good practice? This is the sort of way in which managers and employers can make risk-taking more, or less, dangerous. Other examples include the information and equipment that they provide – or do not provide – for their staff.

Decisions can only be as good as the data they are based upon. Information may be unavailable, or available but of poor quality. For example, data may suggest that someone is 'safe' (e.g. not violent) whilst detained in a hospital. But that cannot tell us whether that person would be violent if not in hospital. It is not just of computers that we can remark 'Rubbish in, rubbish out.' A risk-taker may have to rely upon poor-quality data when making a decision. That decision may lead to success, or at least not to harm. But the presence or absence of harm cannot determine whether it was a good decision. If the decision was based on poor-quality data, for example, it was a bad decision. (There are possible exceptions to this judgement where, for example, it was a dilemma or it was appropriate to rely upon the poor data as this was the best economically available and/or which could be obtained in the time by which the decision had to be made.) Risk decision-makers can – and often are – lucky because good fortune intervenes and prevents harm from occurring. Individual professional risk-takers have a responsibility to consider and seek to learn from their decision-making, and not to rely upon good fortune and the absence of harmful outcomes from their risk decisions. But their managers and employers have responsibilities to help them. They are in a much better position to collate and disseminate relevant, robust information and to ensure appropriate learning from experience. Just as it is their job to identify and promote good staff so is it their responsibility to identify and promote good decision-making.

But how are managers and employers to identify good risk-takers so that others can learn from them if they do not collect and analyse information about the practices of their staff? In your professional experience how often is relevant information about your decision-making collected and used as a learning aid? If it is, is it appropriate information? For example, does your organisation only collect information about risk decisions where harm or criticism, or both, result? If it does then your organisation is behaving inappropriately. It needs, at least, to also know about other decisions where harm does not result. It needs to have a total picture. Without such information it is not even in the most basic position of being able to tell a court or other form of inquiry how often it makes apparently good risk decisions. (There are only ever 'apparently' good decisions since the fact that no harm results cannot prove that that was the consequence of a good decision, well made and implemented.)

You really need to know four figures. Take, for example, an offender being given early release from prison. The risk may be judged to be a success, a good risk decision, if the prisoner commits no offences during the remaining period of his or her sentence, and/or a subsequent period. That would be a 'true positive' in the sense that the prisoner was correctly (truly) assessed as being safe (positive) for early release. You also need to know about assessments that the prisoner is 'safe' (positive) which prove incorrect (false). But the decision may be not to allow early release (i.e. a failure to release) because the individual is considered 'unsafe'. That is still a risk decision because the individual may be wrongly detained. So you also need to know how often offenders are correctly (truly) considered unsafe (negative) and how often they are incorrectly (falsely) considered to be unsafe (negative).

Some people may argue that wrongly detaining an offender in prison is not an example of a poor risk decision. They are wrong. It may be their opinion that offenders should not be given early release, but that is a different point. If, according to the law and good decision-making, the offender could and should have been released, then, by definition, it was a poor decision. Some people may also argue that we will rarely notice such wrong decisions. Now they have a point, unfortunately. We notice harmful consequences of decisions to act – for example, to release offenders or to discharge patients – because we notice positive harm from decisions to act. We do not ordinarily notice the consequence of not taking positive action in such cases. The offenders or patients may remain detained, in prison or hospital, and behave in an excellent manner. That might lead some conscientious people to wonder whether they should have been released earlier. That is suggestive evidence but it does not prove it was a wrong decision not to release.

You need to know these four figures, but it is very difficult to obtain a complete picture. Consider also decisions to postpone a decision. Should those be counted as risk decisions? It is only fair to recognise that managers have a difficult task in obtaining quality data, but that does not justify inaction. Managers should be actively striving to help their staff understand how good they are at risk decision-making, and how they might improve.

Level 5: Dangerous systems

Risk-taking with people in the human services is regularly inter-disciplinary and multiprofessional. The decision-makers, information providers or both often come from several different agencies. Their differences in knowledge and approach provide an opportunity for a richer understanding of each case. But that has to be managed. Different rules or understandings of the requirements of confidentiality, for example, can create problems. Problems can also arise from different professionals having different goals and objectives, such as police officers desiring that a paedophile is tried, convicted and sentenced, whereas social workers are anxious to protect the critical child witness from further distressing experiences such as appearing as a witness in court. If these problems are not sorted out they can make risk decision-making more dangerous. These problems are not the fault of the individual 'risky' client, or of where and how he or she lives. They are not the fault of the individual decision-makers. Sometimes they are not even the fault of the managers and employers. One professional may not give certain information to another professional because the latter is not bound by the same rules of confidentiality or has a different employer. But if employers and professional bodies cannot 'get their acts together', to sort out such problems, how are the people involved in making individual decisions to be expected to cope with them? Those organisations are making risk-taking more difficult, more dangerous.

This fifth 'level' or perspective on risk focuses on the systems and organisations within which risk decisions have to be made. It stresses the contribution that national and local government, public authorities and agencies, including professional associations and similar, can make to improve, or endanger, risk-taking. Consider a mental health service, for example, where the health, social work, housing, employment support and other elements come under different management and organisational structures, which may not even be co-terminous. Clearly risk-taking is going to be more difficult in such a diffuse organisation. There may be good reasons for retaining such a structure but the problems that it causes for quality risk-taking need to be identified and tackled.

It is not just a matter of inappropriate organisational structures. Policies can make risk-taking more difficult, more risky. Some of them have been formalised into law. Take, for example, the role of mental health review tribunals in England and Wales. Under the Mental Health Act 1983 they have to decide whether a patient is to be detained or is to be discharged. That is the risk decision that the tribunals must take. They have limited options. They can discharge but delay implementation. But to discharge someone can involve an enormous step. There is an enormous difference between living in an institution, where the staff have all the powers that go with the right to detain, to living in the community, where their influence is limited. Discharge involves a big step, especially for someone with problems that, by definition, such a patient or client will have. The size of the step makes it more difficult to achieve successfully. Is it any wonder that so many transitions from hospital to community fail? Here the law is making risk-taking and risk management more difficult. Unfortunately, our laws and legal systems are not good at organising small step changes. And a dichotomous (either/or) approach to ensuring procedural civil liberties (detained or not detained, capable or incapable and so on) can make achieving substantive benefits (e.g. better mental health) more difficult. That these problems are recognised, and steps taken to minimise them, demonstrates that the law can be part of the problem.

Another example of 'the law' making risk-taking more difficult concerns policy and practice surrounding mentally disordered offenders. It is widely agreed that mentally disordered offenders should not be imprisoned, especially for minor crimes. Prison is not likely to do them much good, and could make things worse. They should be the responsibility of the mental health or social work support systems, this policy argues. The principles may be sound, the values may attract sympathy, but does this policy work well? The policy effectively teaches offenders that they can offend, at least in a relatively minor manner, without fear of punishment. They, and their offending, will not be taken seriously. The policy may create warm feelings, and be attractive, but it has negative effects. Patients or clients can deny responsibility for their offending and avoid pressure to change their behaviour. The policy, which is in the control of national government, needs to be developed. At the moment it is hindering quality risk-taking.

This fifth level, or notion of risk, also relates to those occasions when official inquiries blame 'the system'. (Consider the report into the killing of Victoria Climbié (Johnson and Petrie 2004; Laming 2003).) The inquiries may identify wrongdoing by some of the people involved but they also contend that 'the system' was at fault. It could be, for example, organisational culture. More will be said about this aspect of risk-taking in Chapter 8.

Rethinking 'danger' and 'risk'

A map, or conceptual overview, indicating how the different parts of risk-taking can and should interrelate, has been described. A five-'level' model of risk has also been outlined. The first, and perhaps the second, of those levels were readily recognised. They are how we traditionally and readily think about risk and danger. The third may be associated with legal perspectives on liability for risk-taking. But the argument is not that one of the five levels provides a better perspective on risk than another. Rather, it is that our traditional definitions of 'risk', and our approach to risk-taking, are dangerously narrow. Improvements could be made at each 'level'.

A reconceptualisation of 'risk' was identified by Steadman and colleagues (1993). These workers were concerned about the risk posed by a very small number of people with mental disorders. They suggested that a focus on the needs of judges and courts was giving way to a focus on the practical needs of risk-takers. That must be welcomed. It also indicated a growing recognition of the processual nature of risk-taking. But neither of these changes or trends means that the law has less relevance to risk-taking. Its approach may have to be different, indeed more appropriate. Instead of just concentrating upon the responsibility, and possible legal liability, of the individual risk decision-makers, this five-fold model could encourage courts to focus upon the responsibility of managers, supervisors and employers for the quality of decision-making processes and support structures. The possibilities for a fresh and more vigorous approach to improving all aspects of risk-taking, emphasising the responsibilities of everyone involved, will be developed in the following chapters.

CHAPTER 3

The Law: From Judging to Supporting Decision-making

Introduction

This chapter explains the key legal concepts relevant to risk-taking. We are conscious that many people believe that the law makes risk-taking more difficult. (This belief was partly responsible for the passing of the Compensation Act 2006, which is described below.) This belief is wrong: although the law requires reasonable professional conduct, it actually supports risk-takers. It can recognise their problems and values, rather than undermine them. In practice competent risk-takers have only one thing to fear from the law: being able to prove the facts of their case. So, whilst this chapter is about the law, the importance of the evidence is emphasised.

Imagine you have taken a difficult risk decision. You are proud of your decision because, despite the intellectual and emotional difficulties, you were rigorous and careful in working your way through the issues. You are satisfied that your decision, and the reasoning process that got you there, would be supported by many co-professionals. But can you prove that? Can you produce evidence to show, to your colleagues or to a court, what information and processes you used and how, in reaching your decisions? If not – ironically – you might lose any litigation or be criticised by any inquiry that results, not because you made a bad risk decision, not because the legal tests were against you, but because cases can be lost on the facts, rather than the law. Although we now proceed to write about the law, *always* remember the importance of being able to prove the facts of your case. Good record-keeping will not only help you prove your version of the facts, if that should be necessary, but it will also help you to work through the complexities of risk-taking and maximise your opportunities to learn from the experience, whether it leads to harm or success.

When describing the law of negligence – which is the key area of law for judging risk-taking – this chapter will distinguish between the 'duty of care' and the 'standard of care'. It is emphasised that, whilst the meaning and the extent of 'the *duty* of care' is determined by judges (i.e. it is an issue of law), in practice 'the *standard* of care' is determined by the professionals concerned (i.e. it is an issue of fact). That last sentence is qualified with the expression 'in practice', because, as will be explained, the courts do reserve a right to declare that professionals' standards are too low. But they very rarely use this power. So it may be declared that, in practice, the standard of care is about matters of fact. Yes, the judges do decide what the standard of care is – how well the risk decision should have been made. Yes, they declare what the professionals ought to have done, or ought not to have done. But they do that as part of their fact-finding, not their law-declaring, role. Judges listen to what the professionals (the expert witnesses on the disputed issue) say. They are investigating what the standard of care, which applies to that case, is. If, as has occasionally happened, a judge declares a preference for a particular standard of care rather than simply finds what the apt standard is, the case will be appealed – successfully. The judge will have made an error of law. His or her job is to find, as a matter of fact, the applicable standard rather than to express a preference.

Why are we making such a fuss over these points in the introduction? First, because they are so important, and yet so often overlooked. Second, because one of our major themes is to help reduce risk decision-makers' fears of being blamed or sued, or both. If risk-takers can demonstrate that their decision and the processes involved in reaching it were, as a matter of fact, consistent with contemporary professional practices, then they have not been negligent. If they can demonstrate that fact with ease then fewer people will begin proceedings against them because it will be clear that they will lose and have to pay higher legal costs. Or if a journalist, for example, wishes to imply that a professional risk-taker should be blamed, then he or she will be able to respond promptly by demonstrating that the alleged poor practice is actually well within professional standards. In order to achieve this it is recommended that professional risk-takers develop 'risk-taking policies', although lots of other expressions would cover the same ground. Chapter 8 includes suggestions for topics which a 'risk policy' could cover.

Although 'risk' is discussed and debated by lawyers (see Steele 2004) as well as other disciplines, it is not a technical term. It is not a 'term of art' for lawyers. We do not have a 'law of risk-taking'. Rather, there are a number of areas of law which affect what risk-takers do. The two legal concepts most closely connected with 'risk' are 'recklessness' and 'negligence'. The former is most closely associated with the criminal law, the latter with civil law. Both of these will be considered but much greater emphasis will be placed on negligence. Both of those concepts are concerned with the quality of the risk decision-making and management. But critical issues also arise in relation to whose decision it is and whose values are taken into account. Issues of capacity and competence to make risk decisions, or to consent to others making them for you, also need to be considered.

'Recklessness'

As authors we are prepared to take a risk. We believe that the likelihood of our readers being charged with a crime for the risks that they take in a professional capacity is so low that we are justified in spending much less time and space on criminal liability for recklessness than on the civil law of negligence. (No, we quickly add, it does not follow that we believe you are going to be sued! Rather, the law of negligence has had such a significant effect on shaping professional risk-taking practices that it deserves much more space.) But criminal liability for recklessness is possible. Risk-takers are sometimes found to have been reckless and are convicted of a crime, including manslaughter. So we must provide some explanation. But the law of homicide, of which it is part, is being reviewed in England and Wales. It needs changing, not least for the sake of professional risk-takers. The Law Commission, a statutory body established to consider and propose changes to our laws, has made recommendations for significant changes (Law Commission 2006). At the time of writing the government is considering the proposals.

In essence, to be guilty of a crime you must (a) cause (b) something that is prohibited (which lawyers call the *actus reus* of the crime) (c) with a state of mind or quality of behaviour (which lawyers call the *mens rea* of the offence), but (d) without special circumstances which would constitute a defence to that crime. Note, first, that you can cause a crime by positive acts of commission, doing something that causes the *actus reus*. But you can also cause a consequence, and a crime, by failing to act. So avoiding risk-taking is not a guaranteed way of avoiding liability, either in civil or criminal law. There will be criminal liability (the other three requirements for a crime being assumed) for an omission to act, including an omission to take a proper risk, if you owed the victim a 'duty of care'. However, you should note that a 'duty of care' in this criminal law context means something very different from 'duty of care' in the civil law of negligence, to be discussed in detail below. In the criminal law 'duty of care' is limited to categories such as very close family relationships, contractual duties to support (which could include some of the professional risk-takers covered by this book), those who voluntarily adopt a duty to care for others, and those who originally caused a risk and failed to remove victims from it. (For fuller details see a criminal law textbook, such as Ormerod (2005)). So criminal liability for a professional omitting to take a risk is also possible, even if unlikely.

Of the four requirements for criminal liability, the most important in practice is the *mens rea*. Note that this can refer either to the mental state of the person accused of the crime (intending to kill is a *mens rea* of murder) or to the quality of behaviour involved (such as dangerous or careless driving). The first category is called 'subjective' because it requires the jury to find, as a matter of fact, that the defendant was 'thinking' in the proscribed manner (e.g. intending, foreseeing or knowing). The second category is called 'objective' because now the jury should pay no attention to what, if anything, the defendant was 'thinking'. Rather, the jury should simply judge the – objective – quality of the behaviour; the jury members should decide whether it was 'dangerous', 'careless' and so forth, according to their standards as reasonable people. So, in order to discover whether a risk-taker has committed a crime, we need – in particular – to discover what the *mens rea* of the offence charged involves.

Murder can only be committed if the defendant intended death or serious injury. Thus it is, confidently, assumed that no more need be said about that crime for this audience. However, some judges have devised a special meaning of 'intention' so that, it may be argued, it is really a category of recklessness (Ormerod 2005). Otherwise 'recklessness' is a key *mens rea* for manslaughter. Notice that negligence is not enough either to constitute recklessness or to justify a manslaughter verdict. Negligence is, exclusively, an objective *mens rea*; 'recklessness' has a subjective meaning of acting although aware of the likelihood of harm, and an objective meaning, but only of a very high degree of negligence. So manslaughter can be committed if the defendant was 'reckless'. That might cover some professional risk decision-makers. The problem is that, at the time of writing, the government in England and Wales is considering the Law Commission's (2006) proposals to reform this law.

Key issues include whether 'reckless' should have an objective as well as a subjective meaning. If someone is aware that what he or she is proposing to do could cause harm to another, and nevertheless acts, then he or she will be adjudged – subjectively – reckless. Under the current, and likely future law, he or she will be guilty of manslaughter if death results. The jury will have been told to be sure, beyond any reasonable doubt, that the risk-taker was aware that harm could occur to a person but he or she nevertheless proceeded, and caused death. But, under current law, it is also possible to be 'reckless' when you behave very badly, even though you are unaware of that. This is an objective test because the jury is told to ignore what, if anything, a person was thinking about and to focus exclusively upon the quality of his or her conduct. Our most senior court has decided that it is manslaughter if a jury considers that someone's conduct, 'having regard to the risk of death involved, ... was so bad in all the circumstances as to amount in their judgement to a criminal act or omission' (Lord Mackay in *Adomako* [1994] 3 All ER 79 at 87) and it causes death. There is no requirement that the individual thought there was any risk, provided that there was an 'objective' risk of death.

This law is in a very unsatisfactory state. Among the problems has been a judicial tendency to refer to a 'serious' risk, or 'the' risk without making it clear whether the degree of outcome, the degree of likelihood or a combination of them is being referred to. Professional risk-takers do, and should, think about the harm that might arise from their risk-taking. Thus they will regularly – and properly – consider potential outcomes, such as physical harm and even death, even though they conclude that those outcomes are highly unlikely. But, unless the degree of likelihood is qualified by words such as 'serious' or (much more appropriately even if it is still vague) 'high', the risk-taker will be liable – if death should happen – because he or she was aware. That is enough to satisfy the definition of subjective recklessness. But risk-takers should be encouraged – not discouraged – from thinking about possible outcomes. The person who does not think about that degree of loss cannot be, subjectively, reckless. Further, the *Adomako* decision by the House of Lords leaves it to juries to decide when they think the behaviour, including the risk decision, should be regarded as serious enough to call it manslaughter. Not only is it, properly, the judges' job to say what is and is not a crime, but juries could be affected by all manner of surrounding factors, such as the defendant's appearance and demeanour, rather than by important conceptual distinctions. However, at least, that test for manslaughter requires that the risk be of death, not just injury.

It must be hoped that, whatever the Government decides about the Law Commission's proposals for law reform (2006), it reduces the risk of risk-taking professionals being unfairly criminalised for their risk decisions. Ferner and McDowell (2006) examined all the cases of doctors charged with manslaughter in the UK between 1795 and 2005. Whilst the numbers are low, and the majority were acquitted, prosecutions have increased since the 1990s. Most were for what the authors argue were slips and mistakes. However, the problem is not just that risk-takers might be criminalised but, much more likely, that they will avoid taking apt decisions because of a fear of criminal responsibility. For example the Law Commission (2006, para. 9.6) is proposing that 'killings intended to cause injury or fear or risk of injury where the killer was aware that his or her conduct involved a serious risk of causing death' would constitute second-degree murder. (We do not, currently, have degrees of murder in English law.) But analyse that proposal more closely. Professionals could, quite justifiably, decide (i.e. intend) to cause a risk of injury whilst being aware that there was a risk that death would result. The risk of injury could be morally and socially justified on the basis of low likelihood, low seriousness of outcome, high level of benefits, high likelihood of benefits or a combination thereof. So it all depends upon what 'a serious risk' means. Given that the outcome has to be death, it must be inferred that 'serious' only refers to likelihood. That is the Law Commission's intention because it goes on to recommend that 'a risk should be regarded as "serious" if it is more than insignificant or remote' (Law Commission 2006, paras 3.40 and 9.12). The Law Commission (2006, paras. 3.36–3.39) considered specifying a level of likelihood for 'serious' but rejected it. It was concluded that it was an expression which juries could understand without the need for any embellishment. We disagree and disapprove, strongly. The Law Commission has, effectively, given the phrase 'serious risk' the meaning of 'any risk'. If that is to be its meaning then 'serious' is superfluous; it adds nothing (other than to exclude the insignificant or remote). It is liable to interfere seriously with professional risk-taking.

Imagine that a psychiatrist and colleagues decide to allow Victor, a patient who has been detained because suicidal and self-harming, to leave the hospital for a day. They do not intend injury to anyone, but they do intend to take the risk of Victor injuring himself, with some members of the care team likely contemplating that he might cause injury to members of the public. They are aware that their risk decision, taken for the very best of motives (professional, legal and moral), carries with it a risk that, although by Victor's own acts, may cause his death. The team members may reassure themselves that, fortunately, that risk of death is not serious, meaning it is low likelihood. But, likely unknown to them (the authorities in rationality and madness), 'serious' actually means anything more than remote or insignificant, so that what they considered to be 'low' was, in law, 'serious'. That Victor killed himself provides no defence. For a crime it is not necessary that your – or the team's – acts were the main, or the last, causes; it is enough that they had an operating effect at the time (Ormerod 2005). Victor did what the detention was designed to prevent, namely injured himself. So being allowed off the hospital grounds must have had some effect. And Victor's relatives might press for an inquiry and prosecution because those 'supposed to be looking after' him took that risk.

It is not just self-harming cases that might fall foul of a new second-degree murder definition. Consider the physician who intentionally takes the risk that a patient will experience side-effects from a drug (i.e. physical injury), and is aware that the risk of death, while not 'serious' in any sensible use of the word, is more than 'remote' or 'insignificant'. He or she is risking prosecution for manslaughter, irrespective of motives to remove pain and so on, when that just-more-than-remote risk of death occurs, as it, by definition, will, within a range of cases.

So, if these proposals are adopted by the Government, and enacted by Parliament, it is important that professional risk-takers are cautioned about the special (entirely inappropriate) meaning given to 'serious' in second-degree murder and that their use of the term in discussions about risk-taking could hold serious ramifications. It may be replied that no prosecutor would bring such a case. But that is a totally inadequate response, however true. Professional risk-takers are likely to wish to obey the law, and should be encouraged to do so. Thus they will be influenced by the actual words, and ascribed meanings, of legal tests. They are unlikely to know the details of prosecutorial discretion, and be unwilling to risk it.

It would be better if an earlier formulation of the proposed offence, by the Law Commission (2005), was adopted. This proposed that one form of second-degree murder would be 'unlawful killings where the offender realised that his or her conduct involved an unjustified risk of causing death but went ahead anyway' (Law Commission 2005, para. 1.38). That word 'unjustified' would have provided the protection that professional risk-takers need. It would be better still if its meaning were made explicit. Risk-takers should be able to justify their decisions by demonstrating that the reasonably predicted degrees of harm, and/or their likelihood, were so low that seeking the anticipated benefits was a justifiable decision, at the time it was taken.

The Law Commission (2006, paras 3.60 and 9.13) also recommend that it be manslaughter by gross negligence, if you cause a death by imposing a risk of death which (a) you were capable of appreciating and (b) would be obvious to a reasonable person. This definition is designed to cover objectively reckless people; it does not matter that they were unaware of the risk that was taken, only that they (a) could have appreciated it and (b) the risk was so clear that reasonable people would conclude it had been obvious. The reference to being capable of appreciating the risk is designed to exclude people whose knowledge or skills are so limited that they could not have appreciated the risk, even if drawn to their attention. Ironically, although a less serious offence, this test is unlikely to trouble professional risk-takers. They are unlikely to be *un*aware of the risks involved. Even if they were unaware of some details, for example of another side-effect, they were still aware that they were risk-taking.

Negligence

Those who are reckless or grossly negligent, and commit a crime, will be punished, if they are proved guilty beyond reasonable doubt. But 'negligence' is also a civil law concept, where different procedures and criteria apply. Those who are negligent, in terms of the civil law, may be sued and required to pay compensation, if they are proved liable on a balance of probabilities. The criminal law is concerned with punishment, with penalising. The civil law seeks to compensate; it provides money compensation to the value considered necessary to put the victim back into the position he or she would have been in if he or she had not been the victim of the other person's negligence. However, notice that the amount of compensation awarded by the courts for civil law negligence is regularly much more than a criminal court would impose as a fine. Because of this insurance plays an important practical role. Claimants (those who sue for negligence) will be advised, by lawyers, that there is little point in suing someone if he or she does not have the money, personally or via an insurance policy, to pay the compensation awarded.

It also makes 'vicarious liability' important (discussed more fully in Chapter 9). Employers are – vicariously – liable for the negligent acts of their employees, provided that those acts are related to their employment (Rogers 2006). This is very important for professional risk-takers. It is the risk decision-maker's conduct that will be investigated and analysed in any proceedings but, if negligence is discovered, it is the employer who must pay the compensation. The rationale is that, but for being employed to do that work, the employee would not have been available to cause the negligence. Hovever, in practice, the more important point is that the employer has the money or the insurance policy, or both, to meet the compensation claim. If you take, or advise others about taking risks, but are not employed to do so, then you should ensure that you are insured in case you are sued. You may believe that you will never make a negligent decision. Even if you are right about that, it does not follow that a court will see it the same way. (The insurance premiums will reflect another risk-taker's estimate of the likelihood you will be sued, and for how much.)

The amount of proving necessary to convict someone of a crime is much higher than for proving someone liable for civil law negligence. To be guilty of a crime, for example manslaughter because of a reckless or grossly negligent risk decision, then the prosecution will have to prove their case beyond any reasonable doubt. However, to sue you in the civil courts for making a negligent decision, the claimant only has to have a more believable version of events than yours, or 'on the balance of probabilities' as it is more technically stated. Notice that there is no baseline requirement; judges cannot dismiss cases just because neither side has much evidence to support their story. Again, the importance of being able to prove your version of the facts is emphasised. In particular, note that you, as the professional risk-taker (i.e. skilled and experienced), will be seen as the person more likely, and/or expected, to have good-quality notes and records. If you do not have such notes, for example documentation to demonstrate all the outcomes you contemplated and how you valued and assessed their likelihood, then that absence is likely to count against you.

The two meanings of 'negligence'

We will now concentrate on the civil law approach to negligence. Unfortunately, the legal word 'negligence' is confusing because it is regularly used in two very different senses. First, it can describe the quality of some behaviour: he drove negligently, she made a negligent risk decision. Second, it can refer to an area of the law, a legal topic such as defamation, crime or contract. The first sense uses 'negligent' as an adjective or adverb; the second sense uses it as a noun, as the title of a topic. Behaving negligently (in the first sense) is just one of *five* critical tests which have to be satisfied for someone to be adjudged negligent (in the second sense). So it is possible to behave negligently, satisfying one of the five tests, but not be liable for negligence, because one or more of the other four tests were not satisfied. It may seem strange but it is perfectly possible to state correctly: 'Liam's risk assessment was negligent, but he is not liable for negligence' or, more confusingly but still correctly, 'Shirley's risk decision was negligent, but she was not negligent.' Liam's negligent behaviour might not have caused any harm, so there cannot be liability for negligence. Shirely may have behaved negligently and some people might have been injured; but Shirley may not have owed any of them a duty of care.

The five requirements of 'negligence'

To be liable for negligence:

1. You must have owed a *duty* of care to the person injured (victim).

2. You must have broken the *standard* of care that applies under that duty of care.

3. Your breach of the standard of care must have *caused* the victim's losses.

4. The losses which you caused must be of a kind that the law compensates.

5. Those legally recognised losses must have been reasonably foreseeable.

If any one of those five requirements (or tests) is not satisfied then there can be no liability in the civil law of negligence. But it does not follow, just because one or more tests are not satisfied, that nothing could be done. In particular focus on test number 2. If Liam broke the standard of care, but did not break one of the other four tests, then he could not be sued for negligence. But it would still be perfectly possible – and proper – to take action against him. Test 2 refers to the quality of the behaviour; was the risk decision appropriate, properly reached and taken? If test 2 is broken then Liam's supervisors, employers, professional bodies and others are entitled to criticise him and take action. It is hoped that they will ensure, at the very least, that appropriate learning opportunities are gained. Employers are not limited to acting only when someone is injured, or something is damaged. They are entitled to act, and really should act, on poor-quality decisions, or other conduct, irrespective of whether harm results.

Breaching the standard of care (test 2 above) will regularly equate with professional misconduct. As will be seen it means that someone behaved in a manner, or made a decision, which no responsible group of professional colleagues would endorse. That would justify, arguably should require, action by others responsible for standards. Perhaps someone (e.g. the pilot on our flight) did behave badly but, by good fortune, nobody was injured. Because test 4, the requirement for legally recognised losses, has not been satisfied, neither the pilot nor his or her employers, can be sued for negligence. But it would still be very proper to act on the bad behaviour. Indeed, failing to do so could cause problems in the future, could contribute to a system or culture that does not learn from mistakes. Equally, as we will shortly discover, there are some groups of professional risk-takers (e.g. child protection professionals) who do not owe their 'victims' a duty of care, in the sense of test 1. They may make a bad decision; they may breach the standard of care that would otherwise arise in terms of test 2. However, they cannot be sued for negligence (see below). But someone should do something appropriate whenever there has been poor professional practice, irrespective of whether anyone can be sued for negligence.

An alternative to suing someone for negligence could be making a formal complaint or establishing a formal inquiry. Such inquiries do not investigate whether there was legal liability for negligence. They cannot award compensation. Nevertheless they are very likely to involve investigations similar to establishing whether test 2, the standard of care, was broken. If it is believed there was negligent conduct an inquiry is not constrained from declaring blame and responsibility just because one or more of the other four tests for negligence is not established. So even if certain risk-takers cannot be sued successfully, because one of the tests other than breach of the standard of care is not broken, they can be identified and criticised in other ways. So it is always best not to breach the standard of care.

Test 1: The duty of care

We are not responsible for everything we do, or to everyone affected by what we do, even though we have been negligent. The first test, the duty of care, determines *who* is covered by the law, *who* can have a remedy. The victim of our negligent action or inaction must have been owed a duty of care. This is decided as a matter of law by the judges. Most of the law of negligence is still derived from the common law so we have to look to precedent decisions of the senior courts, rather than to any statutory definitions. Unfortunately, the test(s) for deciding who is, and who is not, owed a duty of care are not always clear (Rogers 2006). Certain categories are very clear; for example, surgeons owe a duty of care to their patients. But other categories are still disputed. The judges often explain that we owe a duty of care to our 'neighbours', but then they use that word in a manner which ordinary English language users would not recognise. And there are some categories where there clearly would be a duty of care but the judges have decided that 'public policy' requires that there not be a duty.

The principal factors, other than public policy, determining whether there will be a duty of care are proximity, foreseeability and reasonableness (Rogers 2006, p.143). You are driving you car. Who are the people, within proximity to you, whom you can reasonably foresee that you could injure by negligent driving? Clearly you could injure your passengers, other drivers, their passengers and pedestrians, as well as vehicles using that stretch of road. That is easily foreseen. Few would consider that observation to be unreasonable. Indeed, it is rather obvious. That is helpful because you do, when you are a driver, owe all of those people a duty of care. Now let us be imaginative. Imagine that you drive negligently and cause a crash, on that stretch of road, during which a hub cap from one of your wheels flies off and, Frisbee-like, floats over the terraced houses beside the road and lands, injuring someone sun-bathing in a garden. Do you owe that person a duty of care? No. That is not reasonable; in particular, it is not reasonably fore-seeable, and the back garden is not proximate to where the negligence occurred. So whilst most duties of care are now well established, the courts have to decide on matters of degree when new relationships are put to them for decision.

Clearly, professional risk-takers, in the context of this book, will owe duties of care. But not to everyone! They owe (subject to public policy rules discussed below) a duty of care to all those people who are, or will be, closely related to, or affected by, the implementation of their risk decisions or advice. Imagine the issue is whether a sex offender, living in the community, should be publicly named as such. Can we foresee, without being unreason-able about it, that he could be injured by that revelation? Yes. Imagine the issue is whether a patient with a mental disorder and known proclivity for violence should be discharged from a hospital? Can we reasonably foresee that he or she might self-harm, for example? Yes, clearly all doctors, nurses, social workers, probation officers and similar owe a duty of care to their cur-rent patients or clients, to those they are assessing for a service (they could cause loss by a negligence assessment), and to former patients and clients at least for a reasonable period after discharge. Can we reasonably foresee that if we do not do our jobs properly then our colleagues may be injured? Cer-tainly that is foreseeable in hospitals and other institutions and some other circumstances. (If you are unsure about this then clearly you need to watch more hospital and other dramas on television.)

What about members of the public? If we do our jobs negligently is it not reasonably foreseeable that they will be injured? The answer seems obvious; of course they will. But stop; who will be injured? Who will this member of the public be? Can you name him or her? If not, can you find a way of predicting exactly who will be injured? Is this necessary? Yes! Remember that the reason we have a 'duty of care' is to decide who is, and is not, to be protected. In other words it is to limit the duty to some, not to all, people. If we were to conclude that any member of the public might be injured as a consequence of our negligent risk-taking, then there would be no point in having a duty of care because it would cover everyone. We have a duty of care because only some people, not every member of the public, are covered.

Christopher Clunis was discharged, after some treatment for a mental disorder, from a London hospital. Some days later he attacked and killed a man who was entirely innocent and totally unrelated and unknown to him, on a London Underground platform (Ritchie, Dick and Lingham 1994). Was it reasonably foreseeable that the patient would attack that individual? No; indeed, the fact that the victim had nothing whatsoever to do with the former patient, beyond sharing a London Underground platform, made it more unreasonably foreseeable. We may, we should, feel for the victim's partner and we certainly should demand that action is taken in order to learn whatever possible from the experience. But, unless we are going to have a compensation scheme which automatically covers everyone (and a good case can be made for doing so), a line has to be drawn somewhere. And that line, currently, is the duty of care. The particular victim was not reasonably foreseeable. If the victim played a special role in relation to the risk, for example was specially selected to accommodate the discharged patient, then the answer could be different. Just as there is a duty of care to co-workers, as it is reasonably foreseeable that they could be injured and who they are, so it should be with regard to the person with a special role.

Professional risk-takers do not owe a legal duty of care to some victims, because those particular individuals were not reasonably foreseeable. That is one rule. There is another rule, known as 'public policy'. The courts reserve the power to decide that some actors, including professional risk-takers, do not owe a duty of care to the victims of their action, even where there is negligent conduct and the victims were reasonably foreseeable, because there is a more important public policy rule. For example, imagine that an individual is invited to give expert evidence, in court, because the judge or jury need his or her assistance. Is it reasonably foreseeable, if the expert gives poor-quality (negligent) evidence, that one or more of the parties to the case will be injured? Surely yes; so there must be a duty of care. No. The courts have decided (*Meadow* v. *General Medical Council* [2006] EWHC 146 (Admin); *Stanton* v. *Callaghan* [2000] 1 QB 75) that the more important goal is that experts should feel able and willing to give their best advice to the courts. Their primary duty is to the court. So expert witnesses do not owe a duty of care, in the law of negligence, for the quality of the evidence they give, even to the parties who pay them.

There are a number of other areas where the public interest, the judges have decided, requires that there be no legal duty of care. A category of particular importance to us might be termed 'public sector investigators'. We know that this includes some police and some childcare protection investigators, including those who must decide whether to remove or return a child from or to his or her family because of the presence or absence of a risk of abuse. But which particular risk-takers? And will it always be the case? To answer such questions we need to explain the reasoning behind the decisions, and that is easiest by referring to cases involving the police.

It is accepted that the police can be sued for negligent management, or handling, of the people they come into direct and close (proximate) contact with. It is just the same as doctors or nurses and patients, teachers and pupils, social workers or probation officers and their clients. So, for example, police officers failed to pass on knowledge that a prisoner was a suicide risk. A court decided that they had a duty of care and also broke the standard of care (*Kirkham* v. *Chief Constable of Greater Manchester Police* [1990] 2 QB 283). In another case it was decided the police owed a duty of care to a suspect whom they had arrested. But that duty ended when the suspect escaped from their custody, and injured himself in the process. He had taken himself out of their duty (*Vellino* v. *Chief Constable of Greater Manchester* [2002] 1 WLR 218). Notice the proximity or control between the police and the suspects. The police take extensive control over, and freedom away from, suspects when they detain them. That degree of control, or proximity, makes it rather obvious that there will be a duty of care. Analogies can be created in relation to children or clients with disabilities. But investigations are different.

The 'Yorkshire Ripper' murdered 23 women. Relatives of his last victim believed the police were negligent in the way that they investigated the case; that but for police incompetence their daughter would still be alive. So they issued proceedings against the police for negligence. The allegations were never tested in court. The police asked the court to dismiss the claim, because it was not based on valid law. And the courts, right up to the House of Lords, agreed (*Hill* v. *Chief Constable of West Yorkshire* [1989] 1 AC 53). In very clear language it was stated that police investigators did not owe a duty of care to victims of possibly poorly conducted investigations. In particular they argued that it would be wrong if the police were forever worried that they could be sued for making mistakes, that money which could be spent in catching more criminals would be spent in compensating victims. They did not need to make that decision. They could have justified it in terms comparable to the Clunis case (Ritchie *et al.* 1994); the particular victim was not 'proximate' to the police in the sense that she was not known to be at any more risk than other women in Yorkshire, at least of her age range.

That was distinctively different in *Osman and another* v. *Ferguson and another* ([1993] 4 All ER 344). Here, a schoolteacher formed an improper interest in a pupil. He much more than harassed the boy, another boy and their families. The case papers suggest that the police did many things wrong and missed several opportunities to intervene. But it also appears they were acting on the advice of a psychiatrist who had seen the teacher. The teacher was eventually arrested, after he had shot and killed the boy's father and shot the school's deputy head teacher and killed his son. On arrest he is reported to have said to the police: 'What took you so long?' Here, the police could not argue that they were unaware of who was threatened, or who was doing the threatening. There was proximity. But, once again, the courts dismissed the case before there was any inquiry into the facts. The police investigators did not owe a duty of care to the victims, on the basis of the case of *Hill* v. *Chief Constable of West Yorkshire* ([1989] 1 AC 53).

The case was appealed to the European Court of Human Rights (ECHR) on the basis that the decision breached the Convention. That Court found that Article 6(1), which guarantees a fair trial within a reasonable time, had been broken (*Osman* v. *UK* (2000) 29 EHRR 245). But it was a very narrow decision (Hoyano 1999). In essence, the decision was that the House of Lords should never have said 'never'. The ECHR's objection was that the House of Lords was assuming, or deciding in advance, that public policy would always outweigh private interests. The ECHR was not denying the importance of, or the right of, the British courts to declare that some people do not owe a duty of care to others. It insisted that it should be possible for individuals to argue that public policy should not apply to them for very special reasons.

The ECHR decision may appear to be a repudiation of the British courts' decisions in the cases of *Hill* and *Osman*, but little has changed. Duwayne Brooks was with his friend Stephen Lawrence when they were savagely, racially, attacked. A Committee of Inquiry condemned the police investigation (Macpherson 1999). So Mr Brooks sought to sue the police for negligence. But, in *Brooks* v. *Commissioner of Police for the Metropolis and Others* ([2005] 2 All ER 489), the House of Lords decided that Mr Brooks could not sue the police because they did not owe him a duty of care. And, at the same time and on the same day, the judges decided that victims of alleged negligence by child protection professionals could not sue, because they too were not owed a duty of care. *JD* v. *East Berkshire Community Health NHS Trust and Others* ([2005] 2 FLR 284) involved a number of similar cases decided together. In each case a child protection professional had either made a decision to intervene, or failed to intervene, to protect a child. Unfortunately, it proved to have been the wrong decision. One of the five judges in the House of Lords would have allowed the cases to proceed. He wished to see if the victims had any private interests which could be more important than the public policy arguments. The other four judges agreed that the public interest, in those professional risk-takers not owing a duty of care, was clearly more important.

To try to get around this prohibition on claims of negligence lawyers, in 2007, brought claims based upon the Human Rights Act 1998. In *Van Colle* v. *Chief Constable of Hertfordshire* ([2007] EWCA Civ 325) a key witness in a forthcoming trial was killed. The police officer responsible for assessing the witness's need for protection was subsequently disciplined for his inactions. (He was unaware of force rules although it could also be doubted, given the murderer's lack of history of serious violence, whether the actual attack was reasonably predictable.) Anticipating that the court would say the police owed no duty of care, the victim's parents did not sue for negligence. Instead they sued for failure, under Article 2 of the European Convention on Human Rights, to protect the victim's right to life. The Court of Appeal agreed and awarded £25,000 in compensation. However, three different judges, although also sitting as the Court of Appeal, decided *Lawrence* v. *Pembrokeshire CC* ([2007] EWCA Civ 446) differently. There a mother complained that child protection officers had wrongly placed her children on the child protection register, causing her psychiatric injury. Again the mother did not claim for negligence as the court would have said, in line with the cases mentioned above, that she could not succeed as she was not owed a duty of care. Instead she used the Human Rights Act 1998, maintaining that her Article 8 rights to a family life had been violated. The Court dismissed her claim. They decided that Article 8, and the 1998 Act, did not give her the rights to sue for compensation and that to decide otherwise would conflict with the House of Lords *East Berkshire* decision, described in the previous paragraph. Whilst the cases clearly differ, one about the police and the other child protection, one about Article 2 and the other Article 8, the underlying issues and principles are the same. A House of Lords decision is needed to sort out the mess. A good case can be made for all police officers, and all social workers, owing duties of care to their clients and their immediate relatives. But it is indefensible that different legal results should depend upon which heading of law you use.

Professional risk-takers may be relieved to read that not only is their legal duty of care (which is not the same as their moral or, arguably, their professional duty of care) (a) not owed to the world at large, but that the judges will sometimes use their conception of the public interest to protect them by (b) denying a duty of care in certain circumstances. Mental health practitioners and parole decision-makers might wish to argue that they are in a comparable position to child protection workers. They also have to make difficult risk decisions, on behalf of the public, about who needs to be detained because of mental health and continuing danger issues, or where discretionary life-sentence offenders are subject to recall to prison. But, as was stressed above, it does not follow that those risk-takers cannot be criticised or investigated. Litigation for negligence in the civil courts will fail because there was no duty of care. But employers, professional bodies and so on can and should take action against those responsible for a bad risk decision or other unprofessional conduct. Where they are unsure about the nature of the conduct they can and should investigate, such as by establishing an inquiry. So the absence of a legal duty of care does not justify any reduction in the quality of professional conduct. It just prevents a particular form of remedy. So it could be wise for professional risk-takers to assume that they owe a duty of care, and to concentrate upon not breaching the standard of care, irrespective of whether they may be sued.

Test 2: The standard of care

The duty of care is about *who* is covered, about people. The standard of care is about *what* must be done or *how*, about standards of behaviour. It is about doing, or not doing, what reasonable people would do in those circumstances. It is an objective standard. Where the people involved are taking professional decisions then it is the standard of reasonable people in that profession, at the level of the post involved (*Wilsher* v. *Essex Area Health*

Authority [1987] QB 730). The key points to appreciate, for our purposes, are (a) how judges apply the relevant professions' standards and, thereby, (b) how professions can help themselves by articulating those standards. This rule allows the professions concerned to develop a preventive approach towards the law. Instead of being anxious about what judges might decide, practitioners can get pro-actively involved in articulating the values, the principles and standards that ought to be applied to them. This is considered to be so important that Chapter 8 is, substantially, devoted to developing supportive frameworks and ideas.

The judge will, in individual cases, decide whether the standard of care has been broken. But he or she does not apply his or her personal standards or preferences. (When that happens the Court of Appeal overturns the decision (*Burne* v. *A* [2006] EWCA Civ 24; *Maynard* v. *W Midlands RHA* [1985] 1 All ER 635).) The judge has to discover what the standards are that apply to that case. The standard of care is what a responsible body of co-professionals would do. The judge has to discover what that means in the context of a particular case, with reference to the particular type of risk decision. In order to discover what co-professionals would do expert witnesses are called and asked to give evidence about current professional practice. There may be disagreement over what current practice involves. Some witnesses might say that no competent professional, behaving properly, would have done that, would have taken that risk. Other witnesses might, effectively, reply: 'Oh, yes they would!' Judges have to resolve such disputes. Note that it is a factual dispute; would or would not a competent professional have done that? The judge chooses between the parties and their witnesses on the basis of which he or she thinks is correctly describing what current professional standards are, not what he or she thinks the standards should be. He or she is deciding, as a fact, what is professionally acceptable. This is not a lay person deciding for the experts, or any interference with professional standards. It is a case of sorting out a factual disagreement between co-professionals. If the professionals disagree with a judge's decision about their standards, then they should blame themselves. If their standards had been clearer then a dispute would have been less likely, indeed the case would have been unlikely ever to get to court.

> The law here is clearly that the defendant is not negligent if he acts in accordance with a practice accepted at the time as proper by a responsible body of professional opinion skilled in the particular type of activity,

even though there is a body of professional opinion which might adopt a different technique. It is not the court's function to choose between schools of professional thought. (Rogers 2006, pp.251–252, references omitted)

Mrs Partington, an elderly lady, was walking one morning, aided by a stick, when she saw a young woman approaching her. She thought that the young woman wished to speak with her so she stopped. Instead the young woman suddenly pushed her over, causing her to fall on her back and break her wrist. It transpired that the young woman had a learning disability. She was medically described as having autistic tendencies and being 'predictably unpredictable'. One week in four she spent in residential care. During such a week a senior staff member in the care unit had asked a colleague to take the young woman, and another client, for a walk (*Partington* v. *London Borough of Wandsworth* [1990] Fam Law 468).

Was the senior member of the residential unit, who took the risk of recommending the walk and managing it by allocating one member of staff for two clients, negligent? Was the accompanying staff member negligent in the manner she exercised care over the two clients? Clearly, they owed a duty of care to other people using the path that neither they, nor the people for whom they were responsible, would injure them. But did they breach the standard of care?

Why did this case ever get to court? The total claim for compensation was £5080. Many defendants (the local authority in this case) would have decided it would be cheaper, given the legal and other resource costs involved, plus the risk that they might lose the case and then have to pay even more legal costs, to concede the claim and pay up. They could still have insisted that they were not admitting legal liability, and told their staff that they were not accusing them of negligence. Those staff, however, might have felt that, despite the warm words, they were being adjudged negligent and were not receiving support from their superiors. The case would never have reached court if either Mrs Partington's, or the local authority's, lawyers were sure they would lose. But they were not sure because neither side was clear as to what the standard of care, in this case, would involve.

The key legal decision is *Bolam* v. *Friern HMC* ([1957] 2 All ER 118). In this case a consultant psychiatrist risked giving a patient electro-convulsive therapy – without an anaesthetic. Predictably, as this is a compensation claim, the patient was injured. Today it would be clear. Not providing an anaesthetic, in the absence of very special facts, would clearly break the standard of care. *But*, note the date. Practice was different then. Today's anaesthetics were not available then. The judge heard witnesses from the relevant profession. Some would have given an anaesthetic; some would not have done. But that was not the point. It was agreed that a responsible body of co-professionals would have agreed with the decision that was taken. Thus whilst there was a duty of care, it was not broken so there was no liability for negligence. That is the standard – would a responsible body of co-professionals have made the same decision – which applies in professional negligence cases, and which will apply to most, if not all, of the risk decisions contemplated by this book.

Note what the standard does *not* demand, as well as what it does declare. The standard is that of a responsible body of co-professionals. It is not the standard of the best professionals, let alone most of them. A minority professional practice may still – indeed, often will – satisfy the standard of care. Consider how standards change. It used to be that if you attended an accident and emergency department of a hospital you would be seen by a doctor. Nowadays you may be seen and treated by a nurse without ever seeing a doctor. And good thing, where appropriate, too. Someone thinks of a different idea, product, procedure, whatever, and argues that it is better. In this example the original argument was that nurses can diagnose and treat several ailments at least as well as doctors. Sometimes some people agree that the proposals are as good as or better than present practice, and they adopt them. Other times they prove unpopular and controversial. Over time more people may adopt them. Sometimes, from being unusual and the exception, they become normal practice. Indeed, in due course, those one-time radical proposals can become old-fashioned, out of date, reactionary and be replaced by other changes. If the standard of care only meant current professional standards, then improvements, changes, advances, would be impossible. Innovation would, legally, be penalised.

This standard is not perfectly clear. It refers to what a responsible body of co-professionals would do or decide. It is not a simple task of counting up how many people would agree with you, or even what proportion of people. But it seems possible to infer some practical tests. If the practice has been tested, there is supporting quality research, it is taught on a reputable course, is described and discussed in academic or professional journals, then that suggests that it is supported by responsible co-professionals. If it is not regarded as scientific, according to the standards for the appropriate discipline, if it is only adopted or practised by very few people, or in very few places, then that suggests that it would not be supported by a responsible body of co-professionals. The judge, by investigating what the relevant professionals think and do, discovers the standard of care for each case. Effectively the profession, not the judge, lays down the standards. But we must make a critical qualification to this – even though it is of very limited practical significance. If the professions concerned were the last word on the standards then it might be too tempting for them to lower them, artificially. In order to minimise their legal liability they might deflate the standards. So the judges have the last word on what the standards are (see *Bolitho* v. *City & Hackney Health Authority* [1988] AC 232).

The test is objective – what relevant reasonable people would have done or decided – but it varies with the circumstances. The risk of someone losing an eye from doing a particular job may be very low. Thus it could be reasonable to conclude that there was no need for the employers to provide or ensure that staff wore protective goggles. But if one of the employees had already lost one eye the consequences, for him, of losing the other eye would be much more severe than for his colleagues. Thus it could be a breach of the duty of care which employers owe to their staff not to provide him with goggles (*Paris* v. *Stepney Borough Council* [1951] AC 367). That case exemplifies the point that we have been stressing: the law does not penalise sensible risk-taking. However, that case is not binding, even though decided by our highest level of court, as a *factual* example of reasonable risk-taking. Standards can – and do – change. What was regarded as good enough practice in the early 1950s may not be, indeed often will not be, 5, let alone 50, years later. Failing to provide goggles for anyone, however many eyes he or she may have, might breach the standard of care today. Law reports, known to lawyers as precedent decisions, are binding on lower courts with regard to the law that they establish, not on their facts.

The value of the benefits of risk-taking which might be achieved is important in assessing the reasonableness of the particular risk decision. Using a lorry to transport a heavy jack, although not adapted to carry it, would usually be considered negligent. Why else were adaptations designed and usually provided? But what if the jack was urgently required, in order to save the life of someone trapped under a heavy vehicle? That changes things. The courts are alive to the consequence that their decisions might discourage desirable activities (*Tomlinson* v. *Congleton BC* [2003] UKHL 47). It can be entertaining to read newspaper stories which suggest that someone has sued someone else for an apparently daft reason, for example making tea with boiling hot water which could (and did) scald someone. It does not follow that the person suing succeeded (*Bogle* v. *McDonald's Restaurants Ltd* [2002] EWHC 490). Negligence claims can be made for a wide range of reasons, including believing the facts to be different from those found in court or in the belief that, by making a nuisance of themselves, they might be 'bought off' with some money, albeit much less than they claimed.

The standard of care: A discussion

Because of a perception of a 'compensation culture', that people were too readily claiming – and succeeding – in negligence claims, Parliament enacted the Compensation Act 2006. Section 1 declares that:

> A court considering a claim in negligence or breach of statutory duty may, in determining whether the defendant should have taken particular steps to meet a standard of care (whether by taking precautions against a risk or otherwise), have regard to whether a requirement to take those steps might –
>
> (a) prevent a desirable activity from being undertaken at all, to a particular extent or in a particular way, or
>
> (b) discourage persons from undertaking functions in connection with a desirable activity.

But this does not change the existing law! It is a classic example of the then Government's predilection for being 'seen to be doing something' about certain problems, even if that was superfluous and entirely symbolic. The explanatory notes, provided to Members of Parliament as the law was being considered, declare at paragraphs 10 and 11:

> 10. This provision [Section 1] is intended to contribute to improving awareness of this aspect of the law; providing reassurance to the people and organisations who are concerned about possible litigation; and to ensuring that normal activities are not prevented because of the fear of litigation and excessively risk-averse behaviour.

11. This provision is *not concerned with and does not alter the standard of care,* nor the circumstances in which a duty to take that care will be owed. It is solely concerned with the court's assessment of what constitutes reasonable care in the case before it. (Italics added)

Explanatory memoranda have no legal force but it is unlikely that the courts will interpret Section 1 as changing the law. It is disingenuous to argue, as in paragraph 11 above, that the section does not alter the law but, rather, is concerned with how the judges apply it. If it changes how they apply the law it has to change the law! It is also foolish to argue that Section 1 will provide reassurance and reduce fear of litigation. How many people read legislation, let alone to reassure themselves? They could have read court decisions and legal textbooks in order to discover the current law, and be reassured about current law, which this Act does not change. The rest of the Act has useful and important provisions, for example to regulate agencies which handle negligence claims. But risk-takers should not think that Section 1 changes anything, although they could take reassurance from the existence of yet another source which stresses that the courts will be reasonable about judging claims of negligence.

Notice that some lawyers were concerned that the standard of care, especially when applied in medical cases, was *too low.* They thought the standard articulated in *Bolam* v. *Friern HMC* ([1957] 2 All ER 118) should be increased. The House of Lords addressed these arguments in *Bolitho* v. *City & Hackney Health Authority* ([1988] AC 232). Lord Browne-Wilkinson, for the Court, emphasised that professionals could not simply avoid claims that they had broken the standard of care just because they brought a number of expert witnesses who agreed with them. Rather, 'If, in a rare case, it can be demonstrated that the professional opinion is not capable of withstanding logical analysis, the judge is entitled to hold that the body of opinion is not reasonable or responsible'.

The standard must also be reasonable by non-professional standards. So any 'improper' action, such as a deliberate reduction in standards, is liable to be condemned. Some might worry that the judges could use this rule to impose their own standards, their own version of what is 'logical'. For example, given that the feared risk has occurred (which is why the case is before the court), a judge might be tempted to disagree with the decision-makers' assessments of the likelihood. They have the benefits of hindsight which might lead them to disbelieve the original estimates. (This and related problems are discussed further in Chapter 7.) But that should not happen. As the House of Lords emphasised, all that is necessary is that the decision be 'defensible'. Being able to show, for example, that the risk assessors did, really, estimate that likelihood, and for which reasons, should be enough to satisfy a court unless manifestly, obviously, even before the harm occurred, errors were made. The *Bolitho* decision does not make risk-taking any more difficult or legally fraught: 'In the vast majority of cases the fact that distinguished experts in the field are of a particular opinion will demonstrate the reasonableness of that opinion' (Lord Browne-Wilkinson, p.1151).

The *Bolitho* decision supports professional risk-takers. The court expressly approved the approach, adopted in this book, of insisting that the benefits of risk-taking must be taken into account. The judges may have assumed that 'risk' only refers to chance of harm but, since they emphasised that benefits are equally important, that is only a semantic difference.

> In particular in cases involving, as they so often do, the weighing of risks against benefits, the judge before accepting a body of opinion as being responsible, reasonable or respectable, will need to be satisfied that, in forming their views, the experts have directed their minds to the question of comparative risks and benefits and have reached a defensible conclusion on the matter. (Lord Browne-Wilkinson, p.1159)

The risk decision just has to be defendable. Taking into account the importance of the potential benefits, the likelihood of the feared harms, in the context of the quality of the knowledge about the risks and the management plan, can the risk decision be defended?

The key point about *Bolitho* is that the power to declare that professional standards are too low is rarely exercised. Parents will quickly recall the anxieties involved in telephoning a doctor about their child's illness. And doctors will know about the frequent risk decisions they must take on whether to undertake a home visit to make a fuller assessment and diagnosis. That was the issue in *Burne* v. *A* ([2006] EWCA Civ 24). A baby had to have a shunt fitted, when only nine weeks old, to drain fluid from his brain. His family doctor knew this could become blocked, which would be critical. One day, aged six, the boy was collected from school early because he had been vomiting. As he got no better his mother telephoned the doctor. Exactly what was said was disputed at trial but the doctor concluded that it was a relatively minor infection and did not make a home visit. If he had he would have concluded that the shunt had become blocked and he would have had the boy transferred to hospital, thereby preventing the heart attack and brain damage that occurred the next day.

The distinctive feature in this case was that the expert witnesses, *both* for the family and for the doctor, agreed that the GP was correct in only asking open questions over the telephone. This was considered professionally proper because leading, directed or closed questions, such as those that asked about specific symptoms, were too likely to put ideas into the patient's (or the parents') heads. The patient, or parent, would then provide a false report for the doctor to work on. The trial judge was not happy with this, however. He could not understand why it was so impossible or improper for a doctor not to end the conversation with some direct questions which could have clarified, for example, whether the child had a headache, whether it was phlegm or vomit. Explicit answers to those questions, it seemed agreed, would have led the doctor to suspect a blocked shunt, and thus to have visited the boy and had him transferred to hospital. So the trial judge invoked the *Bolitho* decision and decided the doctor had been negligent even though experts *for both sides* agreed that he had done what a responsible body of doctors would have done.

The Court of Appeal disagreed, and ordered a retrial (desperately hoping the parties would settle the case before that took place). They faulted the judge's reasoning on the facts. They also criticised him for using *Bolitho* even though neither of the parties had argued that he should. The trial judge had not given the parties a chance to argue that doctors' distaste for non-direct questions was perfectly proper behaviour, whilst Sedley LJ, in the Court of Appeal, noted that interviewing skills were at the threshold, not merely the centre, of professional practice. He summarised the *Bolitho* rule as being about when professional standards do not 'make sense'. So even if a judge is minded to declare professional standards as 'illogical' or 'indefensible', perhaps because he or she approaches the issues from a very different perspective and/or is too influenced by hindsight, he or she must give the risk-takers in question a chance to explain their different values, principles, standards.

Why didn't that happen in Mrs Partington's case (described earlier)? Perhaps, before proceeding, you would like to guess at the judge's decision. The practical problem, in that case, was that there was no clear, authoritative, statement of what the standard of care should be when deciding whether such clients should be allowed to go on walks and, if so, how they should be supervised. The judge could not turn to, or rely on, clear statements of what was accepted as professional conduct for such professional risk-taking. In the event he decided that the standard of care was not broken, that the local authority was not liable. He was particularly affected by the fact that the young woman was not, just before she pushed Mrs Partington doing anything unusual. There was nothing in her behaviour to lead the accompanying staff member, or Mrs Partington, to anticipate anything remiss was about to happen.

So we ask, again, why did this case get to court? Why were the local authority, their lawyers and witnesses, unable to convince Mrs Partington and her legal team that they were wasting their time and she was risking her money by suing? The problem was that there were few, if any, clear statements of acceptable professional practice, let alone principles or statements of values, which they could argue that the court was almost bound to adopt. Indeed, there was such a vacuum of such authoritative statements that the trial judge said some quite remarkable things. He declared: 'The problem is to try and balance what is best for the handicapped person with what is best for the rest of the world' (*Partington* v. *London Borough of Wandsworth* [1990] Fam Law 468: Schiemann, J., p.469).

He rejected the suggestion that the young woman should have been kept locked up and/or always held, as a child would have been, when taken on walks. But why were such values declared and suggestions ever made, or even given the credence of being mentioned in the judgement? They are, and were, not reflected in professional practice (Wolfensberger 1972). The young woman was not detained under the Mental Health Act 1983. Given that she was only periodically in local authority care (not hospital as the judge suggested at one point), it is highly unlikely that she *could* have been legally detained. And if she could not be detained then there was no legal authority for preventing her (in the absence of immediate concern that a crime was about to be committed) from leaving the residential unit at any time she wished. Equally, there would be no authority for holding her when on walks. Contrary to the judge's seemingly moderate comments there could be no question of 'balancing' her interests with those of other people if that involved depriving her of civil rights, such as free movement, without legal justification. She may have had a learning disability but she remained a citizen with full legal rights until they were lawfully removed.

If only the local authority had been able to point to a clear statement of professional practice, based upon appropriate principles and values (e.g. Wolfensberger 1972), indicating that the care staff were not only acting appropriately but were not allowed, by law, to do less than that. If only such a document had existed, and been 'signed up to' by relevant professionals and, better still, had been adopted by other local authorities and professional groups, then it would clearly have described practice to which a responsible body of professional opinion subscribed. Their lawyers could have directed Mrs Partington's lawyers to that document, and argued that its contents articulated what the professional standard of care was in such cases. Mrs Partington would, of course, still have been entitled to sue, but her lawyers would have been obliged to point out that she was likely to lose, because there was clear evidence that what the local authority's staff had done was within reasonable professional practice. Even an attempt to call *Bolitho* in aid would have been likely to fail. So, to risk overstating the key point, professional groups of risk-takers have the power to articulate professional standards. If they do so, and those faithfully describe at least what a responsible body of current professionals would do, then they can refer to it if and when their risk-taking leads to harm. Chapter 8 elaborates on some of the things that such a statement, which we refer to as a 'risk policy', should include.

Test 3: Causation

The breach of the standard of care, arising under the duty of care, must cause the losses. If there are no losses then the law of negligence is irrelevant. The law of negligence makes a major impact upon professional practice; people are anxious about being found negligent. They alter their behaviour. But the law is only applicable if loss results. It is perfectly possible, indeed common, however, for people to behave negligently but not cause any harm. Just recall some of those times when you were not concentrating on your driving, as you should have been, and drifted too far to one side of the road or the other. You noticed in time and adjusted before having an accident. Phew! Theoretically, you could have been prosecuted for bad driving in such circumstances. Similarly, your employer could take action against you for misconduct at work which, fortunately, does not cause harm. But agencies tend only to act where tangible harm occurs. In terms of accident prevention that does not make (good) sense. Should pilots only report occasions when planes crash? Fortunately, they appreciate the need to report and learn from 'near misses', just as the NHS is learning that it needs to learn from poor practice irrespective of outcome (DoH 2000). The negligence system is concerned with compensation. It is only concerned with accident prevention, or with improving standards, in an indirect manner.

Imagine that the standard of care was broken and harm followed. The one must have caused the other. No, that does not follow. Take *Gauntlett* v. *Northampton AHA* (12 December 1985, unreported but available via the LexisNexis database) as an example. Mrs Gauntlett was admitted to hospital after deliberately swallowing noxious substances. On transfer to a mental health ward she was assessed by a doctor on the consultant psychiatrist's team. Although the patient expressed a desire to die, to cleanse the world, and the doctor thought she was at risk of committing suicide, he risk-assessed her as not requiring constant supervision. That would have required a nurse to keep her in view at all times. Some time later, when visiting, her husband noted that she had acquired a box of matches, with which she could set fire to her clothes. He gave these matches to a staff nurse. The staff nurse took the matches but he did not record either that the patient had obtained them or that he had received them, in the patient's or ward records. The next day the consultant saw the patient. He did not know about the matchbox incident because it was not recorded in the nursing notes. He agreed with the junior doctor's diagnosis and with his risk assessment. Continual supervision was not ordered. The next day the patient went into a lavatory, took out some other matches she had obtained, and set fire to her clothes. She suffered severe burns.

The family argued that the consultant, the doctor and the staff nurse were negligent. Clearly, all three owed the patient a duty of care; that could not be disputed. But neither the consultant nor the doctor breached the standard of care. The trial judge noted that lay people might have approached the issues differently. They might have given more significance to the matchbox incident than the doctors. The judge received evidence which indicated that, whilst some psychiatrists would have put Mrs Gauntlett on one-to-one supervision, many other responsible practitioners would have taken the risk that these doctors did. Thus the doctors did not breach the standard of care. But nobody approved of the staff nurse's conduct in not recording the information about the confiscated box of matches. So he was adjudged to have broken the standard of care and, therefore, to have been negligent.

Wrong! The Court of Appeal had to correct the trial judge's decision. The nurse had a duty of care and broke the standard of care. But did the nurse's breach cause the losses? The injuries came after the negligent conduct, but that is not enough to demonstrate causation. A very useful approach is to ask is whether the injuries would still have happened, even if the breach of the standard had not occurred. In this case it was decided that, if the nurse had actually recorded the incident about the matches, and if the consultant had read them, he would still have decided that the patient did not require constant supervision. So Mrs Gauntlett would still have been able to go into the lavatory, or some other unsupervised place, and set fire to her clothes. The losses would have occurred irrespective of whether there had been a breach of the standard. So the nurse's mistake did not cause the losses and he was not liable for negligence. However, of course, that does not prevent his employers or professional association taking action over his unprofessional conduct.

So it is important not to assume causation and liability for negligence. Risk-takers need to appreciate that they are only responsible for that which they cause, not for everything that happens. If harm results from risk-taking, analyse the circumstances to see if any, or all, the losses would have occurred irrespective of the criticised decision. Indeed, before taking the risk decision, risk-takers should ask themselves what might happen irrespective of their decision. For example, you decide to take the risk and discharge an elderly, unsteady, patient from hospital. As you feared, he or she falls and injures his or her hip. Let us assume your risk assessment was unprofessional, that it broke the standard of care. Were you negligent? Clearly, those injuries are a consequence of your poor risk-taking. No! Do not be so quick to admit liability. What would your patient have been doing if he or she stayed in hospital, rather than been discharged? It is hoped he or she would have been receiving rehabilitation services, would have been encouraged to get up and walk around the ward and hospital. Perhaps he or she would be as likely to fall in hospital as at home, because of this encouragement to be active. So the fall could have happened irrespective of your risk decision. The patient would have fallen and injured his or her hip, at home or in hospital. The only difference would be that healthcare staff could respond faster in hospital than if the patient had gone home. If something is liable to happen, irrespective of whatever decision they make, then the decision-makers should not include that in their decision; it is beyond their control or influence. That goes for benefits as well as harms. But if the benefits or harms are more likely, rather than as likely, then they should not be ignored. In those circumstances your action would make a difference. If the coming storm is going to blow your house down it does not matter whether you leave the windows open or closed.

Remember that you can cause by omission. Professional risk-takers cannot escape liability simply by omitting to take decisions. Failing to detain someone with a severe mental illness, who might injure him or herself, is as much a decision, and the taking of a risk, as would be the positive act of detaining a patient. However, there is an important practical difference. People who are injured will want explanations. Naturally, they will trace the explanation to acts which they think are associated with them, such as the doctor giving them certain medication. However, they will not, in the same way, associate a loss with a failure to take a risk. A doctor's failure to give some medication, unless that omission had dramatic features which give it the appearance of a positive act (such as where there was an extensive debate about whether to give the medicine), is much less likely to be noticed as a cause. In practice people rarely know when they have suffered a loss, or that their life could have been better, if only someone had not omitted to do something. So the risk, of people considering whether they have suffered a loss and making a complaint, may be lower where the problem was an omission to act.

But, although that may be true in practice, it ought not to be. This practical difference ought not to be elevated to acceptable practice, policy or principle. Harm is harm irrespective of whether it was caused by an unprofessional act of commission or of omission. Risk-taking policies and practices should be scoured to ensure that improper advantage is not being taken of victims', or potential victims', ignorance through improper use of omissions to act.

Indeed, this difference ought to be turned around to help professional risk-takers. Imagine you have to decide whether or not a patient should be discharged from hospital. There is a risk; it might be a premature discharge. The patient might fall and break his or her hip or may self-injure. You might be tempted to take an 'easy' way out and avoid making a decision. But you have only succeeded in fooling yourself. Deciding not to take a decision is still a decision. Call it a postponement, a delay, an adjournment or whatever; it is still a decision. And, as such, it might have been wrongly made. It might appear to be an easy decision to take. What could go wrong just by delaying a decision? Quite a bit actually! The patient may want to go home, where life is richer. That is denied, albeit temporarily, by the delay. He or she might become demotivated, lose faith in the professionals. Perhaps these consequences are not very important, relatively. But they exist and should be acknowledged. Yes, they complicate decision-making but they also reinforce one of the key points that has been made repeatedly: risk-taking is about benefits as well as harms; decision-makers have to consider both. So, when the risk-taker makes a decision he or she should not only include the consequences of action, but also the consequences of inaction. A court or inquiry should not be allowed to misinterpret a risk decision as being a choice between possible harms and no possible harms. If inaction could have been beneficial or harmful then that should be brought into the balance.

Tests 4 and 5. Losses: *legally recognised and reasonably foreseeable*

The last two requirements of negligence are (a) that the losses incurred are of a kind which is recognised by the law and (b) that they occurred in a manner which was reasonably foreseeable (Rogers 2006). You do not need to spend so much time on these requirements.

The law only compensates certain losses. For example, it compensates physical injury and medically recognised psychiatric illnesses, such as post-traumatic stress disorder. But it does not compensate mere sadness or disappointment. It compensates pain and suffering, loss of earnings and more. For more details it would be better to consult a tort textbook (e.g. Rogers 2006) than repeat information here which is not especially relevant to professional risk-taking. However, it is important to explain the objective of compensation. It is to put the victim in the same position, as far as money can, as he or she was before the injuries. But this can have confusing results. For example, an elderly person could be killed as a consequence of another person's risk decision, whilst a young parent may be severely injured. We might agree that death is worse than injuries, however serious, and that the age of potential victims will rarely be a significant factor in risk assessment. However, young adults will, invariably, be awarded more compensation than the relatives of deceased elderly people. Quite simply, the former will have continuing needs and expenses. Nobody is claiming that, somehow, death is less serious than injury but that the potential role for compensation is different.

Risk-takers should focus on the immediate consequences of risk-taking and not on the size of potential compensation awards. It is the seriousness, positive or negative, of the consequences that matter rather than how they are compensated. Any professional who assesses a risk in terms of how likely the victim is to sue or how much he or she would obtain in compensation because, for example as an adult with learning disability he or she has been dissuaded or prevented from having dependents, deserves contempt. Professional risk-takers should assess the risk. If a consequence of that is that little compensation would be awarded, for example because the losses would be relatively minor, that is fine. But allowing external factors, such as the likelihood of seeking compensation, or its amount, to affect judgement is improper.

The law will, also, only compensate losses which occur in a reasonably foreseeable manner. This can be a complex legal concept (see Rogers 2006) but, again, it need not detain us. It adds nothing to the risk assessment. Losses which are not reasonably foreseeable are unlikely to receive a significant likelihood assessment.

Whose risk decision is it?

A key legal issue for professional risk-takers concerns *who* is entitled to make the risk decision. We, as capable, non-detained adults, are entitled to take many risk decisions, especially those only affecting ourselves. We are not entitled to risk someone else's life (e.g. by driving our car at them), even if we are entitled to risk our own. We are not entitled, if lawfully detained (which includes those wrongfully detained), to take the risk that would be involved in escaping from detention. But we are entitled to do much else which does not involve a crime or a civil law wrong. We can, for example, kill ourselves, go missing, give all our money away, even though it will cause considerable distress to our families. But there are limits. We have to be adults and to have capacity to make that particular decision. We can agree to take certain risks, for example to participate in drug trials. But there are limits. And if a choice is involved, we have to consent, in a genuine manner.

Risk-takers will need to be aware of the Mental Capacity Act 2005, which came into force in October 2007, for England and Wales. (Scotland made similar changes with the Adults with Incapacity (Scotland) Act 2000). This is another law which does not dramatically change the pre-existing position but it does bring the law into one place and provides important additional detail. An official Code of Practice, required by the statute, has been published. Those who act in relation to adults lacking capacity, such as making or advising on risk decisions affecting them, must have regard to that Code (DCA undated).

The new Act gives statutory effect to the common law position developed by the judges. For example the common law position was neatly embodied in the case of *Re C* ([1994] 1 All ER 819). Mr C was a 68-year-old man with gangrene in a leg. Doctors told him that if he did not have his leg amputated he would die. But Mr C was also a patient detained in a secure mental disorder hospital. And he did not want to have his leg cut off, even if death was the consequence. His surgeons decided, because he was mentally disordered, that he was not able to make a proper decision to object to the amputation. But Mr C had his lawyers apply to the High Court for a declaration that the surgeons were not allowed to amputate his leg. He succeeded: he got the declaration. (It is understood that when he later left the secure hospital, he did so on his own two legs.)

The trial judge, Mr Justice Thorpe, accepted that Mr C had a serious mental disorder. But that was not enough; it is the effects of the disorder that are critical:

> Although his general capacity is impaired by schizophrenia it has not been established that he does not sufficiently understand the nature purposes and effects of the treatment that he refuses. (*Re C* [1994] 1 All ER 819)

The test is of capacity, not of wisdom. Mr C was capable of understanding what would be involved both if the amputation went ahead, and if it did not. He was able to process that information and make a decision. Whether we agree with his decision, whether it was sensible or not, is irrelevant; he was able to understand, make a decision and to communicate it. That he was detained because a danger to other people was irrelevant; it had nothing to do with his ability to comprehend the issues and decide on the basis of that information.

The Mental Capacity Act 2005 adds to this approach by articulating, in Section 1, certain principles which apply throughout the Act. (Note that the Act deals with much more than just decision-making by people who *may* lack capacity to make binding legal decisions.)

- Everyone is assumed to have capacity, until the contrary is proved. Thus adults are entitled to take risk decisions which may injure themselves or their interests, until their lack of capacity is proved.

- Everyone is entitled not to be adjudged as lacking capacity just because their decisions are objectively considered to be unwise, improper or eccentric. (This principle does not stop anyone using that behaviour as a sign of mental ill health.)

- A guide to the Act says that adults must be given all appropriate help in order to demonstrate capacity to make decisions (DCA undated). Actually Section 1(3) specifies: 'A person is not to be treated as unable to make a decision unless all practicable steps to help him to do so have been taken without success.' 'Practicable' is not the same as 'appropriate'. 'Practicable' refers to a question of fact; does it work, can it enable the individual to make the decision? But 'appropriate' includes associations with 'reasonableness'. An expensive system of support may be practicable because it will work. But it may not be considered 'appropriate' because of its cost, even though that does not make it 'impractical' as an aid. The courts are likely to conflate the meanings of the two words.

- Anything that is done for a person who lacks capacity must be in his or her best interests.

- 'Anything done for or on behalf of people without capacity should be the least restrictive of their basic rights and freedoms' (DCA undated). Actually Section 1(6) specifies that 'Before the act is done, or the decision is made, regard must be had to whether the purpose for which it is needed can be as effectively achieved in a way that is less restrictive of the person's rights and freedom of action.'

It is submitted that Section 1(6) requires professional decision-makers to make decisions in at least two stages. The first should require them to think of any way in which they can achieve their goals without taking away their right to make their own decision about the risk. That could involve, for example, instead of taking one 'large' risk decision which the client is incapable of understanding (and therefore incapable of making), making a 'smaller' decision which he or she could understand. Instead of sterilising a woman with learning disabilities, because of a fear of pregnancy and subsequent adverse risks for the child and/or mother, the risk-taking team could take smaller steps such as seeing if her partner is able, willing and consistent about wearing a condom (Carson 1989). If not there are still further 'smaller' steps than sterilisation. Only if the team can devise no less restrictive approach should they go on to consider and make a risk decision. The Department for Constitutional Affairs' 'spin' on the legislative requirement implies that only one decision is made. Against them it should be noted (a) that Section 1(6) begins with: 'Before the act is done, or the decision is made'. That presumes at least two stages. And (b) the Department's view would reduce the meaning and role of Section 1(6) to being no more than that of Section 1(5), which requires the decision to be in the client's best interests. Surely a decision in someone's 'best interests' will – automatically – be the 'least restrictive' possible in the circumstances?

Related principles are elaborated in requirements attached to particular tests. For example, decisions about an individual's best interests must not be merely made on the basis of age, appearance, 'condition' (Section 4(1)(b)), or any behaviour which might lead to unjustified assumptions. The decision-maker must consider all relevant circumstances, including the likelihood that the individual will gain capacity, and when, in the future. The decision-maker (i.e. risk-taker) must: 'so far as reasonably practicable, permit and encourage the person to participate, or to improve his ability to participate, as fully as possible in any act done for him and any decision affecting him' (Section 4(4)).

He or she must also, 'so far as is reasonably ascertainable' (Section 4(6)), take account of the client's past and present wishes and feelings, beliefs and values, and anything else that would be likely to affect the client's decision, if he or she had capacity. He must consult 'if it is practicable and appropriate' anyone the client has 'named' (which would seem to include both those named in the past and at the time) to be consulted on such matters, anyone caring for the client or interested in his or her welfare and any person to whom the client has granted a lasting power of attorney or court 'deputy' (for which provision, and explanation, is made in the rest of the Act).

The core question for professional risk-takers is whether their client is entitled to take the risk decision or whether they must do it for him or her. Notice that the traditional legal approach of imposing dichotomous, either/or, categories onto issues which are inherently relative (i.e. capacity) has been 'ameliorated' slightly, by the principles just described. Before the Act, and afterwards, there were and are only two categories: adults with and adults without legal capacity. Real life is much more complex than the world which the law constructs. For example, capacity may vary from day to day (at least), issue to issue and be affected by who is investigating capacity, and how. But the principles should lead to decision-makers investigating, for example, whether the client can consent to a different – appropriate – risk when it is discovered that he or she cannot consent to another. They must also encourage the client to participate in decisions about risks affecting him or her 'as fully as is possible' (Section 4(4)), even if the professionals must make the final decision. So capacity remains, in law, a dichotomous issue even if the practical consequences have been 'smoothed over'. The experience of clients without legal capacity, when risk decisions that may affect them are being considered and/or being taken, could be little different from clients with capacity – bar who makes the final decision. In that sense the legislation is to be applauded.

But there are 'get-out' clauses. Section 4(9) provides that 'there is sufficient compliance with this section [which specifies the requirements of acting 'in best interests'] if (having complied with the requirements of subsections (1) to (7)) he reasonably believes that what he does or decides is in the best interests of the person concerned'.

Consider, for example, a professional (risk) decision-maker who has decided that he or she has encouraged a client to participate in the decision-making 'so far as is reasonably practicable' (Section 4(4)). Others may, correctly, believe that he or she has barely scratched the surface of possibilities and imagination in finding ways to engage the client. But the professional will have satisfied the requirements of the legislation if he or she 'reasonably believes' that what he or she did was in the best interests of the client. Section 5 provides another defence for decision-makers, if their acts involve the care or treatment of the person thought to lack capacity. (It is difficult to think of a professional risk decision which would not fall within this term.) The decision-maker will not incur legal liability for anything that he or she would not be liable for if the client had actually had capacity and had consented, provided he or she took reasonable steps to establish whether the client had capacity and acted, reasonably believing the client lacked capacity in relation to that issue, in the client's best interests. There is an important limitation to that, however. That will not stop the decision-maker, for example a professional risk-taker, from being liable for negligence in making or taking the decision. It would, however, stop the client from suing for trespass or other civil wrongs.

Under the new Act, which does not apply to those aged under 16 years, an adult is to be regarded as incapable of making a decision if, because of a temporary or permanent impairment or disturbance in the functioning of his or her mind or brain, he or she is unable to make a decision. Inability to understand the relevant information, to retain it, to use or to weigh it whilst deciding, or to communicate his or her decision using any appropriate aids, will be regarded as incapacity (Sections 2 and 3). It is again specified that people must not jump to assumptions on the basis of age, condition or behaviour. By implication an individualised assessment of functional capacity must be made.

Problems are likely to arise because the statute does not pay sufficient regard to the psychology of decision-making. It declares that:

> The information relevant to a decision includes information about the reasonably foreseeable consequences of:
>
> (a) deciding one way or another, or
>
> (b) failing to make the decision. (Section 3(4))

What will be considered the 'reasonably foreseeable consequences' of a risk decision? As has been seen they could be numerous. The qualifying word 'reasonable' is exceptionally important in making it clear that fanciful and remote consequences need not be considered. However, there is nothing incompatible between what is being recommended elsewhere in this book and this legal requirement. Rather, the problem is that humans, whether with or without mental disorders, have a limited capacity to cope with lots of information. Someone could lack capacity, not so much because of his or her mental disorder as the amount of information he or she must cope with in order to satisfy this legal test. It could be very ironic. Again, assuming the absence of a significant mental disorder or learning disability, you might be 'incapable' under this statutory test because you cannot understand, retain and use or weigh all the relevant information. Consider all the information that can be taken into account when we risk buying an expensive bottle of wine. If we try to weigh up and work on it all we are, at least, slowed down and often confused. Compare the complexity and importance of such decisions with some of the risk decisions that this book is concerned with.

It is a pity the new law did not explicitly require or encourage those advising people who might be considered incapable, to break the decision down into appropriate steps. In this way individuals could make a decision on part of the issue (red, white or rosé?), only considering information relevant to that part of it, before moving on, if appropriate. Does the patient understand there is a problem with his leg? If yes, does the patient understand he will die within a specified period unless action is taken? If yes, will the patient consider surgery, at all? If yes, will the patient consider amputation? Professional risk-takers could, and should, think of ways of developing these sorts of algorithms (or decision flow-charts) to help their clients, and themselves, work though the issues. We can all benefit from such techniques. Arguably, the principles stated in the Mental Capacity Act 2005 should require professionals taking, or advising on, risk decisions affecting those who may lack capacity to develop such algorithms. But the 'get-out' clauses are liable to be sufficient to protect those who do not go the extra, practical, step.

However, if algorithms are used, then they must be used properly (see Twining and Miers 1999). It is not enough just to replace one 'overall' question with a few others. In particular (a) the questions must be asked in an appropriate sequence; for example, the choice of which treatment logically follows after the question whether the client will accept any treatment. And (b) the questions must cover all the issues, though not necessarily all the options, involved; for example, if the 'overall' risk issue is whether someone should have a sterilisation operation, then appropriate alternatives should not be ignored. For example, it would be inappropriate to ignore considering the appropriateness and adequacy of action by the partner rather than going straight to forms of possible surgical intervention or invasive female contraception.

Professional risk decision-makers must consider the capacity of the people on whose behalf they propose making risk decisions. If the adult is entitled to take the decision (i.e. it is not about injuring another), and has capacity, then they must let him or her take the decision or be clear that they have authority to take the decision on his or her behalf. The Mental Capacity Act 2005 is designed to challenge paternalistic attitudes and practices. Practices that went unchallenged before the Act should now be challenged. Whilst decision-makers are unlikely to be penalised if they act in good faith, they can still be criticised for not doing enough, or as much as they could, to enable the individual concerned to make the risk decision.

If the person concerned is incapable, and cannot be made capable by the provision of more skilful explanations or by the use of aids, then the professional can take the risk decision. Note that the statute contemplates delays in decision-making to enable the individual to become capable of participating in the decision. Under both the current and the new law the professional must act in the client's or the patient's 'best interests'. Currently, that simply means that the professional must not breach the standard of care that would apply (*F* v. *W Berkshire HA* [1989] 2 All ER 545; Montgomery 2003, pp.240–242). How not breaching the standard of care, a 'good enough' standard, can equate with someone's 'best' interests, has not been explained. Under the new law it will, as outlined above, have a more developed meaning.

If the client or person potentially affected by the risk decision is less than 16 years of age then the Mental Capacity Act 2005 does not apply. The rationale is that the issues should be considered in relation to childhood and development, and not with regard to mental health or disabilities. Professional risk-takers should discover who has parental or other legal authority to make decisions affecting the child (Montgomery 2003). The child may not wish them to consult his or her parents. The key decision in this area is that in *Gillick* v. *West Norfolk & Wisbech AHA* ([1985] 3 All ER 402). Here, the House of Lords decided that doctors could take treatment decisions affecting children under the age of 16 without consulting parents, provided the child was capable of understanding the particular decision. Thus the issues are (a) the competence of the particular child to understand (b) the complexity of the particular decision. Such cases require individual decisions.

Consent

The issue for the professional risk-taker may not be the individual's capacity but whether he or she consents. This related area of law is not affected by the new statute. We all have to consent to things others do to us (e.g. put fillings in our teeth). The core issue is whether the consent was 'genuine'. We may hate it when the dentist drills our teeth, tensing our muscles and retreating as much as the seat will allow. We may not want it to happen, in a very real sense, but we are consenting. Despite our cowering behaviour the dentist is entitled to treat us as consenting. If we were to shout objections, in so far as that is possible with so many implements in our mouth, or try to struggle out of the chair, it would be a different matter. Opening our mouths is enough, although we can always change our minds. It does not matter that we are, regularly, not asked to sign a consent form until afterwards. The consent form is valuable evidence that we consented, but it is not essential, given our clear behaviour, and it can be disregarded if, for example, it can be shown that consent was obtained by force or deception.

Reference is often made to 'informed' consent. It is sometimes said that consent must be informed. The problem is with what 'informed' means. We are entitled to know what we are consenting to – but not to know every-thing, not to be fully informed. So the question is how much are we entitled to? And back comes the answer: what a responsible body of pro-fessionals would give you. The standard for how much information you must be given in order to give a valid consent is the same as the standard of care discussed earlier (*Sidaway* v. *Bethlem RHG* [1985] 1 All ER 643; Mont-gomery 2003, p. 234). How much information should you be given before you risk consenting to having your appendix removed by a surgeon? As much as a responsible body of abdominal surgeons would give you. But you can increase the obligation by asking questions since, even if you do not have to be told everything, you must not be misled. And what informa-tion you are given must be provided in a manner that you can understand.

So, if professional risk-takers wish to ensure they have the consent (where needed) of their patients, clients and so on then they should ensure that they provide sufficient information. It does not have to be everything they know. They can justify withholding information which could frighten their clients, because it is about a very serious, although very unlikely, outcome – unless they are specifically asked about it or no responsible body of professionals would fail to mention it. Once again the law supports professionals making considered judgements about risks.

Conclusion

This chapter began by noting that many people fear the role of the law when it comes to risk-taking. It is associated with blame and a culture of people being more concerned with avoiding criticism than with making the decision they believe correct. It is hoped that you have been shown that these views are wrong, that the law can support professional risk-takers if they will allow it. Certainly, there are minimum standards. The law requires people to be thoughtful and reflective. It protects standards, invariably those that are already recognised by the professions. The problems are more to do with proving the facts, the evidence, rather than the law. Issues can easily arise surrounding what the standards of care are that should be applied, problems about the facts rather than the law. If the standards have not been explicitly articulated, or they have been but it is not clear that a responsible body of co-professionals has adopted them, then cases will have to be taken to the courts for them to investigate and declare them. Professionals should seize the opportunities to articulate the standards, ensuring that they are regularly reviewed, so that the courts can adopt them, although if they are readily known fewer cases will reach court in the first place. This is so important that Chapter 8 returns to this topic.

CHAPTER 4

Risk Assessment

Introduction

It has been argued that 'risk' involves two elements: consequences and likelihood. Both of these are variable; they involve matters of degree. We do not know, because it is a risk, exactly what will occur or, exactly, how likely it is. These two elements are central to risk assessment. Indeed, 'risk assessment' should be understood as collecting information about these two elements. We need information about what might happen as a consequence of taking the proposed risk, how significant (good or bad) that might be, and how likely it is that that will occur. This chapter will examine these, and related issues. We will discover that there are many problems. Although some advice is offered it must always be remembered that since the topic is risk-taking, which by definition involves dealing with uncertainty, nobody can properly promise complete solutions.

Although risk assessment involves collecting information we also need to know how reliable our information is, or how uncertain is our uncertainty. That is another matter of degree. But it relates to the 'dimensions' of risk, rather than to its 'elements'. For example, if we are unsure whether a proposed risk should be taken, one option is to seek more or better information, or both, such as that discussed and recommended in discipline- or service-specific texts on risk (e.g. Kemshall and Pritchard 1995, 1997; Nash 2006; Parsloe 1999; Titterton 2005). We have that option, unless it is a dilemma (see Chapter 1). It is more important to consider those and related issues as part of 'risk management', and so that will be the focus for Chapter 5.

It is always difficult to decide how wide, or narrow, to take a discussion of risk and risk-taking. It has been noted, for example, how risk-taking is a subset of decision-making so that the research on the latter can inform the former. It may be less noticeable, but it is equally the case, that the research on probabilistic reasoning is also applicable. That research indicates when and how we can, and should, infer from what evidence we have. Risk decision-makers have to make an assessment of the nature and likelihood of the outcomes, and their confidence in those inferences. Imagine that you 'know' from a research study that, of 100 people with similar (but not identical) features to Tim, 25 went on to cause harm. You also know that Tim has successfully completed a training programme, which was not referred to in the study of the 100 people. How can you combine that information, of different forms, sources, degrees of relevance and reliability? And how much trust could you put in the resulting information? But, however tempting it may be to draw in references to mathematical and other probability theories, or to the new evidence scholarship which keeps threatening to make a major impact on how facts and evidence are 'proved' in courts and tribunals, it must be excluded for considerations of space and coherence of explanation. However, reference to key texts, such as those by Schum (1994) and Anderson, Schum and Twining (2005), is recommended – but not as holiday reading.

In this chapter the focus is on problems in identifying, analysing and assessing the potential outcomes of a risk decision, and their likelihood. It has been stressed, and will be many more times, that for risk assessment *both* the outcomes and their likelihood must be examined. However, to clarify our argument and simplify the explanation, let us begin with issues related to the outcomes.

Outcomes, consequences: identifying the range

You pause at the side of the road. Why? There is a risk that you might be knocked down by a vehicle whilst crossing the road. Even leaving the likelihood of that happening until later in this chapter, you remain concerned about *what* might happen. The vehicle might kill you outright. It might just injure you. You might subsequently die or recover. The injuries could range from very serious to relatively minor. The vehicle might just give you a shock and teach you to be more careful next time. We cross the road so often, and our usual precautions make accidents so rare, that we rarely think about the risks involved in such commonplace activities. But the risks are always there. The same issues arise with surgery, with crossing bridges, with discharging offenders from prison and so on.

Let us begin with two broad issues. *What* might happen and *how much* harm – or good – might it involve?

Which outcomes should be assessed?

When crossing the road you might be struck by lightning. A serial burglar, whom we take a risk in releasing early from gaol, might kill someone. Strange things can happen when taking risks. Some outcomes of risk-taking are more regularly contemplated, and considered in risk documents, than others. In part, but only part, this reflects likelihood. But unlikely consequences, in particular feared events such as death, are often considered. The reality is that almost anything could happen, particularly indirectly, from a risk decision. The more possible outcomes we think up the more complex will be the risk assessment. But we do not need to do that, and often should not.

A clinical team has to decide whether Jean can be discharged from hospital. The team might decide that the risk of Jean injuring herself is so low (in terms of the amount of harm and/or its likelihood) that the risk deserves to be taken. They may be right; Jean does not injure herself but does injure another person, a consequence the clinical team had not contemplated. Should the risk-taking team be criticised? That depends upon whether the team ought to have considered whether Jean would injure another person. Was there anything in Jean's history, that the team knew about or ought to have known about, which made that outcome a realistic or reasonable possibility? That can only be answered on a case-by-case approach. And it is very judgemental. What would be 'realistic'; what would be 'reasonable' to predict? We cannot answer the individual case.

Let 'reasonable' be your guide

Notice how these criteria, in particular 'reasonable', relate to legal concepts discussed in the last chapter. Quite simply, the law can help to answer these questions; it would have to if a case ever got to court. But we should not rely, entirely, on the law. For example, in Jean's case, the clinicians may not owe the victim a duty of care. Jean's victim might not have been someone whom the professionals needed to be contemplating. (Reconsider the relevant section of the last chapter for more on the limits of the 'duty of care'.) That is the law. The professionals cannot be sued if they did not owe a duty of care. But it does not follow that they should not have thought about other people being injured. The professionals may be beyond legal action but they can still be criticised, possibly severely and with damaging publicity. Disciplinary action might be taken by employers or professional associations; an official inquiry might be established.

A risk assessment only needs, from legal, ethical and professional perspectives, to cover 'reasonable' outcomes. Including unreasonable outcomes will quickly become counterproductive and, thereby, poor practice. A risk assessment is not an excuse for displaying the munificence of our imagination by listing all the things technically possible and the different ways in which they might occur. A goal must be to include as much information, and as many considerations, as is necessary, whilst keeping the decision as simple as possible.

Likelihood will be of great help in this analysis. Certain kinds of outcome can justifiably be ignored because they are simply so unlikely. A parole board could justify ignoring the risk of a serial burglar killing someone, assuming it neither has, nor could reasonably be expected to have, any special information such as reports of the prisoner's stated determination to kill his or her victim. The risk of being struck by lightning when crossing the road may be ignored because it is so unlikely. It does not matter that that lightning might kill us. An unlikely event does not become any more likely just because it could have serious consequences or because, very rarely, it actually occurs. It remains unlikely.

Very unlikely or unimportant outcomes may be ignored
It may be easier to understand the point by using some numbers. Imagine that you can, and do, rate the seriousness of outcomes from a risk as lying somewhere between 0 and −10 on the adverse side, and 0 and +10 on the positive side. In such a scheme the zero would represent a neutral state (i.e. this outcome is neither good nor bad). Technically any outcome which would be rated as zero, neither good nor bad, has no place in a risk assessment. It is irrelevant because it neither favours nor opposes taking the risk. It does not matter how likely it is because it will make no difference, it is neither good nor bad. (Multiplying any number by zero produces zero.) It may be certain to occur but it will make no difference because it is neutral in its effects. However, it can be useful to include references to, and documentation of, these risks. It demonstrates that they were thought about.

In this scheme −10 could represent death. Arguably, there are things worse than death. There are painful and tortured deaths; we sometimes talk of 'living deaths'. And there are problems in deciding what the oppo-site, +10, would involve. But let us delay consideration of those issues and just use this scheme of numbers to explain our current points.

Numbers may also be used for likelihood. If something is impossible it may be described as having a zero, nil, nought, 0, likelihood. If it is certain to occur it may be described as one, 1. If something is as likely to happen as not to happen it may, therefore, be described as 0.5. The likelihood of an event, for example 0.2 or 0.8, may then be fitted into this framework. Clearly, there are many problems with how such numbers are discovered, their credibility and even the propriety of using them. We will return to those problems later in the chapter. But there is sufficient substance, with this basic model for rating the seriousness of a risk, to make the point. For the moment try to suspend any concerns; you just want to clarify this point.

Back to the example about being struck by lightning whilst crossing the road, or how very low likelihood outcomes may be ignored, even if they could be serious. Imagine that you could be killed by the lightning. That outcome is described as −10, the worst possible. But its likelihood is also low. Let us rate the likelihood as one in a million, or 0.000001. Now, combine the two elements, outcome and likelihood (i.e. simply multiply them together). We reach −0.00001 (the minus sign indicates that it is a potential loss). It may be ten times greater (than the 0.000001 likelihood), but it remains a low figure. Now, think of another injury, say, a broken leg which leaves a permanent limp. Let us assess its seriousness as −1. (You may disagree with this figure; actually, it is hoped that you do in order to emphasise that it is a big issue to tackle when deciding how to rate the seri-ousness of outcomes. Rating outcomes and likelihoods is another major issue to return to later on.) That is a relatively low figure. Now let us assess its likelihood as 1 in a 1000, or 0.001. Let us combine, multiply, the out-come and the likelihood and we reach −001. Now compare them: the risk of death is −0.00001; the risk of serious injury is −0.001. Clearly, the risk of death is, despite its much more serious and dramatic outcome, the lesser risk. So it will often be perfectly proper to ignore a risk of death, not because death is unimportant, but because the risk of it could make such a small difference to the overall risk assessment. Small figures make small differences. Small figures are often trivial, particularly when compared with those produced by more relevant risks, even when the margin of error (see later) is considered. So it could be irrational, as well as time-wasting, to

include comparatively small risks in a risk assessment. So it is perfectly justifiable, in law, morality and good reasoning, to ignore risks that, when the
seriousness of their outcomes and likelihood are combined and then compared with other more substantial risks, they are (or would be if the
calculations were undertaken) found to have a trivial effect in any
balancing operation between likely benefits and likely harms.

The same reasoning can be applied to outcomes which are of low value
or seriousness. For example, an outcome may be certain, so it deserves to be
rated as one. But the outcome may be rated, whether plus or minus, as
0.0001. Multiplying that by 1 makes no difference. So, no matter how certain or likely it is, in the overall scheme of things, by virtue of it having a
very low value, it deserves to be ignored. Both elements, likelihood and
outcome, must be considered and if their combination (multiplication
when it is possible to reduce to numerical values) will produce a very low
number it is eminently reasonable to ignore it.

Avoid catastrophising

Some 'professional' risk-takers have been heard to argue that if a serious
outcome, such as death, is possible then it can never be proper to take that
risk and, indeed, any risk assessment is superfluous. (An alternative version
is that risk assessment can continue just so long as they are not involved in,
and/or never associated with, any decision to take that risk.) For once it is
possible to be explicit about this position and these practitioners. They are
acting unreasonably, illogically and unprofessionally! Serious outcomes
are always possible. We can all imagine ways in which people might be
killed by an innocuous risk. But that says more for our fertile fantasy lives
than for the risk. The telephone rings, it is downstairs, I rush to get it in
time, I startle the cat, I try to avoid it but trip and fall down the stairs; I fall
badly and am killed. The message is clear. Do not telephone people. It is
risky.

Rubbish! Unlikely outcomes are unlikely because they are unlikely. It is
perfectly proper to take risks with another person's life – you do it every
time you drive them somewhere – provided it is a low (likelihood) risk.
And that position does not change just because someone is employed to
take risks with other people. Sorry nurses, social workers, prison governors
and so on, you cannot – professionally – avoid being involved in risk
assessment just because a serious outcome is possible. Indeed, if you fail to
get involved, such as by not providing any relevant information and skills

that you possess, you could well be a major cause of the resulting harm. Your colleagues might avoid liability because they acted professionally, but you could break the standard of care by your avoidance tactics. You could end up being the one sued. And your employers and professional associations could take action against you (as they would be entitled to do), even in the much more frequent cases where no harm results. This process, of refusing to get involved for fear of the serious but unlikely outcome, might be described as 'catastrophising'. It has no place in quality risk assessment, not just because it does no good but, more importantly, because it is liable to cause harm.

Responsibilities of expertise
Another argument about whether it is proper to ignore certain serious risks emphasises that risk assessment is subjective, often emotional and can be irrational. Let us return to the case where there is a very low likelihood of something serious, such as death, occurring. Some practitioners have argued that, yes, it is a very low risk, but the problem is that others, including the media, lawyers and judges, do not understand or will not accept that. There was a significant likelihood that a patient, Ian, might self-injure so the risk assessment, and risk management plan, focused on that. Someone mentioned that the patient might kill himself, but everyone involved in the risk assessment agreed, after thinking about it, that the likelihood of that was so low that it did not need to affect their decision. But, guess what? As sometimes happens even with the best assessed and managed of risks, the patient committed suicide.

These practitioners argue that, because this contemplated but highly unlikely outcome did occur, therefore they made a bad decision or, inevitably, that they will be assumed to have done so. But they are wrong. We must always remember that if there is a 1 in 1000 risk of death then, in spite of and not because of, the best of practice, death should be expected to occur once in every 1000 cases. The only exception is if that assessment (of 1:1000) was wrong and the risk-takers should have known that. We cannot – nor can the media, tribunals or judges – properly decide that a risk was badly taken just because the predicted harm occurs. To make that judgement, how the risk was assessed and managed must be examined. (This is perfectly consistent with the law described in the last chapter.) However, if it is conceded that the decision was, or might have been, taken poorly then it must be accepted that others will be happy to jump upon that concession.

Even in that 1 in 1000 case other people, in particular victims, their friends, relatives and advisors, may be expected to be concerned that a death, or other serious outcome, has occurred. We would want that for ourselves, if we were the victim. These other people are perfectly entitled to wonder if (but not to conclude that), a poor decision was taken. They may very fairly hope (even if the decision was properly taken) that we will learn from this event which, possibly, might involve changing our assessments of likelihood of such events for the future. But we should not indulge them by wallowing in self-doubt or sloppy thinking.

If you are a member of the target audience for this book, then you are someone who is employed to take risks affecting other people, often called 'patients' or 'clients'. You are employed, in substantial measure, because you know more about your specialist area of work, for example people who repeatedly commit sex offences, than lay people. You are employed and paid more because, on this topic, you know more than most, if not all, judges, lawyers and members of the media. They are entitled to ask you questions, to challenge you, to check that you used that knowledge and those skills appropriately. But you still know more. They may suggest – a word that lawyers love to use in courtroom examinations – that the risk was much more serious than your risk assessment suggested. If they are wrong, if you still believe in the intellectual basis for your risk assessment, then you should disagree – forcefully if necessary. You may have to remind your audience that a risk assessed at 1 in 100 occurs, on average, once in 100 times even in the best-regulated circles. You may have to explain how you came to your risk assessment, but that is part of the territory of being an expert. You are accountable. We may all guess, like to think, or believe that the risk of a particular outcome is X but we are not entitled, especially if we are judges, lawyers or members of the media or public, to maintain that against better evidence. Professional risk-taking, affecting other people, should be as objective and impersonal as we can make it. (Risk management should be personal.) It is not what we want the likelihoods to be, or guess them to be, but what the best current knowledge tells us. Part of your job entails knowing that best current knowledge and reminding others of that core truth.

So, returning to the main theme, one reason why risk-takers are entitled to limit the outcomes that they are going to include in a risk assessment is that some outcomes are just so unlikely, despite the seriousness of the outcomes, to need or deserve consideration. But if people insist on including them, on catastrophising, then you can go ahead. It will not make a difference, although you will be wasting time and resources that might better be spent on considering alternative, realistic, outcomes.

Only assess outcomes which could be caused

Another reason for limiting the range of outcomes to be included in a risk assessment is provided by the causation rule. Your risk assessment should only be concerned with outcomes that would be caused by the taking of the risk. Consider again the case of the patient who was discharged from hospital, despite a risk of self-harm, who went on to commit suicide. The suicide followed the risk. It may appear, but it does not automatically follow, that it was caused by that risk decision. One useful test is to ask whether it would have happened anyway (i.e. whether the risk decision was actually superfluous). If that is the case there is no legal causation, as explained in the last chapter.

Perhaps John would have committed suicide even if he had not been discharged. Suicide can take place in hospitals. Perhaps the cause of the suicide was a new factor which did not exist at the time of the risk decision and which was not reasonably to be predicted. For example, John's partner, upon whom he relied emotionally, was killed in a car accident and there was not enough time for those managing the risk to reconsider or change the plan before the suicide occurred. You may think that this is clutching at straws; agreed. On the outline facts of this example it is difficult to imagine many circumstances where a suicide would not be caused or influenced, in part, by a decision to discharge the patient. But, and this is the point, it is possible and it is important for risk assessors to think about causation. Risk assessment should not include any outcome which would not be caused by the risk decision being contemplated. If it would have happened anyway, irrespective of the risk decision, then it was not caused by it. The risk decision must have made the consequence, at least, more likely or more serious.

Use 'risk periods'

An aid to considering this causation issue is provided by the idea of 'risk periods'. Consider a significant feature of most professionals' risk decisions. How many risk decisions, per client, patient or comparable person, do they, ordinarily, take? Think about someone who is admitted to hospital. Whilst in hospital a wide range of risks will be taken. Different treatments will be undertaken. Different levels of nursing care could be included, from accident and emergency, through intensive care, to an 'ordinary' ward, to rehabilitation. The reality is that a number of risk decisions will be taken, including the decisions to move the patient through different levels of supervision. And more will occur when the patient is discharged. His or her general practitioner is likely to be advised. Community nurses may visit. The patient may return to the hospital for a check up. Eventually, it is hoped, it will be decided that no further medical or other care is required. That, too, will be a risk decision.

The key point to appreciate is that each of these risks decisions is taken for a period of time. Each decision, except the last in the sequence, is designed – at least implicitly – to last until it is reviewed and another (risk) decision is taken. It is actually quite difficult to think of decisions taken by professional risk-takers affecting their clients or patients which do not fit into this sequencing pattern. One example would be where a professional is asked to investigate whether someone requires a service, for example adaptations to his/her home to help him/her cope with a disability, but the professional decides that there is no need. That would involve just one risk decision. It is a risk because the disabled person may be injured, perhaps getting out of a bath, because no adaptations had been made. But, even with such cases, provision will often be made for a review after a specified period of time. That would be the risk period, for that case.

Decision-makers should only include those risks whose outcomes could occur, and only to the extent that they might occur, within the risk period for the decision they are contemplating. The surgeon and anaesthetist should be concerned with the risk outcomes which might occur during, and as a consequence of, surgery. That should include reviewing the patient's progress and considering any continuing and fresh risks for an appropriate period afterwards. But the surgeon should not, at that time, be concerned with the risks that will occur when the patient is discharged. That is likely to involve other people, for example physiotherapists. Again, it is appropriate for a prison governor to be concerned about the risk of assaults from other prisoners when an offender is admitted to prison. It would not be appropriate, at that stage, to be considering possible outcomes of any risk decision to allow day release. Professional risk-taking involves, quite properly, a sequence of risk decisions.

But what is the 'risk period' for any particular case? To a considerable extent professional risk-takers can – and certainly should – nominate the risk periods themselves. A patient may be under close supervision because he or she is considered to be at risk of committing suicide. The doctor or nurse is likely to decide that the patient should be observed every 15, more or less, minutes. The assessment of the risk should determine how long that period will be. In this example the risk period is 15 minutes. A doctor may decide it is worth taking the risk of discharging a patient. But that decision may rely upon provision for a review of the patient's progress such as in an outpatient clinic, by a general practice doctor or community healthcare practitioner. So the doctor will ask the patient to return for a check-up after a certain period, ask for a community visit by another person or inform a colleague of the relevant facts for the latter to decide when he or she should see the patient. Once again an embryonic risk period is being designated. Each of these reviews implies a risk period.

But the professionals in this sort of case cannot determine the risk period so easily. The patient may not turn up for the outpatient session or may not be at home when the community-based practitioner calls. Prisoners given day release are unlikely to be keen to return before or at the exact time specified. These sorts of issues would be more dramatic in relation to clients or patients who are considered to be a risk to themselves or to others. They could be more unwilling to co-operate. In cases like these the 'risk period' should be understood as the time which the risk decision-makers consider appropriate, for example until the date of the outpatient check-up session, *plus* a reasonable period for getting in contact with the patient should he or she not attend as planned. The risk assessment should only include the outcomes which *could* occur within that risk period.

Risk periods exist independent of clients' or patients' wishes. The doctor may have asked to see the patient in two weeks' time. Two weeks, plus a 'getting in contact' period, is therefore the risk period. The patient, or client, will usually be under no obligation to come and see the doctor again at the end of that two-week period. But that does not prevent the doctor, or other professional, from having a continuing duty, whether legal or professional. He or she should make another risk decision. 'Given that the patient has not turned up, is there such a risk that requires me to take steps to see or learn about the patient?' He or she cannot, properly, argue that as the patient or client is entitled not to turn up for a review there is no outstanding risk. Certainly competent adult patients and clients are entitled to decide that they do not want professional assistance; they can reject further medical or other interventions. That is their right. But that does not affect the existence of a risk, only the ability to act upon it. The decision-makers involved should, at least, take professionally appropriate steps to review the nature and degree of any continuing risk. They need to do this in order to advise the client or patient – enabling him or her to make an informed decision about the risk he or she is taking by not seeking further professional assistance – and for the professionals to discover whether any other person (e.g. children) may be at risk, requiring intervention to protect them.

Risk periods may also be shorter than implied by the last paragraphs. Imagine a team has decided that a client's progress in the community should be reviewed in a month's time. Initially, the risk period would appear to be one month. When deciding whether it is wise to take the risk proposed for the coming month they should include only those outcomes which could reasonably be expected to occur within that month. They should also consider the risk management techniques (see next chapter) which they decide to implement. For example, they might arrange for one of their number, or another professional, to visit the client or patient. That professional might be competent (some professions cannot reasonably be expected to notice signs within the specialised knowledge and experience of other disciplines) to identify any causes for concern suggesting that the risk should be reviewed earlier. That person might be authorised to end the risk then or, for example, to inform others. For example, the Parole Board can decide, quickly, to end a life-sentence prisoner's licence to be out of prison. If this sort of mechanism is established then the risk period may be considered as shorter than the formally agreed review period. However, this sort of mechanism has to be effective. The decision-makers might, for example, ask the patient or client to inform them if there are any problems before the review meeting. But it would often be inappropriate to rely on the client or patient, not necessarily because he or she was considered untrustworthy, but because the nature of the risk involved includes the client lacking sufficient knowledge or insight to be able to advise the professional about all the risks.

Finally, professionals should use 'risk periods' which are related to any research base upon which they are basing their assessments. For example, the excellent research into the risk of violence posed by mentally disordered adults, by Monahan and colleagues in the MacArthur Research Network (Monahan *et al.* 2001) was based on following up patients for 20 weeks. Thus any prediction of the dangerousness of a patient, made in reliance on the authority of this research, should not be for more than 20 weeks. If a prediction has to be made for more than that period then the decision-makers should be clear that they cannot rely upon that research. For example, a court or tribunal may have to decide whether a patient detained because of prior violence should be discharged. The court will want a prediction which lasts for longer than 20 weeks. But any professional giving them evidence should either not rely on that research or explain that it cannot properly be used for a longer period. The court may be displeased but the experts should not go beyond their knowledge base, which is what the law actually requires of them (Dennis 2007; *R* v. *Bowman* [2006] EWCA Crim 417). Other, less research-based, knowledge will have to be drawn upon for predictions beyond 20 weeks. The professionals will have to decide whether that research is sufficiently robust for inferences to be drawn even though it was not the subject matter of the research (Schum 1994). That research, even though being relied upon more than it should be, may be better than nothing.

So, when undertaking a risk assessment the decision-makers should include, and only include, all the outcomes which they reasonably consider could be caused by their decision, and which could occur within the period covered by their risk. They should also be very aware that this is what they are doing, and explain it to others. They may have to 'fight' to make themselves understood. For example, a lawyer might ask a professional in a witness box: 'Is there a risk to my client; yes or no?' They ought, respectfully but professionally, to refuse to answer such questions for several reasons. The one relevant to this part of this chapter is that any answer, such as the one sought, would not refer to a risk period. The court or tribunal is liable to interpret any simple 'Yes' or 'No' answer as referring to the rest of the client's life or another substantial period of time. The witness is unlikely to be competent to say that, and so would have given a false, or negligent answer. Risk-taking for other people is difficult enough without accepting more responsibility, or claiming more competence, than is proper. 'Your Honour; I am sorry but I cannot properly answer that question without limiting my opinion to a specific period of time.'

Outcomes, consequences: identifying benefits

There may be some truth in the observation that in our private lives we tend to concentrate on the benefits of risk-taking (e.g. driving, smoking, drinking, playing sports), but in our professional lives we focus on the harms, what might go wrong. If so it is not too difficult to understand. Being responsible for other people, and making decisions about what might happen to them, is naturally worrying. But it may make us conservative in what we think are risks. Recall, however, that risk-taking is not synonymous with harm avoidance. Risk-taking, in particular in a professional context and for other people, is purposive.

That is an important point. Consider any risk decision with which you are, or were, concerned because of your profession. Perhaps you were involved in a decision to return a child to his or her parents, even though there was evidence that they had avoidably neglected the child in the past. Why did you take that decision? What do you hope to achieve by it? The goals of your proposed risk decision provided you with the potential justification for your action. How else were you going to justify taking the risk that a child may be abused again, or the equivalent, for your risk decision? As individual competent adults we can take risks, affecting ourselves, for the sheer pleasure of it. (However, note that many of the risks we might think of in this context – for example dangerous sports – would actually affect many other people, such as our family and taxpayers, if harm resulted.) Taking risks with other people for our pleasure or for our professional edification cannot be justified. It must be for a purpose. Risk-taking with other people is, or most certainly should be, purposive behaviour. It may involve reacting to a problem – someone is threatening another person with what looks like a gun – but that reaction is still for a purpose.

Invariably, the purpose of professional risk-taking with other people is for potential benefits. The risk is only being considered, and can only be justified, because its likely benefits may be more important than the possible harms. Risk assessment is being undertaken to consider whether this is true. This provides a simple, but exceptionally important, aid to risk assessment. Identify the purpose of the risk-taking. List all the reasons – provided that they are reasonably likely to be caused by the risk decision and arise during the risk period – why the risk should be taken. That should add a lot of potential outcomes, all beneficial, to the list for consideration.

Two of the main reasons why a prisoner is being allowed out of prison for part of the day are to enable him to organise accommodation and employment for when he is released. If he can succeed at this – it not being guaranteed – it will make it considerably more likely that he will not offend again, or so soon, when released. There are several other reasons, such as giving the prisoner increased motivation to plan for release and to prepare for a world outside which might have changed considerably since he was imprisoned. These are all potentially very significant benefits that could accrue from taking the risk decision to release this offender before the end of his full sentence. These potential benefits should be valued (see below) and, when multiplied with their likelihood, considered on the plus side of the rationale for risk-taking.

Professional risk-takers may be unused to this approach (Brearley 1982), although concede the logic. They have become accustomed to regarding 'risk' as only being relevant to potential harms. They, as have so many, have implicitly defined 'risk' as only being about possible harms (Royal Society 1992; Yates 1992). But that is not the only problem. They also become quite competent at thinking of things that might go wrong. The law and legal system does not help. Coroners are only involved because someone has died; people only go to law to sue, or seek inquiries because something has gone wrong. We have procedures and invest an awful lot of resources in examining what went wrong. We do not, certainly at any systematic level, investigate and/or praise successful or high-quality risk-taking.

This is part of what has come to be known as the 'blame culture'. We tend to assume that if the outcome was unsuccessful, if harm resulted, then there must have been fault, and there must be someone who is to be blamed. Sometimes the conclusion will be appropriate. Blame is deserved. But it is important to appreciate that, because of the nature of risk-taking, it simply does not follow automatically. If there is a 1 in 10,000 chance of death then, assuming only that the assessment is sound, you should expect 1 person in 10,000 to die, even if that is a member of our family. That risk of death, or whatever, exists independent of poor-quality risk-taking. Of course, if there is poor-quality risk-taking then there may be more than 1 in 10,000 deaths. So each serious outcome should be investigated to discover whether it was the consequence of a poor or good risk-taking decision. That is appropriate. But it is inappropriate to assume that there was poor decision-making, just because of the negative outcome. It is equally inappropriate to assume that, just because a risk decision led to successful outcomes, that the decision was well taken. It might not have been. It could have benefited from good luck. Unfortunately, the law is not interested in poorly taken risk decisions that do not produce harm that can be compensated. But employers and professional bodies can, and should be, concerned, and they are entitled to take action. Risk decisions need to be judged by the decision processes involved, not by their outcomes.

Those who take risk decisions affecting other people as part of their work should automatically – explicitly and proudly – identify the objectives of their risk-taking as potential benefits. Not only will this make it easier to justify their decisions but it should also begin to have a profound effect on the 'blame culture' and the reluctance of many professionals to be involved in taking risks affecting their clients or patients. The reality is that the vast majority of risk decisions taken by professionals lead to benefits. The more that this is appreciated the more likely it is that a positive culture will develop. For example, teams of risk decision-makers could and, it is suggested, should develop a practice of reviewing the last decision they made before making a fresh risk decision in respect of a patient or client. How did it turn out? Was that due to their decision? Whether successful or harmful, have the reasons for that result been identified? Have those whose contribution was good or bad been identified and praised or counselled? Has the team learnt from the experience? Risk-taking is among the most professional aspects of many jobs. Usually it leads to success. That is what it ought to be associated with. Think how useful it would be, when being cross-examined in court by a hostile lawyer, to be able to respond, truthfully: 'I have kept a record of all the significant risk decisions which I have taken, or with which I have been involved, in a formal manner, in my professional capacity. Only 3, out of more than 1000 cases, have been associated with negative outcomes. And I have taken many more risk decisions informally, because they were less risky, all leading to success.'

Some might respond that this analysis and advice is sound but it would involve too much extra work. Given that most risk decisions lead to successful outcomes, why bother with listing all the potential benefits as well as all the harms which, after all, and being realistic, are what everyone is worried about? First, listing potential benefits ought not to involve much, if any, extra work. Risk decision-makers ought to know what they are trying to do. Thus they should already know what their objectives are. (If they do not then they ought to be ashamed and be prepared accept opprobrium and litigation.) It may not be necessary to re-write these objectives in another risk assessment document. Second, failure to identify and emphasise the potential benefits of risk-taking will not help tackle the 'blame culture' and fear of risk-taking in professional contexts. Third, failing to identify the potential benefits of the risk-taking will make it easier for them to be sued.

Some might argue that there is no point in listing and considering all the potential benefits before the decision is taken: 'Let's wait until we discover the outcome. If harm occurs we will, then, think of all the potential benefits there could have been and we can mention them in our evidence.' Now, consider what is likely to happen if the inquiry team discovers that that is what happened. The team will be bound to condemn the decision-making! Any risk decision-makers who deliberately failed to identify, analyse and assess, the existence, potential value and likelihood of benefits of risk-taking would manifestly not have done their job properly. A risk decision may be justified in itself (so that no claim for negligence would succeed), but the way that it was taken may deserve condemnation (leading to action by employers, professional bodies and official inquiries). The potential benefits of risk-taking should be an integral part of risk assessment, never just an afterthought.

Someone might also argue that, in his or her line of work or in respect of a particular decision, there are no potential benefits to be had. This must be challenged rigorously. It has been heard to be said that there are no benefits for consideration in relation to risk-taking with high-security patients or prisoners. That is wrong. First, with such examples there is the question of whose benefit? There is both benefit to the public, who could be at risk, as well as benefit for the offender or patient. Second, there is the question whether those who make such points are speaking descriptively – there are, in fact, no benefits to be had – or normatively, i.e. that such people ought not to receive benefits. If they mean the latter they are being unprofessional and possibly acting unlawfully; it is not for them to punish offenders or patients. But there will usually be potential benefits. For example, it ought to be possible to work towards offenders requiring less supervision, albeit still within a secure perimeter, or from their only being allowed plastic cutlery to being allowed proper utensils and so forth. A consequence of that could be increased motivation and co-operation by the offender or patient. A consequence of that could be, over time and after regular rigorous testing, placement in less secure, less expensive, settings. In reality it ought to be impossible *not* to be able to think of potential benefits of risk-taking.

What about end of life risk-taking? What benefits can professionals working in geriatric, in particular psycho-geriatric, services place into the risk equation? Death may be imminent. The individuals concerned may lack capacity to express preference and their lives retain little if any privacy or dignity. Life's length may be extended – it is not being argued that longer life is necessarily a benefit, although within many belief systems that is an explicit or implicit article of faith – and its quality retained. It is doubtful if there is a state of affairs where we could not say, if we were the patient or client and could communicate effectively, that we would not want something to happen. If that is realistic it is a potential benefit. Dignity is, of course, an exceptionally important value. There may be few, if any, tangible benefits that are achievable; we may have to think in terms of reducing the speed of a terminal patient's decline. But it should be possible to identify some benefits.

Outcomes, consequences: how much?

The discussion to this point has assumed that it is relatively easy to describe the outcomes of risk-taking. In reality it can be very difficult. Several examples, up to this point, have been about the risk of death. That has not just been because it is dramatic and attention-grabbing, but also because it is relatively explicit. We are either dead or alive. Actually, this might be contested as we sometimes refer to 'living deaths' and there could be problems with unconscious states. But death is still relatively dichotomous; it is one thing or the other. Compare it with concepts such as 'injury', 'motivation', 'happiness', 'pain'. These are much more relative. Injuries may be very serious, life-threatening, or minor, trivial. Motivation may be essential, for example in the sense of necessary if a further step in rehabilitation is to be achieved, or simply nice, useful. Quality risk assessment requires us to think about the amount of harm, or benefit, which might be achieved.

This is difficult and can lead to exasperation; it is difficult enough predicting what kind of thing could happen without having to specify exactly to which degree it may happen. But the problems should not be overstated and we should recall that we are concerned with risk-taking which, by definition, involves uncertainty. Recall what the law of negligence, discussed in Chapter 3, requires. It does not require professionals to get it right every time; they only need make such decisions as a responsible body of co-professionals would make. But that should be understood as referring both to (a) what they decide and (b) how they decide it. Risk decision-makers should make reasonable decisions. They should identify and include reasonable potential outcomes. In practice it could be more important that they think about responsible ways of making their decisions.

For example, consider a case where a client or patient might suffer physical injury as a consequence of a risk being taken, say, after a fall. How serious might this be? It could be very serious, perhaps a broken hip causing lots of pain, incapacity for some time and requiring surgery. Or it might just involve a bruise. How much harm – or benefit – should be taken into account when assessing this risk? One approach would be to list every conceivable degree of harm or benefit and assess the likelihood of each. But that would be entirely wrong, as well as time-consuming. First, we should identify separate outcomes, for example distinguish physical injury from damage to property. Second, we should identify a reasonable degree of benefit or harm for each, separate, outcome. Third, we should rely on the reality that degrees of harm, and benefit, develop in a 'sequence'. We can assume that all broken hips will involve bruising but all cases of bruising will not include broken hips. Stabbing someone, for another example, entails a number of lesser injuries; a serious injury necessarily involves lesser injuries.

We need to fix on a reasonable degree of loss, or benefit. This should be appropriate to the case. For example, we should anticipate that the degree of injury to an elderly person from falling will be greater than to a younger, sturdier individual. Professionals should be expected to have better knowledge than lay people as to what these outcomes are most likely to be. In practice it will regularly be wise to identify the degree of outcome considered to be most likely, most realistic. It should not be a case of finding the mean or 'average' outcome, within a range, but rather the mode, the most likely to occur. There may be concern that a patient will kill him- or herself. But it might be much more likely that this individual will neglect him- or herself within the risk period concerned. Only separate outcomes should be included. It would be appropriate to assess the risk that this individual might injure him- or herself and might injure another, because both of those could occur within the risk period. But it is inappropriate to assess both the risk of the individual killing, as well as neglecting, himself or herself, since the former 'includes' the latter.

It will be easier to understand the rationale for doing this if likelihood is included in the examples. Consider the comparative likelihood of falling and being bruised, or of falling and breaking your hip, of killing or injuring yourself. The less serious outcome has to be more likely than the more serious. This has to be the case, in the vast majority of situations, although modern surgical techniques can frustrate this analysis. It appears possible, now, to perform major internal surgery with minor impressions upon the skin. However, ordinarily, you can only 'get to' the more serious outcomes via the less serious. In law if you have committed grievous bodily harm on another person (Section 18 of the Offences Against the Person Act 1861) you will also have committed actual bodily harm (Section 47). But if you have caused actual bodily harm you have not necessarily also committed grievous bodily harm. It has to be actual bodily harm before it can be the more serious offence of causing grievous bodily harm. It has to be more likely that one person will be injured than that three will be. Every time risk decision-makers choose a reasonable outcome to assess, likelihood will be attached in due course. If they choose a serious outcome, such as death, then their likelihood assessment will be lower than if they chose a less serious outcome, such as serious injury. It is *not* being suggested that there is a direct, mathematical, relationship between the two. But there is a 'logical' or commonsense relationship which risk-takers should adopt to help them both to make difficult risk decisions and to justify them.

If a lawyer was to criticise a risk-taker for not assessing the risk that the victim would die, which is what happened, the decision-maker ought to be able to promptly, and correctly, reply that – actually – death was foreseen but, for the reasons specified, it was considered more realistic to assess the likelihood of serious injury. The risk-taker should go on to explain that that outcome was given a higher likelihood assessment than death would have been given, if that had been chosen as the possible consequence. The higher likelihood of lesser outcomes 'balances' the lower assessment or valuation of more serious outcomes. The relationship is not perfect; the degree of likelihood does not increase in a proportion exactly related to how the seriousness of the outcome reduces. But decision-makers would be entitled to draw upon that relationship both to explain and to justify their choice of the outcomes to assess. They cannot justify assessing the value and likelihood both of death and of serious injuries occurring (let alone more alternative outcomes along the general range of physical injuries) and taking both (or all) of them into account. Decision-makers should have little to worry about if the process is rational and the assessments reasonable.

Outcomes, consequences: assessing values

Once the potential outcomes, beneficial as well as harmful, are identified it is necessary to assign them values. It cannot simply be concluded that a risk is worth taking just because there are more potential benefits than there are potential harms. Nor the converse: failing to take a risk cannot be justified just because we can think of more possible harmful outcomes than benefits. One outcome may be so potentially harmful that 20 or more potential benefits may come nowhere close to justifying it although, of course, this can also be concluded after taking likelihood into account. But how are we to value outcomes; where are we to find authority for our assessments; how are we to express them?

Whose values?

Think of a risk decision that a professional may have to take for, or with, a client or patient; for example, whether to perform surgery or to advise that a couple with significant learning disabilities should not be discouraged, let alone prevented, from living together without other support. Whose values should be taken into account when assessing such risks? If the patient and couple are adults, are legally competent to make the decisions and it is not a decision about protecting others' interests (e.g. whether someone should be detained to protect other persons) then, in the last resort, it is their values which matter. (See Chapter 3 for the law on capacity, competence and consent.) The doctor may believe that surgery is the obvious way forward, that there is little risk involved, that those side-effects that he or she mentioned to the patient would not be at all serious even if they occurred. But if the patient is legally entitled to make the treatment decision then the doctor is powerless to do anything other than seek to persuade. Does it follow that, in such a case, risk assessment is superfluous? It is the patient's decision and that can be made on irrational grounds. No. The doctor, and anyone in a similar case, is obliged to advise the patient or client about the risks involved.

The professional's duty of care, not just in the law of negligence, would include giving appropriate advice, and in an appropriate manner (particularly where the Mental Capacity Act 2005 is involved) for the client or patient to make an informed decision, if he or she wished. Whilst the professional must concede that the patient or client has the last word on whether the risk is taken, it is the patient's or client's values that count. But the professional need not adopt the patient's or client's value system. He or she should explain and assess the risk in 'objective' terms. The professional should identify the outcomes that he or she considers appropriate, both positive and negative, and a reasonable degree of severity. For example, if the risk included the possibility of side-effects from a drug the professional ought to use his or her specialist knowledge of other patients who have experienced these side-effects, research studies and other relevant knowledge when considering which side-effects to mention and how seriously to rate them. The patient may have little, if any, or mistaken knowledge of the significance of these side-effects or other possible outcomes. He or she may reject the professionals' information and advice but sufficient information must be provided. A failure to give responsible advice about any risks, according to the standard of care in the law of negligence, could mean that the patient did not give legal consent (*Sidaway* v. *Bethlem RHG* [1985] 1 All ER 643; Montgomery 2003).

It is different if the patient lacks legal capacity to make the decision (see Chapter 3). It is also different if the risk relates to, or includes, possible harms to third parties. Offenders cannot consent to the risk of them harming members of the public and thereby effect their early release from prison. Parents cannot decide that they pose no risk to their children, so that they must be returned from social services' care. Patients with a mental disorder, even if adults with legal capacity, cannot require that they be allowed to leave hospital if they are considered, by legally relevant people, to be a sufficient danger to themselves or others that they have been legally detained. In these cases the professionals are not advising the clients or patients, they are taking the decisions for them.

Which values?

Where are risk decision-makers to get their values from? They cannot just adopt their own personal, non-professional (which is very different from unprofessional), values. Rather, they should first seek to identify any 'legal values' by which they are bound.

Some 'legal values' exist. For example, in relation to risk-taking with reference to child protection, the Children Act 1989 specifies, for England and Wales, that the child's interests are paramount (Section 1(1)). But it seems as if a number of other things are almost as paramount and the section has lost the explicitness it seemed originally to have. Also, there is the Mental Health Act 1983, which specifies levels, or degrees, of risk which must exist before certain action, such as detaining patients, is permissible. For example, under the 1983 Act, there has to be a 'serious risk' before a hospital order is permissible, whilst a mere 'risk' is sufficient for a treatment order. The difference between the two orders relates to who is empowered to discharge the patient. Despite this significant consequence the difference between a mere 'risk' and a 'serious risk' is unclear and could depend entirely on individual judgements. No further clarification is provided in the Act, such as whether 'serious' relates to the possible outcomes and/or their likelihood. The values articulated in the European Convention on Human Rights would also be very appropriate, not least because the Human Rights Act 1998 requires that public authorities give effect to the Convention. But the general language, and provision for exceptions, is liable to make it difficult to apply the values in specific cases.

It would also be appropriate to consider any 'implicit' legal values. For example, the law values individualism. It is a premise of the law of contract that individuals may make their own bargains. We may all, overwhelmingly, be of the opinion that Grant got the better of the bargain with Phil. We cannot understand how Phil was so stupid as to accept that bargain. But, the law insists, provided that Phil did not lack capacity to make that contract and Grant did not use false, forceful or cheating methods, it is up to them. We may worry about the consequences for Phil's family, but that is not a relevant consideration.

After any 'legal values' have been considered the decision-makers should draw upon values respected by their, and by cognate, disciplines or professions. Whilst this would be professionally appropriate it is also legally wise. If there is to be litigation then the court or inquiry will, invariably, be examining whether the decisions taken accorded with the practice of a responsible body of co-professionals. Chapter 7 will develop these ideas and make the case for the development of 'risk policies' or 'protocols'. These should articulate a range of values considered important within the discipline in question. This is particularly important where the values are vague, or third parties, such as lay judges and members of the public, are liable to disagree with the values or not appreciate their importance.

Include values that others might not appreciate
Take the example of 'motivation'. How important is it that a client or patient is motivated to work with the professionals involved? Ask a lay person how important it is that an offender should recognise the nature of his or her problems and become motivated to change? Lay people may be reluctant to acknowledge the importance of motivation at all, preferring punishment to rehabilitation. But, given that the professional risk-takers are required to seek rehabilitative goals, that is not the issue. Nevertheless, when required to concede that motivation is relevant, they are liable to rate it as little more than something generally desirable, as a good thing. But relevant professionals are likely to declare that it is exceptionally important, indeed critical. Motivation to change is one of the most important things that they can achieve.

Why is this difference so important? Imagine that a risk decision was made, that harm resulted, that an inquiry is being held. The professionals may declare that one of their objectives, and a potential benefit of taking the risk, was to increase their patient's or client's motivation. So far so good, but they could be referring to 'motivation', meaning something exceptionally important, critical to progress, whereas the lay members of the inquiry understand something much less important, that it was just a useful thing to achieve. It is very important that risk decision-makers identify goals, objectives or values which mean something significantly different, even if only in degree, from how other people are likely to consider them. They should keep asking themselves whether they value the risk outcome under consideration (whether potentially beneficial or harmful) significantly more or less than lay people are likely to do so. If they do then they need to take steps, such as articulating that explicitly in any risk policy they develop. Now they will be in a much better position to make it very clear to judges and other inquiries, if necessary, that this is how they value the significance of that outcome.

Someone with a mental disorder may declare: 'I am going to kill myself.' Hearing that lay people are liable to be anxious and worried; they will find it difficult to understand why mental health professionals do not always respond to such statements with as much anxiety as they do. But, to professionals, it may not be so significant (recall *Gauntlett* v. *Northampton AHA*, described in Chapter 3). However, if the harm occurred, the patient committed suicide, any clinician coming to an inquiry and saying: 'But it means something different to us,' is liable to be interpreted as trying to avoid blame. If outcomes are valued differently by professionals, they should make this clear, explicit and provable in advance of deci-sion-making. It would be better if the clinician could, truthfully, say, 'I refer you to the current risk-taking policy which we use to inform and improve our decision-making. See paragraph 14 where we articulate how important it is, in our line of work, to get patients motivated to work with us.'

Include the intangible

The outcomes of risk-taking do not have to be tangible. Clearly, pain could as easily be a consequence as a broken bone, even though it may be much more difficult both to prove and to quantify that pain. Risk-takers are not limited to considering consequences for which the courts would award compensation. For example, risk-takers should, where appropriate, take into account outcomes such as dignity, rights, freedom, privacy and so on. Risk-taking can increase, or diminish, these consequences. So it can be useful to put ourselves into the position of the people we are advising, or on whose behalf we are taking the risks. How, for example, would we like it if our legal right to manage our property was taken away from us? How would we enjoy the loss of the practical power to make a range of choices? We might, jokingly, respond that it would be nice to be relieved of the responsibilities, but a little consideration should lead us to appreciate the significance of the relative powerlessness of being in that position. Perhaps we could cope with one night in prison – knowing that we will be released the next day. But what about coping for three months; how much would we hate that?

Exercise: exemplifying the importance of articulating values

A useful exercise for members of a team involved in risk-taking with patients or clients involves identifying a number of possible outcomes, both harmful and beneficial, that could occur from the kinds of risks they take or advise upon. It is particularly helpful if this exercise involves people from different disciplines within the team, who can call upon their differential knowledge, experience and working philosophies. They should seek to identify outcomes which are specific in the sense that everyone will have a good idea of the degree, or extent, of the consequences involved. One outcome could involve a broken limb which requires treatment in casualty for three hours, wearing a cast for a month and two weeks off work. Another could be losing control over your personal income, bank accounts, savings and so on for six months. Once a series of contrasting outcomes have been listed, each person in the team should be invited to assess, in secret, how significant he or she considers each outcome to be. This could be done in terms of a scale where −10 is the equivalent of one person's death, zero is neutral (i.e. is neither good nor bad) and +10 is the opposite of death, if there is any such 'equivalent'. An alternative mechanism would be to take one beneficial and one harmful outcome and then rate everything in comparison with them. For example, a broken leg might be rated as three times worse than a broken arm, losing control over your income as ten times worse.

When everyone has made their assessments they should be made public. Keeping them secret at this stage avoids letting anyone change his or her mind when he or she hears what others have concluded. It is important to avoid 'group think' where people fall in with what appears to be a majority, given, or just historically accepted position. Why one individual thinks very differently from another could be as important as discovering why, for example, nurses rate certain outcomes significantly differently from doctors. An individual with a very different rating from the majority may have misunderstood the exercise (perhaps wrongly included an assessment of likelihood) or he or she may have a valuable perspective which others should consider.

This exercise will show that people disagree. That should not be surprising and it is not a problem. We are dealing with an area of work where differences of values and opinions both abound and are legitimate. (The standard of care, in the law of negligence, is that of *a*, not *the*, responsible body of co-professionals.)

The focus should, first, be on the extent to which there is a degree of consensus, and only then on the extent to which this might differ from how lay people might complete the same exercise. There may be little consensus on how the same outcomes are rated by different people. But is there a degree of consensus in how people comparatively rate the outcomes? Three outcomes, (a), (b) and (c), may be described in different ways or given different numerical ratings by different people. But do they all, or almost all, agree that (a) is more significant than (b), which is more significant than (c)? That much agreement could be very valuable. Does the exercise 'tell us' something significant about the professions involved? For example, one of the authors of this book ran such an exercise and discovered that an audience of psychiatric nurses (with considerable internal agreement) regarded the seriousness or significance of detaining a mentally disordered patient as three times more serious than he did. That, as an example, may appear unimportant and say more about the author than anything else. But imagine that the author was actually a member of a tribunal reviewing a risk decision, such as whether to detain a patient for a month. Those nurses could simply state that they had regard to the seriousness of depriving the patient of his or her liberty for a month. But would the judge or tribunal 'really' understand how seriously those nurses took that deprivation of liberty? They, like the author until he undertook the exercise, may think they share the same values but be unaware that they differ, by a factor of three. This sort of exercise is very valuable for ensuring that any 'special' values, which might differ from those of lay people, are identified. Only if they are identified does anyone have a chance of drawing them to the attention of those who judge risk-takers' actions.

Risk-taking: an inexact science
Readers may be disappointed with this part of this chapter. You may have expected and want more certainty, less disagreement, and want to be told which outcomes you are to take into account and how you must rate them. Sadly, it is not possible for anyone – outside of legislative instruction – to tell you how and what you are to think, and it would be grossly improper for us to attempt to do so. You are the professional; you are the one with special knowledge about both how serious or valuable outcomes can be and about how your colleagues think about them. Turn to your professional books and colleagues for guidance. Remember the law. To avoid breaching any standard of care that applies you have only to make a decision with which a responsible body of professional colleagues, not all or the best of them, would agree. The law does not require consensus, only

that you come within the range of values and decisions that responsible colleagues would make. If you can demonstrate that you made a 'rational' decision (see *Bolitho* v. *City & Hackney Health Authority* ([1988] AC 232) discussed in Chapter 3) then you should be safe. Being able to demonstrate that you thought about, considered and debated how to value outcomes, how you consulted colleagues, will be seen as more 'rational' than failing to do so.

The consequences of risk-taking for whom?

Obviously, we are concerned about the consequences for the patient or client concerned. But should we think of others? The question, for example, is whether child protection officers should take the risk of returning a child to his or her parents. Should the outcomes for the parents be taken into account? No, not directly, for this is a special case. It is the child's interests that the professionals must focus upon. If taking the risk will affect the parents positively (such as by maximising their willingness to work with social workers) or negatively, that is likely to affect the child's interests or experiences. If the effects upon the parents are liable to rebound on the child then they are certainly relevant to consider, but because of their effect on the child. A partner might benefit from an offender's early release, for example, to permit a marriage to be saved. A secure marriage, at least in the sense of providing accommodation and some social support, should reduce the risk of re-offending. To that extent the partner's interests are significant but beyond that they are unlikely to be relevant to the risk decision.

If we risk discharging this hospital patient then it will free up a bed for someone else, to that person's benefit. Can we take this into account when assessing the risk relating to the first patient? Here we should distinguish between private and public services. It would be unrealistic to ignore this factor with regard to public services. Professionals in the public sector are, inevitably, also involved in rationing and maximising the value of the resources available to them. Indeed, many will regularly find themselves having to take risks forced by competition for resources such as hospital beds. Prison officials may have to consider taking more risks because there are insufficient places in the total prison system for all those being sentenced by the courts. Taking account of the consequences to others is perfectly appropriate in this sense. The real issue is the extent to which it is valued. The issue remains the appropriateness of taking the proposed risk for that client, patient or offender, not other people. The rights of other patients and clients who are owed duties of care must be considered separately, even when they overlap and intermesh. They are all individual people, cases and individual risk decisions.

But risk-taking in the private sector should be different. Here, however, 'private' should refer to functions rather than financing arrangements. A charitable or for-profit hospital, prison and so on may have to make risk decisions which could affect members of the public, for example discharge someone who might act violently. But a for-profit hospital which was simply deciding whether to risk the discharge of a private patient should only take the patient's interests into account. That they might make more money through discharging that patient and admitting another should not be a relevant consideration for that risk decision.

Include the consequences of inaction

Naturally, when thinking about risk assessment the focus is on the consequences of taking the proposed decision. But think also about the consequences of inaction. Should the doctor prescribe a medicine which might treat the symptoms but might also cause side-effects? Certainly the risk posed by that medication should be investigated. But what would happen if the risk decision to give the medication was not taken? Of course cases will differ greatly but continuation of the symptoms for some time is likely, indeed, is implicit. It is not a 'simple' decision of whether or not to take that risk, the medication, but rather it includes a comparison of the consequences of action and inaction. Should Jane, an elderly patient, be discharged? If she goes home then she might fall and break a hip and have to be re-admitted to hospital. Against is that Jane wants to go home to a more familiar life with more independence and dignity. Is that the simple choice? We need to investigate what the consequence of inaction would involve. For example, it is likely that with continued hospitalisation Jane will lose some skills in independent living, such as mobility and self-care. Indeed, special programmes, involving resources, may be needed within the hospital to maintain those skills. And Jane might be as likely to fall and break a hip during those hospital-based activities. (The difference would be in the speed with which someone could assist and tackle the pain and other injuries.)

So, when listing the potential outcomes of a risk, decision-makers should ensure that they include the consequences of inaction. What is it reasonable to contemplate could occur if the risk is not taken? Any existing 'problems', such as symptoms, are very likely to continue.

Although here the focus is on the *outcomes* of risk-taking it is worth noting that the likelihood of an existing problem continuing because of inaction will regularly be certain. The patient being treated for a mental disorder may lose motivation if not allowed to leave the hospital grounds for a day. The treatment team may decide to postpone deciding whether to take that risk. The likelihood of that patient being disappointed, by the (risk) decision to postpone the decision is certain. This is appropriately referred to as a likelihood of one. So, to make the point mathematically, the continuation of a relatively minor outcome (rated as $-.1$) is ten times more serious than a low likelihood (say, 0.001) of a very serious (-10) outcome ($-1 \times 1 = 1$ compared with $-10 \times 0.001 = 0.01$, assuming a common risk period).

As has been stressed, professional risk-taking with or for other people should be purposeful. It is designed to bring about a different, better, state of affairs. So it will be a rare case where inaction will have no costs or consequences. Notice that this is another way of identifying more potential benefits of risk-taking. Including these outcomes in the balance will, regularly, make it much easier to justify taking a risk. Failing to identify them, not assessing their significance and likelihood, would be poor practice. Should we risk allowing an offender day-release in preparation for formal release? In addition to the potential harms of the offender re-offending whilst on release and not returning to prison there are the potential benefits of making future re-offending less likely. And there are the consequences of inaction. What harms and benefits are reasonably likely to arise from inaction? It is easy for the media to advocate, and for a government minister to decide against, allowing early release of offenders but failure to seek benefits has its consequences and costs.

Some might argue, particularly because it is risk-taking with other people, that it is wise to be conservative. Thus they might argue that it is appropriate to ignore the consequences of inaction, to concentrate on harmful outcomes rather than benefits. But they would be wrong. It may be appropriate to be conservative about risk-taking but that should occur at the time of making the decision, not at the time of collecting the information needed to make it. It may, depending upon the case, be appropriate to decide that a risk should only be taken if the potential benefits greatly exceed the possible harms. That can only be decided upon once information has been collected about those likely benefits and harms, and the potential for risk management has been considered. Possible outcomes, whether beneficial or harmful, should only be excluded if irrelevant, if, for example, they do not relate to the risk period, or are of so little consequence, whether because so unlikely or of so little significance, that they could make little difference to the overall decision.

Likelihood

Risk assessment involves collecting and assessing information about both elements of risk-taking: the outcomes and their possibility. The first part of this chapter has concentrated on the outcomes and several problems were identified. Fortunately, there are fewer – conceptual – problems with assessing likelihood.

Whose likelihood?

It has been emphasised that legally competent adults are entitled to decide whether to take a risk which does not threaten harm to others. They may be clients or patients but, if legally competent, it is their ultimate decision. Any professionals involved should still advise them about what they consider the risks to be, but they are not entitled to force their views upon them. It is the clients' and patients' values that matter, however much we might regard them as unwise and improper. However, even though it does not make a difference to the final decision, there is an important difference between outcomes and likelihood.

If a competent adult considers embarrassment to be much more serious than, say, two broken legs then, it is hoped, professionals will try to help him or her over the problem with being embarrassed. But, in the end, that adult is entitled to make decisions based on that unusual and strange judgement. Professionals can and should explain if, for example, they think the patient has an exaggerated fear of a side-effect of a drug or treatment of which they have considerably more experience than the patient. If they fail, they must allow the patient to make his or her own judgement. But contrast that position with the patient's 'misjudgement' of the likelihood.

Imagine a patient believes that he or she has a nine in ten chance of experiencing a particular side-effect, but the doctor knows that the best research puts it as a 1 in 100 chance. That is different. The doctor has a duty to correct the patient, irrespective of whether he or she is legally competent. This time the patient is wrong. The error is one of fact rather than value. The best knowledge, based on current science about this drug, rather than a value judgement, tells us so. Professionals are not entitled to impose their value judgements on the legally competent because their values are not more correct. But they can, and should, point out and explain when and why they believe a competent patient or client is using wrong likelihood information. However, in the last resort they cannot impose their information because it is the legally competent adult's decision. But they can, and should, insist that they know more and better about the likelihood – of course, only if they do.

Measuring outcomes involves value judgements. Assessing likelihood does not. We need to know how likely it is that the offender will re-offend, the patient will experience side-effects or not return to the ward and so on. We can wish that something is very likely, that it be virtually impossible, or whatever. But our wishes can change nothing. The likelihood of the outcome is given (subject to risk management: see Chapter 5) even if we do not know it to any exact degree. But we should not, and professionals cannot, give up at the first sight of a little local difficulty. We may not know what the likelihood of the patient committing suicide actually is, but certain predictions are plain stupid; some appear sensible but others are considered the best. The risk assessor's duty is, within the time and resources reasonably available, to identify the best statement of likelihood. This should not be a guess; this should be based upon the best science (knowledge) available, applied to the particular risk proposed and the surrounding circumstances. That the harm feared does occur cannot prove that the prediction was wrong, or negligently assessed. The issue is whether the likelihood assessment was within what a responsible body of professional risk-takers would have considered.

Likelihood knowledge from where?
The knowledge source for the assessment of likelihood will depend upon the type of risk involved. The quality of that knowledge will also vary. To an extent this is inevitable. It is, for example, easier to undertake high-quality research into the risk of side-effects of medicines than it is

into the likelihood that sex offenders will re-offend within a particular period. It is much easier, and more ethical (e.g. to provide placebo treatments), to control the relevant variables in healthcare settings. There are so many other factors which could influence an offender's behaviour.

It is useful to adopt the cognitive continuum model initiated by Hammond (1978) (but see also the explanation by Hamm (1988)). This model suggests that we can, and should, distinguish six 'levels' of 'knowledge' that can support a risk decision. The key points, for us, are first that different levels of knowledge will exist for different risk decisions. Second, when making a risk decision, we ought to utilise knowledge from the 'highest' level available. The lowest level of knowledge is 'intuitive judgement'. This refers to an individual decision-maker's knowledge, experience and attitude towards a decision. It could include 'gut feelings', where people claim a 'feeling' or 'sense' based upon experience. Next is 'peer-aided judgement'. Here, two or more people will share knowledge, intuitions, experience and discuss their assumptions and predictions. It draws upon the popular saying that 'two heads are better than one'. It could cover decisions where one person makes the decision but, after genuine consideration of others' recommendations, makes the decision (e.g. where a psychiatrist is legally responsible for recommending a patient's detention, but asks colleagues, including other disciplines, first). 'System-aided judgement' would include any appropriate process for aiding the decision-making. This book offers many system aids, for example ensuring both benefits and harms are assessed, and that outcomes and likelihood are both separately analysed before being jointly considered. It would also include the use of risk factors. Of course, the quality of these system aids will vary considerably; some lists of risk factors are little more than a checklist based upon an individual's imagination, experience, or both, whilst others are based upon high-quality, controlled, empirical research.

The next three categories are 'quasi-experiment', 'controlled trial' and 'scientific experiment'. These are three levels relating to the quality of scientific research involved in making the risk assessment. Clearly, findings from a rigorous scientific experiment, in which there will have been both test and control populations, are more reliable than those from a quasi-experiment, let alone an individual's intuitive judgement. They will be even more reliable if based upon a large research population which has been replicated, to similar conclusions, by other researchers in different parts of the world. But a major problem for professional risk-takers is that knowledge is not always available from these highest levels. High-quality research can be, and regularly is, undertaken into, for example, the efficacy and side-effects of drugs. Indeed, it must be undertaken before the drug obtains a licence for use. There the researchers can impose considerable controls with, for example, some patients receiving the drug being researched and others receiving a placebo, which may have a psychological, but will have no pharmacological, effects. Even the treating doctors can be kept in the dark about which patients are receiving the drug so that they cannot, even innocently, influence the results. But such research is not possible, and if it was often would be unethical, with regard to many other forms of risk. It is not lawful to detain someone who has not committed an offence in a prison or hospital (although changes in the law with regard to some people with personality disorders have been proposed) just because that would permit researchers to have a control group for their research.

The value of the cognitive continuum is that it reminds us that different levels, or standards, of knowledge exist. When making an assessment of likelihood we ought to use knowledge from the highest level, providing it is relevant knowledge. It used to be considered appropriate to consult the Delphic oracles, or to cut open a chicken and examine its entrails, or both, in order to make a decision. That is no longer an acceptable way of informing or assessing a risk, even if it might be said to constitute 'system-aided judgement'. Nor is astrology.

Are risk decisions being made with intuitive judgements or guesses when appropriate research data are available? If they are then that is, in the absence of special factors such as the lack of time and/or other resources for obtaining the information, poor practice. Is a risk assessment being made without consulting peers? A doctor may be responsible, ethically and legally, for making the risk decision but his or her failure to consult other peers or colleagues who may have relevant information, including other disciplines that may have more information about different aspects of the patient, is poor practice. Failure to use risk factors (system aids), presuming that they are professionally regarded and relevant, will be poor practice. If harm results from taking the risk then failure to use an appropriate source of knowledge could constitute the poor practice leading to a finding that the standard of care was broken. Even if it is decided that it was appropriate to take the risk decision, so that there cannot be liability for negligence, employers and professional organisations are entitled to, and should, condemn the process of decision-making. The method or process was improper.

Likelihood in this case

It may be objected that this approach – emphasising the importance of relying upon the best scientific knowledge available – removes or diminishes the contribution that the professionals can make. It may seem to be suggesting that risk-takers should simply seek likelihood information 'from the books' and apply that. But that would be a misunderstanding. Risk-takers should seek the best knowledge available as a starting point and then apply it to the particular case. The best research available might, for example, clearly indicate that the individual in question is exceptionally dangerous. But that must be considered in the context both of the individual's immediate circumstances and the potential available for creative risk management. The risk factors from quality research may proclaim that the individual is very dangerous, but what if he is immobile because both his legs and arms are broken? The research does not cover for such detail, nor should it be expected to do so. The research provides a starting point; applying it to the individual might lead to a revision up or down. What if this very dangerous individual, detained in a prison, wishes to attend his mother's funeral? The starting point is that he is very dangerous, but are there resources available to manage the risk? Will he agree to wear a body belt; are there enough staff, and further back-up staff, available to accompany him? As the next chapter will emphasise, it is not being argued that just because the risk can be managed that it must be. The point is that we should use the best knowledge available to provide the starting point for both risk assessment and management.

Actuarial is for assessment: 'clinical' is for management

There is a continuing, often controversial, debate between proponents of 'actuarial' and 'clinical' risk data. Some (e.g. Hare 2002) argue that background information, such as gender, age, past behaviour and key offence, are the best predictors of future behaviour. Others (e.g. Maden 2002) insist that the focus must always be on the individual concerned and include factors not covered by the empirical research which produces actuarial data. It would be possible to fill several pages of this book discussing this dispute. But the dispute is unnecessary, if not misguided.

Both 'sides' have important information to offer risk-takers. The issue is not *which* is better but *when, where* and *how* the information should be utilised.

Consistent with the cognitive continuum, it is proposed that actuarial information should be used, where available and applicable, to make initial risk *assessments*. Information about the individual, for example the extent to which he or she is motivated to work with others towards achieving the goals of the proposed risk, should then be taken into account in developing the risk *management* proposal. Car insurers use actuarial data, for example age, gender and number of prior accidents, when deciding how low an insurance rate they can risk offering. We could plead for lower rates on the basis that we are nice people and never break the speed limit, but it would fail. The insurers know that the actuarial method is the most accurate and appropriate approach to making such initial risk decisions. They also know that they must manage the risk or we may take our business elsewhere. So they offer us 'no claims bonuses' and similar. Actuarial data should be used for risk assessment; clinical information should be used for risk management.

Conclusion

This chapter has identified a number of problems facing those responsible for undertaking risk assessments affecting other people. It has emphasised the role of values in assessing the significance of different outcomes, and how, usually, it will be the client's or patient's values which will determine the decision. By contrast it has noted that assessment of likelihood should involve the best knowledge currently available. That exact agreement, whether on the seriousness of the outcomes or the degree of likelihood, is highly unlikely has been acknowledged. But that is not necessary. We are dealing with risk, which is defined by uncertainty. All that is needed for a legally justified risk decision is that the assessments follow a process and be within a range that responsible professional colleagues would support. How we might describe and communicate assessments of risk were not discussed; that will take place in Chapter 6. But first let us examine the role and contribution of risk management.

CHAPTER 5

Risk Management

Introduction

It has been established that a risk has two elements: outcomes and likelihood. These are the two core factors in risk assessment. It has also been stated that risk has a number of 'dimensions'. These relate to the context of the risk decision being considered. They relate to risk management and are the subject matter of this chapter. One way of looking at it is that the elements (e.g. what the formerly abusive parents might do and how likely that is) are beyond the direct control of the risk-takers. But the dimensions are, to an extent (e.g. the frequency with which skilled social workers review the case) within the risk-taker's control. Risk management can, thereby, affect the risk (what might happen and how likely).

Risk assessment may tell you, for example, that the offender recently convicted of a series of serious offences is too dangerous to be allowed release from prison to attend his mother's funeral. The amount of harm that could occur, multiplied by its likelihood, is so serious and so insufficiently offset by the likelihood of benefits that the risk should not be taken. That conclusion should be drawn from the best risk assessment information reasonably available. But, if the prisoner agreed to be placed in a body belt, was surrounded everywhere he went by, say, six wary and competent prison officers, and was taken to and from the churchyard in secure transport, then it might be safe – that is it might not be dangerous – to let him attend his mother's funeral. So risk management is concerned with how the risk decision is implemented. Risk judgements, the decisions taken, should consider risk management as well as risk assessment. Risk assessment provides the setting, and key information, for risk management to focus upon. But just because, as in this example, risk management might justify taking a decision which risk assessment did not support, it does not follow that it should be taken. Better use might be made of the six prison officers' time, for example. Risk management may show that a risk *could*, justifiably, be taken; it does not follow, from that, that it *should* be taken.

Kirk Heilbrun (1997) developed the distinction between risk assessment and risk management, with particular reference to forensic risk decisions. He emphasised how risk management has received much less attention, both in empirical research and policy analysis, than risk assessment. And yet risk management provides more powerful tools for controlling risk-taking. His approach may be affected by his therapeutic concerns and assumption that 'risk' only relates to negative outcomes. He is concerned with predicting and managing the violence of people in forensic settings. He focuses on risk reduction and notes (Heilbrun 2003) developments such as individualised analyses of risk (including individualised risk factors based upon an individual's history), tools which include risk management components, identification of treatment needs which will affect risk and emerging standards of professional practice.

Here the importance of risk management for not just reducing the likelihood of harm but for maximising the degree and likelihood of benefits is emphasised. The authors entirely agree with Heilbrun on the importance of direct risk management interventions with clients, for example providing substance abuse programmes before taking certain risks. But it is stressed that risk management has a major contribution to make to the decision-making process and with more situational factors (which Heilburn (1997, 2003) agrees are undervalued) where the emphasis would be on altering the 'setting' (rather than the client), such as arranging and supporting employment. Risk management strategies which individual clients or patients can adopt to make their lives easier are also included, but these could be more effective if negotiated with and supported by professionals. For example, Ryan (2000) identified people living with mental illnesses who would self-mutilate in order to prevent or minimise the risk they felt they were to other people. They also took steps to make it more difficult to give way to command hallucinations, for example making it difficult to leave a house when being instructed to throw themselves in front of a car. Not only were these people not being given medals for their selfless conduct, but they were often not getting support with such strategies from professionals. We now need comparable attention to be paid to risk management as was paid to risk assessment by skilled and properly resourced researchers such as the MacArthur Research Network on Mental Health and the Law (Monahan *et al.* 2001). That should incorporate both service and client strategies. Heilbrun's advocacy of risk management, which is relevant to all other areas of risk-taking, deserves wider appreciation (in relation to social work, see Titterton (2005)).

The dimensions of risk

Risk has a number of 'dimensions'. The common feature is that they are all forms of resources, although they may not all initially appear as such. They are all things which can, or cannot, be invested in the proposed risk. Sometimes those resources, six skilled prison officers in the example above, exist and can be utilised. Sometimes they do not. Sometimes they exist but the cost of using them is too high. It is not the nature or existence of these resources that matters so much as the potential for making effective use of them. Professional risk-taking will sometimes involve 'one-off' risks, for example letting a young offender go on a cross-country run from which he might abscond. But it is, perhaps, more often dynamic. A risk decision may be taken, for example, to discharge a patient from hospital despite his or her record for self-harming. Part of the plan for implementing the risk decision, that is its risk management, could be that a skilled person (e.g. community psychiatric nurse) visits the patient within a certain period. This person will be able to manage the risk (to an extent), for example by providing support, by recommending a change in medication or by ending the risk by arranging for re-admission to hospital.

Poor risk assessment can lead to harm, inquiries and litigation. Good risk management, because it comes after the assessment, could prevent a poor risk assessment from causing harm. It is that important. But good risk assessment cannot prevent poor risk management from causing harm. A risk assessment might have demonstrated, consistent with contemporary professional standards, that it was appropriate to return a child from his or her foster parents to the natural parents. But the way in which that decision was implemented may have been inappropriate, have been the cause of the problems. There can be liability for poor risk management as well as for negligent risk assessment.

Time

It may be difficult to think of time as a resource, but it is. Time is exceptionally important to risk-taking in a number of different ways. Indeed, it is worth distinguishing some of them. First, there is the time during which a risk decision is being taken. More was said about this risk period in Chapter 4 because it is a key feature of risk assessment. It is the outcomes, beneficial or harmful, which could occur during the risk period, the time for which the risk will last, that matters. It is what may go right or wrong, and how likely, during this treatment, this flight, or from this decision to the next time that it is reviewed or renewed, that matters and should be assessed. It is inappropriate to make professional risk predictions for many years in advance; the science rarely justifies it.

Second is the amount of time that is available to make a risk decision. Recall the discussion in Chapter 1 about the difference between a 'risk' and a 'dilemma'. One of the differences, it was suggested, was that with a dilemma there is not the luxury of time to consider the risk assessment or make the risk decision. The absence of time to make a fully considered decision is one of the factors that make it a dilemma. It is a resource in short supply. The point is important in law. The standard of care required of a professional (whether risk-taker or whatever) is lower when he or she is acting in an emergency or dealing with a dilemma (*Wilsher* v. *Essex Area Health Authority* [1987] QB 730). The absence of time in which to obtain more information, get more or better resources, to think about it and so on and the requirement to take action to reduce harms such as continuing pain and loss of blood puts it at a premium. Those who face up to a dilemma deserve to have that reality taken into account with the result that they are judged by lower standards than would apply if there was not a dilemma or emergency.

Third, there is the time available to intervene in the implementation of a risk decision. This is the meaning most readily associated with risk management. What time is there, for example, to intervene in a risk decision to stop it from failing? A child has been returned to his or her natural parents. But things have begun to fall apart; relationships are deteriorating. If a social worker visits the family twice a week, rather than twice a month, then he or she will be in a much better position to manage what is happening, to make any changes that are necessary. The relevant child protection team might have decided to take the risk and review the case in three months' time. The risk period determining the risk assessment would be that three months plus another period appropriate in case the patient, client, family or whoever could not be contacted immediately. But, as part of the risk management plan to be implemented, the team may have agreed that one or other of its members would visit once a month to check on progress. That person may have the power, on his or her own or by organising a special meeting, to ensure that the risk is ended, or otherwise changed, before that three-month period is completed. That could include reducing certain restrictions if things are going well. In this way time is a resource to be used creatively.

The relationship between risk assessment and risk management is, or should be, dialectical, interactive over time. Professional risk assessment should be undertaken with an eye to the possibilities for risk management. The resources available for risk management could suggest what the risk period should be. That would then be used in the risk assessment. It is a potentially creative process. The availability of particular risk management resources in one county could, quite properly, lead to a different risk proposal being assessed from that in another county that does not have those resources.

A risk assessment may have been made on the basis of what might happen in the next month (i.e. a risk period). However, that assessment might produce the judgement that the likely benefits are not sufficiently greater than the possible harms to justify taking the risk. Rather than giving up, which would be inappropriate and unprofessional if the next step proves possible, the risk assessors could reconsider the risk proposal. Two of the easiest, and quickest, things they could do would be to reconsider (a) the risk period they had been considering, and/or (b) the extra risk management resources they could put into more timely interventions. How much greater are the likely benefits than the possible harms if the risk is only taken for a fortnight; that is, if a fresh risk decision is organised for two weeks later? Each side of the 'risk balance' cannot simply be halved. The seriousness of the harms possible in two weeks will rarely – and if so only because accidental – just be half of what they would be in four weeks. Rather it may be easier, in two weeks, to identify things that are going wrong – and intervene to stop them – within that period than it would be in four weeks. It will depend upon each case. And, of course, the value of the likely benefits will also be reduced. Altering the risk period and the intervention periods are resource tools which *may*, not necessarily *will*, help decision-makers to work towards a risk decision that they can justify.

People and their skills

People are another major resource for risk management. It is not just the number of people but their qualities. The number of people able to visit to check on how a risk decision is going will be important. But having those people will be of little advantage if they are not sufficiently knowledge-able, skilled, or both, to identify problems and opportunities, and to make appropriate interventions. This can be seen in the management of offenders through multi-agency public protection panels (Nash 2006).

In practice, the essential factor is the degree of control that risk management permits. How quickly and effectively can those responsible for taking and monitoring the risk decision intervene to control it? Risk management, here, should be thought of in terms of shaping, encouraging, discouraging, facilitating and using opportunities to affect what happens. It is not just about terminating the risk, such as by exercising a legal power to return an offender to prison. It is about finding ways to make the predicted benefits more likely to occur and/or prove more beneficial than predicted, and to make the feared harms less likely and/or less harmful. Ideally, risk-taking becomes a dialectical process of continuing changes.

This might pose a challenge to the traditional image of risk-taking where there is one, or just a few, dramatic decisions. But change is needed. The traditional image is substantially caused, or reinforced, by what happens in the few atypical cases where harm results. Courts and other inquiries into risk-taking focus on the time and/or place where things 'went wrong'. They focus on a stage or decision which might deserve condemnation. But that is for the practical needs of compensation claims and inquiries. It cannot deny the reality of professional risk-taking which, it is suggested, invariably involves a sequence of decisions. Certainly there will, and should, be times when progress is reviewed and learnt from; when fresh goals are decided and possible harms identified and guarded against. But these are the 'ups and downs' of implementing a risk.

It may be useful to think of a 'risk path'. (This idea was introduced in Chapter 2 but it is worth reconsidering it here in its primary context of risk management.) Imagine that Robert has a mental illness and is detained in hospital because he is considered to be a serious risk to himself. Robert could be subject to constant supervision, not allowed access to anything that might be used to self-injure. The first risk assessment and management plan decided that these restrictions were necessary. But that decision will have envisioned, and be designed to work towards, a better state of affairs.

In due course, it is hoped, Robert will require less supervision and be trusted with more opportunities for self-injury (not that that is the goal). Eventually, Robert will be discharged, whether from that ward or hospital to a rehabilitation ward or community care, and new professionals will join the team making, or advising on, risk decisions. So a sequence of key decision points may be identified. These will usually appear to be a roughly straight line from extensive control (detention in hospital under close supervision) to being in hospital under few controls (being in the community encouraged to make a full range of decisions for himself). But, if you look more closely, you are liable to see that the path travelled zig-zagged, to and fro, as things went well or less successfully and even when there was mishap or relapse. One weekend Robert was observed to be rather frustrated and tense so the decision to let him walk in the hospital grounds unaccompanied was delayed. Overall, and usually, the detailed zig-zag shape does not matter; it is the big picture that is important. The problem is that, sometimes, one of those detailed changes might lead to harm and be alleged to constitute negligence. For example, after being allowed to walk unaccompanied in the hospital grounds for an hour Robert absconded and went into town where he stabbed someone who he thought was laughing at him.

The decision to allow Robert unaccompanied time outside the ward has become the focus of attention. As the last decision before the harm it is legally significant. However, if anyone cared to examine the case holistically, that decision could have been the most appropriate, whether in terms of the risk assessment (likely benefits over likely harms), the risk management (the steps taken to maximise the potential benefits and minimise the likely harms) or the risk decision-making procedures adopted. But that decision will be the focus, and other decisions, both past and prospective, are liable to be ignored, at least comparatively. The point is that this will often be very unfair and inappropriate. Concentrating on that one decision may create a false impression. Robert's clinical team, including psychiatrist, psychologist, nurses, social worker and more, may have decided that a nurse could be authorised to allow Robert to go off the ward, provided there were no contra-indications. That could be represented as demonstrating that the other professionals did not take the decision seriously, rather than that convening a committee to make the decision would have made no difference and been a waste of resources.

So if your experience of professional risk-taking is that this 'zig-zag' risk path is the reality, you should feel entitled to stress this to any court or inquiry. Risk-taking is a very practical undertaking. The media and books, including this one, tend to put the emphasis on risk assessment and decision-making. Recall an incident in the news recently, for example where an offender, on probation, commits a serious crime. The focus of the reports will be on individual, discrete, decisions. The argument here is not that that is inappropriate but that it is incomplete and unrepresentative. The interactive, dialectical, nature of making decisions and implementing them in practice is under-represented in descriptions and explanations, and it is undervalued. The risk-taking path is rarely straight. But it is unrealistic to expect it to be, and courts and inquiries would be better informed if they appreciated this. Risk decision-making ought not to be taken out of this context.

Opportunities

If you travel to an adjoining town then you have opportunities to enjoy facilities that you do not have at home. That is a rather simple example but it can make a key point about risk-taking. If the professional risk-takers are trying to take their patient or client somewhere along a risk path then opportunities will arise at different stages. So if it proves possible to place an offender in employment then several opportunities, such as fresh friendships, will arise (Bain 2004). The point is that it is valuable to identify possible opportunities and to use them to justify both a risk decision and the particular way in which it is managed.

In order to think about risk management opportunities you should imagine that at least some of the potential benefits have been achieved. Recall that seeking goals is a core part of professional risk-taking. What opportunities has your success opened up? Imagine that one of your goals to motivate a client has been achieved. What opportunities has that success created? What more can be achieved because of that? But, of course, there are also opportunities for things to go wrong.

Opportunities are equally important in the negative. Consider a risk assessment and management plan which is evenly balanced. There is anxiety about taking the decision because the likely benefits do not clearly outweigh the possible harms. But now consider the opportunities which will be *missed* if the risk decision is *not taken*? Have they been taken into account? They should be. These are potential benefits. Unless the client is allowed to do what it proposed, for example, you will not discover whether he or she will be motivated to engage with the proposed programme. If he or she does respond then many other benefits will be possible because that opportunity has been realised. Inaction prevents those opportunities being realised. Of course, these may already have been identified as goals and so should not be double-counted.

Knowledge
Another dimension of risk-taking is the quantity and quality of knowledge available to the assessors. This can relate to the type of risk-taking in question or to the particular case. We have lots of good information about several forms of risk-taking, for example the effects of drugs on humans, but much less data about other forms, for example the behaviour of offenders. This should not be surprising. It arises from the ability to undertake the necessary quality controlled research, which in turn depends upon the degrees of control possible for quality control. We should be careful not to make the mistake of criticising one group of risk-takers just because they have poor, or less, information to work upon than another. That may be inevitable because of the type of risk involved rather than any negligence or lack of attempts to obtain quality data. It is possible to undertake methodically exacting research with drugs. We cannot do similar research in many other areas of risk-taking, not least because it would be unethical. We cannot decide to release certain offenders from custody, or detain certain non-offenders, just so that they can be a control group for others.

Before making their decision, professional risk-takers should consider what they know, its quality, plus what they do not know, and its significance (Moore 1996). A risk assessment may have been prepared on the information to hand. But is there more information which could, and perhaps should, be obtained? There will always be incomplete information; that is a central characteristic of risk. It is not suggested that there should be a constant search for more information and a continuing dread of decision-making. It has to be proper, because it is risk-taking, to make decisions with incomplete information. The issues are the nature and value of the missing information, the time and other costs there would be in obtaining it. The risk decision-makers have to make preliminary risk decisions about (a) whether further information is likely to make a significant difference to their assessment or management plan, and (b) whether –

presuming it is not an emergency or dilemma – it is appropriate to wait until they can obtain more and or better information.

Additional information may add little to what is already known, and that may be reasonably predictable in the particular case. It will always be possible to undertake more research. But a decision needs to be taken. The key question is not the existence of further knowledge, but its likely significance. The decision-makers might like to ask themselves: 'If we obtained this information, and it told us what we are anticipating, what difference would that make to our decision?' If it would make little difference then, other things being equal, it would be reasonable to ignore it. For example, it might be possible to consider a more detailed list of risk factors. But would that increase the quantity or quality of your knowledge sufficiently? Some risk factors are much more powerful, are more predictive and useful than others. Those may already be available. It may appear to be better practice to use a more detailed list of risk factors but, given time and cost and the limited extra yield of extra information that they would provide, that could be a waste of valuable resources.

Control

Knowledge is a form of power which, in turn, enables degrees of control. Risk management concerns the implementation of risk decisions. People and knowledge are ways of exercising control but there can be others. An important source can be the law. It can provide powers to require patients or offenders not to do various things, such as leave hospital or breach a curfew, and it empowers or authorises action if there is disobedience. Those powers can be used in risk management. However, the law can also create many problems. The media, and lay people, regularly assume that professionals have more legal powers than they actually possess: 'The police should have stopped it – even if no crime was involved.' 'The psychiatrists should have prevented that suicide, even though there was no mental illness.'

These are problems which occur after the risk has been taken and harm has resulted. They concern managing the public response rather than any risk. It can only be recommended that professional risk-takers are forewarned and forearmed for these problems. We also recommend that they identify the limits of their legal, professional, ethical and moral powers to intervene and control the risks they take. These limits should be declared in the documents associated with the risk policies that are recommended in

Chapter 8. These documents should be distributed along with the risk policies to opinion formers, such as the media, which are likely to report on professional risk-taking. Then, when harm results from professional risk-taking and the media demands a response, it will be much easier to convince opinion formers of the difficulties of risk-taking, including the lack of legal powers to intervene or control a risk. The risk-takers, or their spokespersons, will be able to direct the media and other poor risk analysts to documents that were sent to them in advance.

Money

All the resources that have been identified as being available for risk management cost money. With more money available to organise and purchase resources for better risk assessments and risk management plans a better job can be done. That is stating the obvious, but an important point needs to be made. Risk assessment, in marked contrast to risk management, can be, and regularly is, portrayed as 'non-political'. It is about a decision; do the likely benefits outweigh the likely harms? Of course, as has been demonstrated and stressed, it is not that easy. But that is the focus: on the quality of a decision; on an intellectual exercise. Thus it is easy to associate the quality of risk assessment with the quality of the decision-makers. It is not the lack of resources which led to the risk assessment being of poor quality, it might be argued in a particular case; rather, it was the incompetence, the lack of professionalism of the decision-makers. It is hoped that you will not be associated with such simplistic reasoning. Quite simply the absence of resources, or monies to make them available, can affect the quantity and quality of information available for risk assessment. Risk assessment is not as apolitical as it is often portrayed.

But risk management is fundamentally about resources and, therefore, about politics. Even if a good risk assessment can be made on limited resources (there must be some, such as a professional knowledge base), a good risk management plan presupposes adequate resources for carrying it out. Improving risk assessment may, substantially, be achieved by improving skills and knowledge. The costs of doing that may be hidden in general or others' budgets, for example in general education rather than for the particular service. But, quite simply, risk management can be improved with more money, with better resources. And that requires funds from the services concerned. So risk assessment can be *portrayed* – simplistically – as purely professional, but risk management *is* political. However, it is totally artificial, and contrary to good practice, to separate risk assessment and risk management in this way.

Conclusion

A good risk decision requires both good risk assessment and good risk management. Indeed, good risk management can protect against the consequences of a poor risk assessment, because it concerns the implementation of the decision. But a good risk assessment cannot protect against poor risk management. Many risk decisions will be successful irrespective of poor risk management. In the absence of loss few people will think to complain (although professional associations and employers ought to), and none will sue, as it is legally impermissible. But that will be due to good fortune. Reliance on good luck ought not to be a management tool. At every opportunity we should emphasise that risk assessment and risk management need to go together and that therefore money matters. Quality risk decisions need practical support, not just fine words.

In Chapter 2 a five-level model of risk was proposed and it was argued that if risk-taking is to improve then we need action at all five levels. Level 2, the setting within which the risk is taken, and Level 4, the support provided by managers and employers, are particularly relevant to risk management. This model is developed further in Chapter 9, which is concerned with organisational causes of good and bad risk-taking.

CHAPTER 6

Risk Communication

Introduction

It is perfectly possible to undertake a professionally exemplary risk assessment and to design a risk management plan that will ensure the benefits are maximised and the potential harms reduced to little more than theoretical possibilities – and yet for everything to fall apart. Poor communication can ruin the best-laid risk plans. Poor communication about risk must be expected to become a popular basis for negligence claims.

You can stand at the side of the road and assess the risk (likely benefits and harms) of crossing the road. You can decide to manage the risk by moving to the pedestrian crossing, as cars are more likely to slow down there. You make those decisions by and for yourself. But the kind of risks which professionals have to take, in particular the kind that have been discussed in this book, have to be communicated. A parole board, for example, needs to obtain information from several sources, and probably receives it in many different forms. Different people in the child protection team need not just tell what they know, but should explain to their colleagues why their professional experience, and disciplinary perspective, leads them to emphasise different points. Information that is not understood by the risk decision-maker might just as well not have been given. Actually, given that it may be *mis*understood, its effect may be worse than if it had been omitted. Quite simply, everyone involved could be doing his or her best but, because one person describes a risk as 'X', but another hears or understands that person to mean 'Y', it could all fall apart. It is a mistake waiting to happen. That is the concern of this chapter. It is so easily done, but there are a number of practical steps that can and should be taken in order to minimise the likelihood of error.

To fully appreciate the importance of this topic you should undertake a little experiment.

Describing likelihood

Find some colleagues and ask them to translate the meaning of certain words concerned with likelihood into numbers. Ask them to tell you what they understand to be the corresponding numerical meaning of the word (see Table 6.1). Initially, work in percentages. For example, ask them to tell you what percentage they would use to correspond with the meaning of 'possible'. If they think that it has the same meaning as 'impossible' (which logically it cannot) then they should say '0 per cent'. If they think that it has the same meaning as 'certain' then they should say '100 per cent'. If they think it corresponds with the meaning of the phrase 'as likely as not', then they should say '50 per cent'.

It might help if you gave your colleagues a context. Imagine a weather forecaster has said that it is 'possible' that it will rain; that a doctor has said it is 'possible' that the treatment will have side-effects; that a probation officer has opined that it is 'possible' that the offender will re-offend, and

Table 6.1 Putting a value on words

Phrase	Your assessment	Colleague no.						
		1	2	3	4	5	6	7
'It is possible that…'								
'There is a chance that…'								
'It is likely that…'								
'Almost certainly it will…'								
'Almost certainly it will not…'								
'It is certain that…'								
'It is foreseeable that…'								
'It is quite likely that…'								
'It is probable that…'								
'It is highly likely that…'								
'It is evens that…'								

so on. Having been given a figure for 'possible' use other words and phrases, such as: 'It is probable', 'There is a chance...', 'It is virtually certain...', 'It is foreseeable...', 'There is a risk...', 'It is highly likely...', 'There is a real chance...', and 'It is evens'. Except for phrases like 'evens', 'as likely as not', 'certain' and 'impossible', you are almost certain (by which we mean 'around 99 per cent') to find that people understand very different things by these words. We have yet to find an audience where everyone understands the words and phrases – other than 'as likely as not' and so on – to have the same numerical likelihood. Greater consensus has been found over certain expressions, usually those expressions with meanings closer to the extremes, but there are still major differences. It is not uncommon for one person to associate an expression with 40 per cent likelihood when another believes that 80 per cent is best.

If someone told you that it would 'possibly' rain tomorrow, what would you understand that likelihood to be in percentage terms? For example, most people would understand 'certain' to mean 100 per cent and 'impossible' to mean 0 per cent. (It is suggested that you limit yourself to 5 or 10 per cent variations.) If you think the word could be represented by several percentages then just write down the one that you think is closest – which will usually be the median. Then ask your colleagues what they think. Make sure that they cannot see, and are not influenced by, your or others' assessments.

The implications of this should be obvious – and frightening. Imagine someone told you that he or she thought something was 'likely' to happen. He or she might have meant 40 per cent, but you could have 'heard' 80 per cent. You may have been influenced by his or her assessment; you may act upon it. You may agree with your colleague's verbally expressed assessment, not realising that you actually disagree quite profoundly. You believe that you have communicated because you clearly heard what your colleague said. But you have not communicated effectively because you did not understand. Now, imagine that someone has been injured as a consequence of this risk decision, and a lawyer has discovered that you and your colleague meant very different things by the same words:

Lawyer: Do you agree that effective communication is essential in risk assessment?

Risk-taker: Yes. (What else could you say?)

Lawyer: Have you read any books or guides which stressed the impor-
           tance of accurate communication?

Risk-taker: Yes. (Because you certainly have now.)

Lawyer: Did you follow any special procedures or take any special
           action to avoid or minimise the risk of miscommunication?

Risk-taker: No.

Lawyer: But you had a serious miscommunication?

Risk-taker: Yes ...sorry.

You may be thinking that is unfair. Words are vague, especially the many words and phrases relating to likelihood. It would be wrong, it might be argued, to penalise people because they use ordinary words of the language. There is no law or rule (legislative, social, moral or literary) which prescribes that 'possible' (which, strangely, may mean something very different from 'clearly possible') has to mean 20 per cent, 60 per cent, or whatever. A dictionary might articulate a quite specific meaning but the dictionary editors are reporting what they understand to be contemporary usage, not laying down immutable, correct, meanings. Dictionaries aim to reflect common understandings and can only prescribe meanings in the very weak sense that it is socially sensible to use terms in ways that listeners and readers are likely to understand.

There are at least two separate problems. First, most likelihood expressions are relatively vague; their meaning is inexplicit. That is a communication problem. Second, most assessments of likelihood are uncertain; their accuracy is unclear. That arises from the nature of risk and risk-taking. First, we have problems in deciding how likely it is that, for example, X will re-offend within the next month or that Y will experience side-effects of drug treatment. The problem is that we do not know, and can never be sure, how likely it is. However, we do know something. We know that some predictions are better than others, are more likely to be accurate than others. We may conclude that it would be unhelpful and inappropriate to describe the risk of side-effects from taking a drug as 'likely', 'probable' or 'highly probable', preferring 'chance' or 'possible'. We may not know that the likelihood is 23.742 per cent (as confirmed by research studies), but we do know that it would be positively foolish to think in terms of 80–100 per cent and not even very sensible to think in terms of 40–50 per cent.

In order to make an assessment, and then a decision, you need to fix on a statement of likelihood. You do not need a very precise figure. Indeed, given that you are dealing with the uncertainties that are involved in risk-taking that would be inappropriate. But some figures, and some expressions, are better than others. You do not need a single figure; you might conclude that it is almost certainly somewhere between 20 and 30 per cent, possibly 15–20 per cent or 30–40 per cent, but claiming that the likelihood is higher than 50 per cent would be unreasonable. Note that word again. It would be 'unreasonable' to suggest a likelihood of over 50 per cent but 'reasonable' to suggest 15–40 per cent. If a responsible body of co-professionals agrees that that would be reasonable then that assessment would not breach the standard of care owed in the law of negligence (assuming only that the courts do not exercise their right – using the case of Bolitho v. City & Hackney Health Authority ([1988] AC 232) – to decide that that standard is too low).

It is possible to be more precise with some risks because there is more and better information available about them. For example, extensive high-quality research is undertaken on the introduction of new drugs. That makes it easier to be more precise about the likelihood of side-effects for a particular patient. But some risks involve human agents, people, with the rights and the ability to exercise freedom of choice and to be awkward and 'unpredictable'. (Their behaviour is not really 'unpredictable' in the sense that no predictions can be made. It is just more difficult to predict in such cases.) Indeed, as emphasised in the discussion on risk management (Chapter 5), it is important to identify and explain the quality of the knowledge used in risk assessment. It is not just a case of the likelihood involved – in the particular risk under consideration – but the likelihood that that statement of likelihood is correct.

It may be tempting to throw up arms and eyebrows in protest at the difficulty of it all. But that would be unprofessional, defeatist and negligent. Nothing has changed, just because these points have been made and you have been encouraged to undertake that exercise. Risk-taking involves, by definition, uncertainty. Recognising the problems does not change them, although it may remove any excuse for inaction. There are (have to be because it is a risk) limits on the accuracy of likelihood predictions because of the current state of our knowledge. We can recognise that. You may have to declare that your best estimate of likelihood is 15 per cent, whilst emphasising that that is what it is, all it is and can be, a best estimate. Provided that that estimate is one that a responsible body of co-professionals would endorse, then the standard of care, for the purposes of the law of negligence, has been satisfied. If the law of negligence is satisfied then any other tribunal or inquiry, including the court of public opinion, should be too. But you should not then proceed to spoil it all by miscommunication of that best estimate. If you use an expression by which you mean 15 per cent, but other people hear and act on a distinctively different estimate, say, 25 per cent, then that not only could constitute negligence (no responsible body of professionals would communicate in that negligent fashion), but you have wasted all the hard work that you put into identifying that estimate.

One 'solution' to the communication problem is to use numbers. Where words are vague, numbers are certain. You know that a 20 per cent likelihood is twice a 10 per cent chance. But many people respond to this suggestion with horror. They stress that it is impossible to be that precise with estimates. Risk-taking, it has been emphasised, necessarily involves uncertainty. But that objection is misconceived. Quite simply, the risk assessor will have a best estimate of likelihood, say, 10 per cent at the very least in the sense that other figures are not as good, not as sensible, not as reasonable. Thus it is much wiser for that risk assessor to say 10 per cent than, for example, 80 per cent. So the risk assessor should say that his or her best estimate is 10 per cent and should immediately go on to emphasise that that is only a *best* estimate.

Many risk assessors are reluctant to use numbers because they *appear* so precise, so certain, so sure, when the assessors do not *feel* certain or sure. So risk assessors should not give that impression of certitude, as it would be false. They could go on to explain that, whilst 10 per cent is their best estimate, they would not be at all surprised if it was between 5 and 15 per cent; or that they do not mean 10 per cent, exactly, but 'around' 10 per cent, or '10 per cent, give or take 5 per cent'. Of course, those listening may respond by asking for more precise information, which the risk assessor would have to refuse to provide because he or she simply cannot be more precise. But a request for more precision would be a success story, not a failure. In such an instance the assessor would clearly have communicated to the other person both what he or she thinks (that it is around 10 per cent) and just how relatively (un)sure he or she is about the reliability of that figure. The key point is that even if we cannot, because of the state of the science and the fact that it is a risk, surmount the problem about the precision of the prediction, we can – and should – do something about the communication problem.

Another approach would be to use a limited number of likelihood expressions to which working definitions are added. Take, for example, the following words and phrases. There is no magic in the particular choices. More or less could be adopted. Others words and phrases might be preferred.

- foreseeable
- chance
- possible
- real possibility
- good possibility
- evens
- likely
- very likely
- probable
- real probability
- highly probable.

What is important is the hierarchy into which they are placed. Do you agree that they have been listed in an order – from those expressions which express least likelihood to those, as was intended, which express highest chance? This is not a claim that we are correct, knowing only too well from exercises like the one at the start of this chapter that people use these expressions in different ways. Some people might argue that 'foreseeable' refers to a higher likelihood than 'possible', that 'real probability' means it is more likely than does 'very likely'. They may be right, in terms of how most people in our community, profession, work group, or whatever, use those terms.

It would be very useful if there were words and phrases that fell into a natural hierarchy. If so they could be adopted and you could do likewise. Until then the key point is that both speakers and listeners could agree (a) to limit their assessments of likelihood to these expressions and (b) to understand them as being in a hierarchy of likelihood. For example, everyone working in a specific child protection service, irrespective of profession, could be required to adopt such a scheme. When describing a risk they would be required (i) only to choose likelihood expressions from the prescribed list and (ii) to give them their prescribed meanings. Thus, when a social worker comments that he or she thinks it is 'possible' that a particular child will be abused, the listening paediatrician will know that he or she means (for example) that it is more likely than 'foreseeable' but less likely than a 'real possibility' and certainly, it is not 'probable'. Note that for such a scheme to work it is essential that this hierarchy of words and phrases, and the importance of adopting it, is widely disseminated. Such a scheme could involve many different services, disciplines and professions which do not share the same managers or employers. And it would, in due course, need to be explained to 'outsiders', such as judges and tribunals of inquiry.

One possibility would be to adopt the following hierarchy of expressions. Staff would be told to use only these expressions (in their professional roles), and to use the one that *most closely* represents their understanding of the likelihood. When speaking to others who are not aware of these arrangements they should be required to explain that (and why) they are deliberately limiting themselves to a few expressions which fit within an explicit hierarchy and reflect the whole range of likelihood.

- Foreseeable: by which mean in the range of 0–10 per cent likelihood.
- Chance: by which mean in the range of 10–20 per cent likelihood.
- Possible: by which mean in the range of 20–30 per cent likelihood.
- Real possibility: by which mean in the range of 30–40 per cent likelihood.
- Good possibility: by which mean in the range of 40–50 per cent likelihood.
- Evens: by which mean in the range of 45–55 per cent likelihood.
- Likely: by which mean in the range of 50–60 per cent likelihood.

- Very likely: by which mean in the range of 60–70 per cent likelihood.

- Probable: by which mean in the range of 70–80 per cent likelihood.

- Real probability: by which mean in the range of 80–90 per cent likelihood.

- Highly probable: by which mean in the range of over 90 per cent likelihood.

You could stick with a hierarchy that is just the list of expressions in the previous paragraph, omitting the percentages. However, someone, quite likely a lawyer, is going to enquire whether the words and phrases chosen represent equal 'steps' in the hierarchy. If your answer is 'No' then the rejoinder is going to be, 'Why not?' What is the point of having a hierarchy if it only covers the equivalent of 0–25 and 60–70 per cent? How are your colleagues supposed to understand you when you wish to explain that you think there is a 40 per cent chance? So it is suggested that you take the next step of associating each expression with an equal proportion range of likelihood and cover the whole range. In that case it could be appropriate to exclude the expression 'evens' and all equivalents, although it does help to explain the hierarchy and method. Alternatively, it could be allowed to represent 45–55 per cent.

You will have noticed (a) that 10 (or 11) expressions were chosen (b) to cover the full range of likelihood. Clearly, this was done so that each expression could be associated with a 10 per cent range. Some risk-takers might wish to use more, or fewer, expressions and focus on particular parts of the range. For example, Sir Kenneth Calman (1996), when he was Chief Medical Officer at the Department of Health, proposed a range of expressions, but all for likelihoods of less than one per cent. His concern was that public perception of risks (more accurately of likelihood) was often irrational and led to poor health choices. A study could report that the side-effects of one drug were twice those of another, leading to patients refusing to take the 'more risky' medication. Whilst the *relative* risk might be that one was twice as likely as another, the *absolute* risk of both could be very low. If the likelihood of side-effects from one drug or procedure is 0.00001 it is a very low risk, even if another drug has a likelihood of 0.000005.

Calman (1996) wanted to enable patients to make more informed risk decisions. So he proposed identifying 'risks' as high if the likelihood was more than one per cent. As a sort of marker, he noted that this was an appropriate expression for the likelihood of transmitting measles or chickenpox to susceptible people within a household. Other expressions which he used were: moderate, low, very low, minimal, and negligible. These related to 1 in 100 to 1 in 1000; 1 in 1000 to 1 in 10,000; 1 in 10,000 to 1 in 100,000; 1 in 100,000 to 1 in 1,000,000, respectively. Associated examples included a road accident as 'low', a polio vaccination as minimal and death from smoking ten cigarettes a day as 'moderate'. Other approaches have developed to express such ideas (e.g. Adams and Smith 2001). That they have not 'caught on' with the public and the media, as their authors hoped, may tell us a lot about public attitudes to risk-taking. But it does not follow that professional risk-takers can ignore these ideas. Even if they are not allowed to make the risk decision because a client or patient is legally competent and entitled to take the decision for him- or herself they still have to give 'proper' advice and information. Even if they feel sure that the client will 'hear' 90 per cent whatever expression they use to try to communicate 5 per cent, they must still try. They must put in as much effort to communicate the information about the risk as responsible co-professionals would.

There is, of course, no problem about adding Calman's terminology to the words and phrases outlined above for more likely outcomes. We would, however, caution against use of any word which is liable to confuse because it implies more than just likelihood. For example, the label 'moderate' may lead to the risk being misread as 'moderate', when Calman's, our and similar systems are *only* concerned with the likelihood element of risk-taking. Before judgements can be made, for example as to whether the risk is 'moderate', the nature of the outcome must be included in the equation. A 'moderate' likelihood of death, and a 'moderate' likelihood of a headache, are quite different.

Some non-medical professional risk-takers might complain that, for many good reasons, there is limited reliable research that can give them precise information. They would complain that they cannot fairly pretend that they can offer assessments that would be accurate within a 10 per cent range. Their problems are appreciated but the appropriate response would not be to reject such suggestions but to adopt them and tell those who need to know, for example 'Unfortunately, the research basis for such predictions, in these circumstances, is limited and I can only say that my best assessment is that it is "possible", by which I mean there is a 20–30 per cent chance, but my colleagues and I would not be surprised if it was 10–20 or 30–40 per cent.'

One of the virtues of choosing a limited number of likelihood expressions would be a 'public' demonstration of how the professions involved believed that it was both impossible and improper to imply that greater exactitude was possible. Some disciplines (see BMA 1990) are capable of more exact predictions and so they could use more words and phrases to reflect more levels in their hierarchy. But it is submitted that a range of about ten mutually exclusive expressions of likelihood is the most suitable. Imagine a discipline or profession which claimed that it could only assess likelihood in terms of, say, 'possible', 'chance', 'probable' and 'likely'. Is it not liable to be considered so unhelpful or underdeveloped that its contribution to making risk assessments should be questioned? It is also guessed that a court or committee of inquiry would expect there to be a minimum of ten expressions to cover the whole range.

A combination of words and numbers is recommended. 'I think it is likely to happen, by which I mean about 55 per cent.' That provides a clear communication of what that individual is thinking. It avoids miscommunication. But the person giving that assessment should continue and provide an explanation of (a) how accurate that assessment is (that is how likely it is to be 55 per cent) and (b) how confident (and preferably why) he or she is that that figure is correct. That should avoid miscommunication as well as providing a reasonable explanation. If the risk assessor lacks confidence in the assessment he or she can use a wider range or fuller explanation of why it is appropriate to lack confidence in the assessment.

Assessing the likelihood of benefits and of harms
Should the likelihood of harms be assessed in the same manner as benefits? Some have argued that, in order to be 'safe', harms should be assessed as being more likely than they 'really are', whereas benefits may be assessed as being less likely. We totally disagree. The risk-taker's duty is to obtain the most likely to be accurate assessments of likelihood. Introducing any 'safety' factors is deliberately introducing errors, the effects of which are difficult to control, especially if several contributors of likelihood

information add their own bit of bias. The place for including any notions of 'playing safe' is at the risk management and risk judgement stages. The decision-makers may choose to decide that, even though the likely benefits clearly outweigh the likely harms, they are unwilling to take the decision. There could, for example, be fear of a particular outcome or concern about the implications of investing so much in risk management for a particular individual. There are enough problems in risk assessment without deliberately adding errors.

It could be useful to check whether this bias is being introduced unconsciously. A technique for examining that possibility is to re-run the exercise shown in Table 6.1, but this time to add some further information. For example, ask some of your colleagues what they think is the percentage equivalent of 'likely to be killed' and then the same question for 'likely to gain motivation'. The answers ought to be the same. Differences in the outcome should not affect the assessment of the likelihood. But it is suspected that many will give different answers.

Whose assessments of likelihood?
Some people have said, when given an example, that they would rate the likelihood as 'possible', meaning in the range of 20–30 per cent, but immediately add that others, such as the public or judges, would say it was 'likely', meaning in the range of 50–60 per cent. They may be correct, with respects to others' predictions. That may inform their cynicism about being fairly judged by others if harm should result from their risk-taking. But their jobs are (a) to state the likelihood that they believe is most accurate and (b) to explain why others, who think differently, are wrong. In particular, they should be quick to insist that just because they rated the likelihood as, for example, 1 in 100, the fact that the feared harm has occurred does not prove, of itself, that the prediction was wrong. They gained their jobs because of their specialist knowledge and skills. It would be unprofessional for them to refuse to use that knowledge and, instead, use estimates which they believe others would – wrongly – assume.

Describing outcomes
There are also problems, but of a different character, in describing the outcomes, or potential consequences, of risk-taking. Here both the potential benefits and harms must be described accurately, and we must ensure that that is what is communicated. Likelihood is, in one sense, easier

to communicate because it is only concerned with one 'dimension'. Likelihood varies from impossible and very unlikely through many gradations to highly probable and certain. But outcomes can come in many different shapes and sizes. With one risk, for example, someone might be killed, another injured, a third party shocked, someone miss an opportunity, and yet another have some property damaged. Clearly, these are not equally important, but how are we to describe or compare them, at all? It is not just the problem that we do not have a common comparator, but that we may value these outcomes in very different ways. How bad is it, for example, that a child of ten years lives in a house where there are no books to be read? How can that loss be compared with physical abuse of the same child? Then there are the issues of different individuals' perceptions and value systems.

As was emphasised in Chapter 3, on the law, non-detained and competent adults (and children on some issues) are entitled to make risk decisions affecting themselves. It is their values that matter. In such cases professionals should, in particular where they believe their clients or patients are misinformed or are making very inappropriate decisions, explain why they reach different conclusions. They must also answer questions and give advice. But otherwise it is the individual's decision. Does this mean that much of what follows in this section might appear irrelevant because it is the client's or patient's decision and not the professional's? No. This section is still very relevant and important. It applies when it is a decision which the professional has to make, and it should also be useful in helping professionals to identify when their competent patients or clients may be making 'errors' in their own assessments, so that they can give them appropriate advice, even if they cannot compel the patient or client to accept it.

Which outcomes?

First things first, what are the possible outcomes? They may appear obvious. The question, for example, is whether the child who was taken into social services care should be returned to her parents – everyone is worried about the risk involved. The fact is that we do not have sufficient information. For how long will the child be returned to her parents; are we contemplating hours, days or weeks, for example? Under what conditions; what opportunities will there be for managing this risk? Before assessing the risks it is essential to have a clear idea of what is proposed; everyone involved must be contemplating the same risk decision. The risks, both in terms of the outcomes – what might happen – and their likelihood, will be affected by, among other things, how long the child or other person will be 'at' risk. Only when it is clear what the proposed risk involves can we begin to assess it.

How can we compare outcomes?

How are the different outcomes to be compared, let alone communicated? With some 'simple' risk decisions (simple in the sense that there are relatively few issues to consider, but they will be raised in the next chapter about decision complexity) it may be appropriate just to think about the information collated. For example, the ultimate issue may be X chance that the patient will gain in motivation against the Y likelihood he or she will be disappointed by failure. But it will, regularly, be more complex and involve outcomes of very different natures. The drug proposed is very likely to remove, or at least greatly reduce, the symptoms. But it may also cause nasty, life-long, side-effects. (And that is not a particularly complex, in terms of the number of issues to be considered, decision.) How are we to compare these? We need a common denominator for comparing outcomes.

If harm was to result from the risk decision then the quality of the risk assessment and its management could be examined. If the applicable standard of care, and other requirements of the law of negligence, were satisfied then compensation would be payable. Here is a potential common denominator – money, lucre, compensation – would be awarded by an independent court using long established principles (Rogers 2006). But this approach – even though the case may end up in such a court – must be rejected. When harm results from negligence the courts decide the amount of compensation that must be paid. The courts have done the comparisons; some families are compensated for relatives who have been killed, some victims are compensated for loss of limbs, some for post-traumatic stress disorder, for pain, for loss of functions. This shows that it can be done, that we can devise a common denominator which, even if it does not receive universal approval, is widely accepted. And it has been used as a basis for risk decisions. Companies can calculate the likely cost of compensation they would have to pay (or buy insurance to cover) and compare that with the cost of making safety improvements. They can decide which action is economically the more rational and in the best interests of their shareholders. Many would argue that that is a perfectly proper business practice, but only if we accept the limits imposed by business values.

Compensation is paid *after* the event; it is concerned with 'righting' a wrong. Risk assessment is undertaken *in advance*; it is concerned with prevention. Compensation is designed to put victims back into the position they would have been – in so far as money can – if they had not been the victims of negligence (Rogers 2006). Compensation reflects the victim's needs, not the perpetrator's degree of negligence. A small degree of negligence can lead to a very large compensation award; a great deal of negligence can lead to a small award, or even none at all if, by good luck, there was no victim. Causing quadriplegia to a young person at the start of his or her career and family life will lead to a very large award as both current and future needs, and earnings, are taken into account. Killing a young person before he or she has any dependents and avoiding any life-long requirements for nursing support and so on will lead to a much smaller award. That is an understandable approach for a compensation scheme; it is not an acceptable basis for a scheme concerned with prevention. It is hoped that few people would argue that it is appropriate to regard the risk of a child's death as less serious than the same likelihood of risk of a young parent's death – let alone several times less serious. It might be argued that preventing a child's death is more important than preventing an older person's death, but surely not the converse. We might have to accept that having adopted such economic systems it is appropriate for commercial organisations to undertake cost–benefit analyses and balance the cost of greater safety measures against the cost of paying compensation. But would it ever be appropriate for a social work, health or criminal justice organisation, for example, to decide that it would be cheaper and therefore better to pay compensation to injured clients, or patients, than to employ more staff?

Other techniques have been devised to create a common denominator. For example, quality-adjusted life years (QUALYs) were devised to support a rational system for allocating health resources (Schwartz and Aaron 1988). Some medical interventions will produce more years of (quality-adjusted) life than others. Other things being equal, and where there is a limit to what can be provided, those treatments should be preferred over treatments that produce fewer years. The method acknowledges that the quality, and not just quantity, of years ought to be taken into account.

Naturally, it is not as simple as it may appear. New forms of treatment will produce few QUALYs until the science and skills develop. But for that science, and those skills (e.g. heart transplants), to develop there have to be cases. But the motivation for, and sense behind, QUALYs is understandable. In its context it is certainly defensible.

How exact must the assessments be?

That is a key point. Perfect systems are not possible, not least because we are concerned with values. Differences of opinion are rife, proper and, indeed, desirable in a pluralistic society. How are we to compare emotional abuse with physical abuse, let alone with losses of opportunities for life-enhancing experiences? These are exceptionally difficult questions. But there is a very 'easy' answer. We do not need a perfect system. Lord Browne-Wilkinson, speaking for the whole House of Lords in the leading case on the standard of care required in professional negligence cases (*Bolitho* v. *City & Hackney Health Authority* [1988] AC 232), emphasised that doctors (in that particular case) could not avoid being found negligent just because they produced expert witnesses who approved of what was done in the case being litigated. But he went on to specify (italics added):

> In particular in cases involving, as they so often do, the weighing of risks against benefits, the judge before accepting a body of opinion as being responsible, reasonable or respectable, will need to be satisfied that, in forming their views, the experts have directed their minds to the question of comparative risks and benefits and have reached *a defensible conclusion* on the matter. In the vast majority of cases the fact that distinguished experts in the field are of a particular opinion will demonstrate the reasonableness of that opinion. ... But if, in a rare case, it can be demonstrated that the professional opinion is not capable of *withstanding logical analysis*, the judge is entitled to hold that the body of opinion is not reasonable or responsible. (pp. 1159–60 (emphasis added))

Note that a 'defensible conclusion' is required. It has to be justifiable, capable of being defended. Lord Browne-Wilkinson is not specifying that there is only one conclusion with which the judges, let alone everyone, would agree. But it has to be based upon an arguable system in the sense of being rational and objective rather than capricious and unpredictable. (It might have been better if he had referred to 'rational' rather than 'logical' analysis, since the latter might be narrowly interpreted as referring to the principles of formal logical deduction.)

All that is required, first, is a system which 'makes sense' within the goals, principles and values of the services and professions concerned. These need not coincide with lay or majority public views; the involvement of a 'profession' implies specialist training and knowledge. For example, child protection services might regard the absence of stimulation in a household as more serious than certain forms of abuse. Others, including judges, might not have come to the same conclusion on their own. But that is not fatal. The professions concerned should be able to defend their position in a sensible manner. They might be able to show, in particular by referring to research and experience that lay people and judges are not aware of, how the absence of stimulation causes long-term damage to a child. In such a way the professionals can defend their system of values, priorities. Thus their standards should be, in the terms of Lord Browne-Wilkinson, 'defensible'.

Second, that system of values should be applied consistently. It would be inappropriate to treat similar cases differently – unless, of course, there are good reasons showing that they are not really similar. This does not mean that the value system must remain unchanging and inviolate. On the contrary, it would be important to demonstrate that the system is open to change and development as knowledge and views change. Evolution is defensible; haphazard change or inconsistent practice invites criticism. The point about having different disciplines, specialities and professions is that we cannot all know the same things. So it is understandable that specialists may well come to different conclusions from the rest of us. But they should not breach the law and, if their values and standards are counterintuitive (in particular, if they are different from what judges and others would initially expect), then time should be spent in being prepared to defend them.

Rating outcomes, as well as likelihood
One productive approach involves 'rating' outcomes along a scale. We could think of harms as running from zero, which would represent neutral, neither good nor bad, to −10, which could be equated with death. Benefits would then run from 0 to +10. But we run into problems immediately. Arguably, there are states worse than death (e.g. 'living deaths'). We do not need, indeed, cannot have, a perfect system. Unless there is something special about the kinds of risk decisions you take with your clients, for example you regularly torture them for several years before casting them to

the lions, then any rating system you adopt which equates 'death' with 'living deaths' is likely to be considered *defensible*. The courts authorise using a relatively broad brush; they neither require nor encourage us to worry about neat distinctions, however accurate they may be.

If death is rated as −10 then what is the equivalent of +10 in terms of benefit? That is another interesting question and, since it has been stressed that risk-taking must include considering the likely benefits as well as likely harms, it must not be avoided. But the mistake is to assume that there must be an opposite; there are lots of benefits of risk-taking but perhaps none are so beneficial as causing death is so harmful. There does not need to be an equivalent opposite. The scheme may get no higher than +8. Surely we can live with that. You can still justify taking the risk of killing someone. Remember, always, that you have to combine likelihood and outcome. You regularly justify crossing roads, for example, even though you know that you may be (indeed, many unfortunately are) knocked down and killed. The seriousness of that death, if it occurs, may make the reasons for getting to the other side of the road appear trivial. The bereaved family is likely to regret that those reasons were thought to be enough. But that comparison ignores the critical importance of likelihood. It is because the exceptionally high likelihood of obtaining the benefits of crossing the road, multiplied by their value, so greatly outweighed the readily admitted seriousness of the death, but multiplied by its being exceptionally unlikely to occur in that instance. Some people might be prepared to exchange a lost limb for certain benefits, to exchange one of their kidneys for money, to give their life for that of their children; but we are getting too remote from our context of how professionals could and should rate alternative outcomes of risk-taking.

Such 'philosophical' problems may suggest that rating scales are simply too problematic, but this is not the case. They are, at the very least, exceptionally important for communication about risk. Just as with assessments of likelihood there are problems in communicating words that sufficiently and accurately describe outcomes. For example, everyone might be agreed that the likely benefit of taking a risk, resulting in enhanced client motivation, is 'very important'. But what does 'very important' mean? Even if the professionals concerned have a common understanding of how important enhanced motivation is, other people may neither understand nor appreciate it. A judge, for example, might hear 'very important' and think, in his or her comparable lexicon, 'significant'. But the risk assessor – if only he or she knew how the judge would interpret the term – might wish that he or she had added: 'Unless we get the client motivated he or she will not be willing, let alone keen to work with us and a co-operative client is so very different from an indifferent one.' Failure to communicate what is really meant – be it about an outcome or likelihood – is a frequent cause of many problems with risk decisions.

The value of articulating values

To help them with these problems, services could devise their own scales. They could, for example, identify ten common benefits and ten common harms that arise from their types of risk-taking. These should contrast in importance or seriousness. Then a group of relevant professionals, acting in that capacity rather than any other, should consider this list. (It could be beneficial if the group included a range of people, in terms of experience and seniority, in order to maximise opportunities for learning about a range of practical matters.) First, the group members should be asked to place the outcomes in a hierarchy, from least to most serious. Any extensive disagreement should be investigated. (It might reflect different disciplines, degrees of seniority or even personal experiences which are preventing individuals from considering the issues professionally.) Second, each individual should allocate a number – representing what he or she considers to be the most accurate, reflecting his or her professional views as to the seriousness or value of the outcomes – say, from –10 to (say) +8. Then the individuals should work as a group to iron out differences between them. It is very important that all the individuals identify their opinions before there is any group discussion. It is only too easy for people to change their opinion when they discover that, unless they do so, they will be in a minority. Group dynamics can introduce error. Individual differences, reflected in the numbers chosen, could reflect differences that deserve open discussion. For example, differences between individuals could reflect different understandings of the outcomes concerned.

Note the potential of this practical device for turning statements of principle – and vision – into something concrete and meaningful. For example, if a profession declares that it regards a particular outcome as very important, for example a patient's consent, then that ought to be reflected in its list of values. If a child's interests are declared to be more important than an adult's, then any scheme which assessed parents' rights more highly than a child's would demonstrate hypocrisy. This device should also prove exceptionally valuable for inducting staff into the service; it demonstrates commitment to values via concrete examples rather than vague generalities.

Then this document should be circulated to all colleagues to encourage consensus and to support decision-making. Comments could be sought to ensure understanding and agreement. If consensus is forthcoming it should be formally noted, as that could prove very useful, in legal terms. The support of a substantial body of people could go a considerable way towards demonstrating professional standards. So, for example, the group might have proposed that 'gaining the client's motivation to work with us' was to be rated as +5. Lay people, who have little or no experience of that line of work and who have not studied in those disciplines, might have thought that gaining motivation was only worth +2. Those lay people could include judges in negligence trials, or members of committees of inquiry appointed to examine a particular case where harm occurred after professional risk-taking. If that is the case then it is both very important, and very proper, for those professionals involved to make sure that the judge or committee knows about their statement of sample values. They should cite it as an example of contemporary professional standards of practice. Recall that the standard of care, in the law of negligence, is what a responsible body of co-professionals would do, which includes deciding. Nobody can guarantee what the courts will decide, but the fact that several professionals have agreed this statement should be very powerful evidence – especially where a witness may have to try to convince a judge that, contrary to what the judge may have long assumed, his or her profession regards things differently.

Finally, the document should be used. Whenever any professional has to make a risk assessment, he or she should have regard to the list of outcomes and their valuations. It is, of course, quite possible that the outcomes which have to be considered in relation to the particular risk decision proposed are not included in the list agreed by the group of professionals. That is not a major problem. The outcomes on the formal list can be used as markers. The particular risk decision-makers can ask themselves, and their colleagues, whether the outcome under consideration is more, less or equally valuable or serious than the items on the list. They might decide that the particular outcome should be located somewhere between outcomes on the formal list but that does not matter. The list – provided that the items on it are spaced well along the continuum from least to most serious or valuable – will have done its job. It will provide an indication of value. Precision is neither possible nor required; serious thought is. This approach will demonstrate it.

Which outcomes, and to which degree?

There is another problem with the seriousness, or value, of outcomes. An investigation might suggest that someone could get injured. But injured in which ways? Injuries can be so slight as to be trivial; they can also be so serious as to be life-threatening and with permanent effects. At least, you might be tempted to sigh, with death you know where you are (in a manner of speaking). You (actually someone else) are either dead or not dead. But even that is arguable, for, as has been noted above, we sometimes refer to 'living deaths'. However, there is an important point. Injury, damage to property, pain and so on are all *relative*, from slight to serious. Death is *categorical*, or dichotomous. Risk assessors need to focus upon a particular *degree* of harm or benefit. But, of course, it being risk-taking, they cannot be sure. The 'answer', once again, is to be sensible and reasonable, to develop a defensible practice. Risk assessors should, for practical reasons, think about a 'sensible' degree of harm, or benefit, which is likely to occur. Perhaps they are concerned about a car accident. What is a sensible, or reasonable, degree of harm to anticipate from a car accident? We know that most car accidents do not end in death so that would not be 'reasonable', even though it is certainly possible. Equally, we (or most of us) do not know the most common degree of injury from different activities. So let us 'fix' on a degree of physical injury, say, a broken leg. With that degree of injury in their minds risk assessors can now 'fix' on the likelihood of *that* outcome.

Why should we do this? We can break a fingernail, a hand, an arm, a leg, two legs, a back and so forth in a car accident. But it would be inappropriate (daft even) for the risk assessor to predict the likelihood of each and every one of those possible degrees of outcomes. That would become impossibly complex for humans. But that is not the critical objection. It is entirely inappropriate to add the likelihood of every possible outcome together. If injury, or benefit, occurs from risk-taking then it will be at a certain level or degree. You may have thought that the most likely degree of harm from taking a risk was a broken leg but, in the event, what occurs is a broken arm. It could have been more serious; it could have been death. It could have been less. This is risk-taking; you cannot know in advance. You can only do your best; the law requires that you do as well as a responsible body of colleagues.

Here is a useful aid. Note that we invariably rate the likelihood of less-serious outcomes as being more likely than more-serious outcomes. Serious harm presupposes (you cannot have it without) minor harm. To get to the life-threatening injuries you have to 'go through' minor and serious injuries. Generally speaking, more serious outcomes are less likely to occur than minor injuries. (There could be incidents, such as the escape of highly volatile materials, aircraft crashing, where serious harm, e.g. life-threatening, is more likely to result than minor. But this will be unusual.) You can cause actual bodily harm (the lesser degree) without causing grievous bodily harm (the greater degree). But you cannot cause grievous bodily harm without causing actual bodily harm. The more serious implies the less serious; the less serious does not imply the more serious. This is convenient. You may be anxious, when you decide upon a degree of outcome (e.g. a broken leg from a car accident) that you have chosen the incorrect degree of harm. The *likelihood* of minor injuries from a car accident (or other risky activity) is higher than serious injuries. So if you decide to predict a minor injury from a risk, you will (properly) give it a higher likelihood rating than if you were predicting, say, death. So if you are wrong about the minor injuries (e.g. in the event that a leg was broken). your likelihood rating – of the minor injuries – was higher than you would have used if you had predicted the broken leg.

Remember there are two elements to a risk: the outcome and the likelihood. Ideally, you predict both correctly. But if you get one wrong there *may* be 'compensation' from the other. In the above example the outcome was underpredicted but the likelihood was overpredicted. This is important for your reassurance and for you to use to attack inappropriate criticism. If a lawyer, for example, wanted to make cheap points he or she could point out that you predicted minor injuries when major injuries occurred. You should not fall for that bad argument. You need to point out that – assuming it is true – your assessment also included a prediction of likelihood. If you had based your risk assessment on the actual amount of harm that did occur, then you would have rated the likelihood as lower. You 'compensated' for fixing on a lower amount of harm than actually occurred, by having a higher likelihood. As both elements of risk-taking, likelihood and outcome, must be taken into account when risk-taking the overall difference is not as great as might be thought.

Let us use some simple mathematics to make this point. Imagine you thought that the most likely degree of harm (or benefit) to occur was equivalent to −2. And you assessed the likelihood of this occurring as being 60 per cent, or 0.6. Multiply the two elements together to reach −1.2. But what actually occurred was much more serious, deserving a rating of −6. If you had predicted this outcome you may be able to convince the court you would have rated the likelihood as 20 per cent, or 0.2. Multiply the two elements together to reach −1.2. Of course the numbers were rigged in this example; it was an illustration. But real-life cases could be like this. If this happens you need to be able to explain to others – like the awkward lawyer above – that even though you underpredicted the particular outcome, your risk assessment was still correct. Even if the figures in your case do not balance so magically you may still be able to demonstrate that your assessment was broadly comparable to what occurred.

But this is not fail-proof, or fool-proof. The degree of likelihood does *not* vary at a rate that is directly equivalent, and in all cases, to the rate at which the degree of outcome varies. But it is worth noting and reminding anyone who seeks to judge your risk-taking. When thinking about outcomes choose an appropriate degree of benefit or harm, usually by thinking of what is the most likely amount. Then use that to assess likelihood.

Communicating outcomes and likelihood

Outcome is only one of the two key elements of risk. Likelihood must also be considered. Refusing to cross a road because of a risk of death would be indefensible if the likelihood is low. (Try not being sacked because you think the risk of death from travelling to work is too high.) It may be understandable that people are frightened of being criticised, of all the publicity and inquiries and critical media coverage that could result from someone dying as a consequence of them taking a risk. But that would be unjustifiable. The problem is poor protection of risk-takers when harm results, a topic that is returned to in Chapter 9. Employers and managers must be prepared to respond, publicly, promptly and forcefully, that risk-taking, even if death occurs, can and regularly *is* justified. Risk-taking should be judged by the quality of the decision-making processes, not merely by the outcomes.

Communicating outcomes 'x' likelihood

There are two elements to a risk: the outcomes and their likelihood. We may speak of, for example, a slight chance of a broken limb or of an almost certainty of a critical improvement in patient or client motivation. And for many professional risk-takers that will be a suitable place to leave it. But, if the outcomes and likelihood have been translated into numbers, it then becomes clear that the significance of each outcome should be multiplied by its likelihood. Not only is this proper but it halves the amount of information that has to be coped with. Then the product of all the beneficial and negative outcomes can be added together and compared.

Please note that it is *not* being suggested that, just because the total of all the positive outcomes exceeds the total of all the negative outcomes, the risk can be justified. Risk assessment is a guide to action. Decision-makers must have regard to the size of the difference (e.g. how much greater the potential benefits are than the possible harms), the reliability of their data (e.g. is the difference between potential benefits and harms greater than degree of concern about reliability of the data used) and the potential of their risk management plans to control the consequences. Even then that is not the end.

Although percentages were used above when discussing likelihood, it is wiser to use the conventional method of zero to one. It is easy to translate from percentages: zero per cent remains as zero; 100 per cent becomes one. Thus an even, or 50 per cent, chance becomes 0.5. There is no similar convention for measuring outcomes but it is suggested that any scheme adopted should not imply more knowledge, sophistication and certainty than is possessed. It may be appropriate for some services to use a scale of 0 to +100 and 0 to −100, but it is unlikely that any of the professions which this book targets would realistically have so many different levels. In practice it is suggested that most could cope with 0 to −10 and 0 to +10, but envisaging that some assessments might involve half and quarter positions between whole numbers. Decimal points are much more likely to arise with likelihood assessments because a one in a million chance will be translated as 0.000001, which, when multiplied with death rated for seriousness as −10, produces a product of 0.00001, which clearly demonstrates that this is – still – a very low risk, even though the word 'death' has been mentioned. And a nil likelihood of death, –10, of course, when multiplied, produces 0, or no risk.

As has been stressed throughout, numbers are only recommended because they improve analysis and communication. Any numbers (just like words) chosen for a risk assessment are best estimates. Risk assessors should be quick to stress that despite the appearance of exactness and precision that numbers can suggest they are merely tools and referents for assessments 'in the head'. They must say the same about the product of likelihood and outcomes. Those, too, are best estimates and the assessors will have a range, or band, of confidence in them.

Conclusion

This chapter has highlighted the importance of risk communication and offered some practical suggestions. It may seem strange, even redundant, to focus on the importance of risk communication because you are so used to taking risks in your own life. Unfortunately, language is often vague and that can lead to confusion and miscommunication. Where professionals have to communicate with one another to take or to advise on a risk affecting another citizen it is important that they actually communicate their meanings and not just exchange words. This is liable to become an area where critics and lawyers increasingly focus their attention. If it is argued that risk-taking should be judged by the quality of the processes involved, not just by the outcomes, then risk communication must be paid more attention as a key process.

CHAPTER 7
Risk Procedures

We have to accept that, owing to the nature of risk-taking, harm will sometimes occur, even in cases where the best-quality decision is made. It has been argued that risk decisions should be judged by the *processes* involved, not by the *outcomes*. The other 'half of the equation' is equally important. Harm may be avoided by virtue of good fortune, even though a risk decision was poor. This chapter will identify some possible problems with the procedures that can be adopted for making risk decisions, and make some practical suggestions.

A wide range of things can go wrong. For example, whilst it is perfectly proper to use a list of risk factors to help assess a risk (indeed, it may be negligent not to do so), such a list may be a source of error. Risk-taking requires a lot of decision-making, but decisions are another potent source of errors. A substantial body of research has identified a number of ways in which we regularly make mistakes (e.g. Kahneman *et al.* 1982; Rachlin 1989). Risk-takers should be alive to these problems in order to avoid errors or to minimise their effects. Although this might make it appear that this chapter is going to be an inventory of items to terrify risk decision-makers, it is emphasised that perfection is not required. However, when and where we know that errors can originate, then and there should we act. If a responsible body of practitioners would act to avoid these well-known errors, it may constitute negligence (remember there are five separate tests to satisfy) not to do so.

Decision complexity
In the last chapter, the judicious use of numbers as communication aids was advocated. It was pointed out that it is proper to multiply the value of each reasonably possible outcome by its likelihood, which it is easier to do with

numbers than words. You may continue to say 'very high likelihood of minor harm', but you may also say – if this is what you have decided you mean by such terms – 'an 0.9 chance of a 0.05 loss' or 'my best estimate is around 0.045'. Being able to reduce the amount of information that risk assessors must consider is very important.

Imagine you are concerned about the risk to a child of him or her remaining with parents who may be abusive. Not only must you consider the potential harms of the child remaining with the parents but the almost certain (but it is hoped less serious) harms of taking the child into local authority care. And there are the potential benefits of leaving the child with the parents, such as maintaining bonds, and of taking the child away, such as having time to work with the child on a more one-to-one basis. Considering these different risks is liable to produce an awful lot of information. And then when you have collated it all you have to think about its accuracy and its significance, and compare them. The task becomes inhuman. Humans have 'bounded rationality' (Gigerenzer and Goldstein 1996); there is a limit to the amount of information they can cope with without the assistance of aids.

Imagine you obtained all that information about that child and family; that you are doing a very thorough job. That is great but will you, or could others, or both, be able to cope with the sheer amount and complexity of the information? Rather than being overwhelmed humans adopt heuristics, or techniques for simplifying the task (e.g. Slovic 2000). But these devices can quickly lead us into error (Janis and Mann 1977). Imagine the frustration of collecting a lot of valuable quality information necessary for a risk assessment, only to make errors when making decisions based upon it. There have been extensive developments over recent decades in developing risk assessment in all the professional areas covered by this book (e.g. Nash 2006), for example in producing ever better lists of risk factors to consider. But there have not been equivalent advances in improving risk decision-making processes (Titterton 2005).

Just as individuals may be sued, or otherwise professionally embarrassed for poor risk assessment, so they may be sued for poor use of quality information. (This could be an area for legal developments!) The courts may be expected to provide professional risk-takers with considerable latitude when assessing the differential seriousness and likelihood of different outcomes. But it will be more difficult to justify failing to adopt decision-making aids such as those identified above for communicating about risk, and those listed below, which are designed to minimise the likelihood of error. Note that the presence or absence of decision aids will be more visible, more evident, than improper professional judgements about seriousness and likelihood. A court or inquiry will be able to see for itself whether risk-takers had, or made use of, decision-making aids. This is an area where responsibility, and liability, may fall directly on supervisors, managers and employers, because they have failed to provide decision aids when they could not, sensibly, claim they did not know of their importance.

Risk factors

A wide range of risk factors have been developed to inform particular types of risk-taking, from lists of potential side-effects of a drug to lists of factors that should be considered when deciding whether an individual (e.g. patient, prisoner, parent, partner) is liable to be violent. You cannot comment upon the appropriateness of particular sets of risk factors, not just because there are so many but because you are not qualified to express judgements outside of your professional experience. But, presuming responsible co-professionals approve them, it is perfectly proper to use these lists. Indeed, it would be negligent not to use them if no responsible body of co-professionals would fail to do so. The concern is that risk factors can be misused. Here are some problems that can arise.

Double-counting

Lists of risk factors are unlikely to have been drafted as if they were a legal document. That is understandable but, as a consequence, they may be ambiguous or vague. For example, the same concern may be addressed in different ways. A list may enquire whether the individual has committed a violent offence, a property offence, a sexual offence. But someone who has committed a sexual offence has almost certainly, by nature of the offending behaviour, also committed a violent offence. Should his (it will invariably be a male) offence be recorded twice, as if he has committed twice as many offences? If someone has committed robbery has he or she committed both violence and the property offence? (Robbery requires both that theft is committed and violence used in effecting it; Section 8, Theft Act 1968)

  The answer to these questions will depend upon the particular risk assessment document, its quality and objectives. It would usually be appropriate to note the nature and frequency of significant past behaviour rather than how it is legally characterised. But the information may have been recorded for legal purposes. It is fine for a checklist to use different techniques to prompt risk assessors to recall and consider a wide range of information. However, it would be wrong to count some behaviour twice simply because of how the list of risk factors describes it. To minimise this problem you could analyse any lists of risk factors you use. Does it, innocently, encourage double-counting? Alternatively, when undertaking a risk assessment, identify the evidence that you are relying on in relation to a risk factor. Does that evidence justify you in making all those different and separate predictions, some or just one? Evidence for risk should not be made to bear more than it could, in reality, bear.

Factors for risk assessment or risk management?

Many lists of risk factors are strong on features relevant to risk assessment, but weak on factors relevant to risk management. For example, the list may identify reasons for concern that a prisoner, or defendant seeking bail, will abscond. Taken together these may suggest that the proposed risk should not be taken. But, irrespective of that initial impression, there may be information available to indicate that the risk of absconding may be managed with relative ease. Recall from Chapter 5 how risk management is concerned with the nature, quantity and quality of resources available for use in order to make it more likely that valuable benefits will be achieved and feared harms avoided. Lists of risk factors can only help as far as they go; they cannot answer questions that they were not designed for. Can you identify a list of risk factors which encourages you to think about how you might manage the risk; how you might influence or control the consequences and their likelihood? Could you and your colleagues, at least over time, develop one?

Risk of benefits

Risk factor research, and the consequent lists, are – invariably – biased. The lists usually identify causes for concern, likely harms; that is, reasons why risk should not be taken. This is not too surprising given the continuing tendency to think of risk as only relevant to potential harms. The rationale for the research into risk, and the development of risk factors, has been the avoidance of losses. But it is hoped that the earlier chapters have successfully made the case for 'risk-taking' being understood as balancing likely benefits and possible harms. It would be perfectly appropriate for researchers and practitioners to undertake work to identify factors predictive of benefits from risk-taking. There is already research, in various disciplines, on 'protective factors' (e.g. Dillon *et al.* 2007). But that is not what is meant and it is not enough.

'Protective risk factors' usually means the features of a case which can make it less likely that *harms* will occur. For example, the fact that an offender has recently been married may make it less likely that he or she will offend again. It 'protects' him or her. If that is the case then it is very relevant. It should be used to reduce the assessment of the likelihood of the feared re-offending. But, whereas that is beneficial, it is not a benefit in the sense referred to in this book. It is a reduced negative rather than a likely positive. Risk factors which encourage risk-takers to think about, for example, the kinds (and likelihood) of benefits that can accrue from an offender are needed, for example not being incarcerated, a patient not being medicated, a child not taken into local authority care. This is not romantic or wishful thinking; you can make better decisions both by becoming better at identifying benefits (risks) which will succeed as well as harms (risks) which will fail. Could you and your colleagues, at least over time, develop lists of possible benefits of risk-taking so that these, too, may be used by risk assessors?

This is particularly important in relation to risk decisions that may find their way to a court or other inquiry. Because of the pervasive association of risk-taking with harm avoidance, plus the fact that these are only ever involved because harms have occurred, they are less likely to think about the potential benefits. So it is incumbent upon professional risk-takers, if they want their decisions to be respected, to identify the potential benefits and show how they influenced their decision.

Risk factors: equal importance?

Think of a list of risk factors, within your discipline or area of practice, which identifies things that risk assessors should consider. Is each item on that list equally important? The first problem is that those who use risk factors may treat each item on the list as of equal importance. For example, one item could be the number of previous violent acts, if any, that a person has committed. Another could relate to whether the individual has a steady job. Both could be relevant predictors but, if the risk concerns future dangerousness, then the first item is many time more important than the second (Campbell 1995; Monahan *et al.* 2001; Walker 1996). Some risk factors have much greater predictive power, are much more relevant, than others. To consciously treat unequal items as if they were equal is to make a deliberate error.

This can be confusing. It has been argued that there are two key elements in risk: outcomes and their likelihood. Is a third, the importance of the information, being suggested? No. Consider, for example, a case whether there is concern that a client might be violent. Risk assessors have to investigate what they anticipate he or she might do, and how likely that is. But, in undertaking that investigation, they should utilise risk factors which the research, and/or good professional practice, recommends. If those risk factors contain an item, for example the nature and frequency of previous violence, which is much more predictive than another item, such as marital status, then they must pay much more attention to that more *powerful* predictor. If there is plenty of evidence both to indicate a frequent and ferocious violent past but equally a very stable marriage, there should be no question of the one cancelling the other out. When making their risk assessments the decision-makers should be able to demonstrate that they accorded different risk factors the appropriate degree of emphasis and attention. Do you know which risk factors, in any list that you regularly use, are the most predictive?

There is a major problem, however. Many lists of risk factors do not identify the more powerful or reliable factors. Researchers are often reluctant to identify what they consider to be the relative power of different factors. They might feel that the quantity and quality of research conducted to date does not make it proper to do so. That may be appropriate but, equally, it may also involve professional anxiety. If pressed those researchers may be prepared to indicate which of the risk factors they think are the most predictive. (They may be able to work on their data to investigate which factors predict most cases.) They may not wish to articulate their opinions without undertaking more research. This could be unfortunate. Those researchers' 'mere' opinions, as yet unsupported by solid research, are liable to be much better informed than others' guesses. They may avoid making the sorts of mistakes that others, without their background knowledge, would make.

Some lists of risk factors encourage their users to add numbers according to the amount of evidence there is to support each factor listed (for example Webster, *et al* .1997). This might appear to be a means of recognising the differential importance of each factor. To an extent it is. It concerns the degree of evidence for that item. If there is no evidence, for example, *for* that factor then that factor will not count against (or for) the client concerned. Only those evidenced factors, and to the extent that they are evidenced, will be taken into account. But that does not involve a differential according to the *nature* of the factor. Returning to the example where the concern is someone's future dangerousness, there could be plenty of evidence of previous violence and of poor current marital relationship. In terms of evidence available they may be equal. But in terms of predictive power and importance they remain very different (Webster *et al.* 1994).

Degrees of detail

This point is related to the last. Some lists of risk factors are much more detailed than others. There may be a tendency to conclude that the more detailed the list the better it is. But such reasoning is dangerous. The longer list of risk factors may include a number of considerations which are of very limited predictive power – and could exclude, or distract attention from, some of the most significant considerations. Size is not always important. Two alternative lists could include the same most predictive points. The longer list may be of little, if any, greater predictive power. This point may need to be explained to courts and inquiries. It is 'natural' to assume that using the longer, more detailed, list of risk factors will be more complete, more thorough. Choosing a shorter list could be represented as being lazy. It could be counterintuitive. It could be perfectly proper professional practice, and in terms of the most efficient use of available resources, including time, it could even be better practice to use the shorter list of risk factors – providing always that it, too, contains the most powerful factors.

Different ways of counting the same thing

A problem can arise when a list includes items which are really just different ways of asking for the same types of information. For example, a key consideration for a particular type of risk could be a disorganised lifestyle (Jeyarajah Dent 1998). Thus, the list of risk factors might produce questions about rubbish left lying around dustbins, torn clothing, ownership of an old car and so on. All of these types of question could relate to the one concern: disorganised lifestyle. The list of ideas is very handy as an aide-memoire to encourage risk assessors to think of the evidence available to support an assessment about disorganised lifestyle. It helps us to think of the evidence, its quantity and quality. But that is only the starting point. What is relevant is the chaotic lifestyle, not the untidy dustbin. It is the second question, 'What does this evidence of chaotic lifestyle tell us about what may happen, its seriousness and likelihood?', that is the relevant issue.

There is a real risk that some lists of risk factors will tell us more about their authors than about the risks that they are concerned with. Some authors will have good imaginations and will be able to come up with lots of different ways of asking about the same thing. But we need to know about the person, or thing, at risk – not about the author. So judge lists of risk factors by their value and by the nature and extent of their research base. It is quality, and not size, that matters. Checklists of risk factors are designed to encourage, facilitate and improve your thinking. You should not stop thinking just because they exist. They should be treated critically. As a means of tackling these problems try the idea of a 'risk factor filter funnel'. But this is just an aid; it is not a substitute for careful analysis and assessment.

Risk factor filter funnel

The role of a filter is to ensure that only proper things pass through it: the wine and not the lees. The role of a risk funnel is to ensure that only proper information gets through and goes to the right place. Each piece of information provided or suggested by a risk factor should be perceived as being added into the top of a funnel. The lower part of the funnel should be directed towards the relevant part of the risk assessment or management plan. So, if the information suggests that there is a likelihood, or an increased likelihood of someone's arm being broken then the funnel should be directed to the harm side of the equation, and, in particular, to the degree of likelihood of an arm being broken. If the information relates to potential benefits then, of course, the funnel is directed to the other side of the equation. However, it does not follow that any or all of the information passes through the funnel. Two questions must be asked of each piece of information offered to the funnel.

- Does, and if so how does, this information add to, or otherwise affect, the amount or degree of harm or benefit possible?

- How does this information affect the likelihood of the different outcomes?

These questions 'filter' the information and control what passes through to affect what is already there. So, for example, an assessment might already have been made of the nature, degree and likelihood of harm that could arise from a client having a disorganised lifestyle. More information arises which shows that the client has an untidy dustbin. To what extent, if any, does that extra information affect the likely outcomes already considered because of disorganised lifestyle? If the answer is that it has no effect then none of the information should 'get through'. If it provides a 'fuller picture' and, for example, indicates that the implications of the disorganised lifestyle are more significant than previously thought, then some of the information – to increase the seriousness of the outcome, or its likelihood, or both – should be allowed through. But as the problems arising from disorganised lifestyle have already been considered it will rarely, if ever, be appropriate to allow all the information through.

Equally, an assessment of the risks arising because of the client's previous violent offence may have been made. A fresh risk factor may tell the risk assessor to consider previous sex offences. If the previous offence was a sex offence it may be inappropriate to 'double-count' that incident just because this listing of risk factors has not dealt with the overlap between sexual and violence offences. However, the fact that it was a sexual offence may, sometimes, according to the particular risk, justify increasing the assessment of the seriousness of the harm and/or its likelihood. It is important to be able to demonstrate thought. It is just too easy for a lawyer to criticise a risk assessment where the assessor has used the risk factors as a checklist and naïvely just counted up how many ticks he or she has made.

Risk factors are an aid to thinking, not a substitute for or a limit to it. Other considerations, beyond those which the list seeks to cover, may be relevant. Risk-takers should be able to show that they used appropriate risk factors to the extent possible, but also thought about issues that list did not cover.

Decision errors

It is not just that some decision-making, such as risk-taking, is complicated. It is particularly complicated when lots of different pieces of information (such as risk factors) of different levels of relevance and degrees of reliability have to be considered all at the same time. Thus it is not surprising that decision-makers make mistakes. It is also very easy simply to blame anyone who makes a mistake; mistakes should not happen. But not only is that a very unforgiving attitude, it may also be unhelpful. For example, the 'mistake' may only be evident after the event, with the benefits of hindsight. If that is the case then the question should be whether the 'mistake' could have been avoided; whether wisdom both could and should have been provided before the event. And it is critical to stress that not all mistakes deserve blame, at least in the sense of being considered negligent in law. It will often be the case that a responsible body of co-professionals would have made the same decision, the same mistake. Again, the nature of risk-taking should be emphasised; it means – inherently, necessarily and by definition – that sometimes harm will result. That harm results does not, necessarily, mean that there was a bad risk decision. The quality of the decision-making process needs to be examined. But we should still want to reduce errors.

The key point is that there is a science of decision-making (Janis and Mann 1977; Kahneman *et al.* 1982; Slovic 2000) and risk-taking is one kind of decision-making (MacCrimmon and Wehrung 1988; Royal Society 1992). This research has demonstrated that we are all prone to make decision errors. It has identified a number of ways in which we regularly make similar mistakes. Professional risk-takers need to identify these types of error and be able to show that they are acting to minimise their occurrence or effects. It is one thing for a judge to conclude that although a risk decision may have been made erroneously, nobody is to be blamed because the decision-makers acted consistently with current professional standards. But it should be an entirely different thing for a judge to notice that the error was of a kind the risk-takers knew was both commonplace and capable of being avoided or minimised with relative ease.

Professional risk-takers need to heed the research on decision errors and learn from it (Greene and Ellis 2007; Heilbrun and Erickson 2007). Recall from Chapter 3 that judges are reluctant to interfere, via the law of negligence, with professional statements of the standard of care. But they have reserved the right to do so (*Bolitho* v. *City* & *Hackney Health Authority* [1988] AC 232) where they consider the rationale for the decision not to be 'defensible'. Thus they may be more willing to interfere with regard to these types of common decision error which are not discipline – or profession – specific. They could expect there to be evidence that the risk-takers recognised the possibility of these research-informed errors arising, and took appropriate action to minimise them.

This is an area where supervisors, managers and employers have an important role to play. They may 'stand back' from the immediate decision-making role of the front-line professional risk-takers. They may not be directly responsible for individual decisions. But they are responsible for the processes and systems involved in reaching and implementing them. They are responsible for the training and competence of their staff. They are responsible for designing and investing in systems that will determine the quality of information which their staff must work with. They have the responsibility to review the quality of risk decision-making by their staff, and to realise opportunities for learning from and improving it.

Availability of information

Assessments of likelihood are influenced by the amount of information you have about them, not just the content or quality of that information. Some events are read or heard about quite regularly. Other events we hear about relatively rarely. This is a consequence of the 'news agenda' adopted by the media. For example, a death caused in a train crash will almost certainly receive national attention, whilst a suicide achieved by jumping in front of a train will receive little attention. The former is perceived to be more newsworthy, and interesting, than the latter, even thought the latter is a more serious social problem. Because you hear more about some rare events you can overestimate their likelihood.

To emphasise this point consider the following questions before proceeding. Which is more likely: (a) homicide or (b) suicide by a mentally disordered person? Which is more common, deaths in (a) airline, (b) railway or (c) road accidents? It is hoped that the readers of this book will know that suicide by mentally disordered people is more common than their causing a homicide. But how many people know that? In particular, how many decision-makers, such as judges, or opinion-formers, such as journalists and politicians? We know that it is more likely that a mentally disordered person will kill him- or herself than kill another person, but how many times more likely? A lot of people working in mental health services will know there is a difference, but not its degree.

The Samaritans (2007) estimates that, each year, over 6000 people in the United Kingdom and Republic of Ireland kill themselves. And this is liable to be an underestimate because of the reluctance to admit or report suicides and attempts. The National Confidential Inquiry into Suicide and Homicide by People with a Mental Illness (2001) investigated 6367 cases of suicide by people with current or a recent mental illness between April 2000 and December 2004. That was 27 per cent of all suicides. It was estimated that there are over 1300 suicides by patients with a mental illness each year. There were some 850 recorded homicides a year in England and Wales (886 in 2000–2001) (Simmons 2002). The National Confidential Inquiry into Suicide and Homicide by People with a Mental Illness (2001) found 249 cases of patient homicides translating to 52 a year. So, in relation to patients the ratio appears to be, on average, 52 homicides to 1300 suicides a year or, roughly, 1:25. Does this ratio reflect either the hysteria that often follows a homicide by someone with a mental illness, or the investment of resources to tackle problems?

Many people may know that one outcome is more likely than another, but they consistently underestimate the degree of difference. This is true of many areas of professional practice. You may be right that X is more likely than Y. But is it good enough to be partly right? How 'right' is it to know that there are more Xs than Ys when, in fact, there are 25 times more Xs than Ys? The use of numbers helps to dramatise the degree of difference. There are some 3500 deaths on our roads each year (DoT 2004). That leads to road safety campaigns and television advertisements. Somehow we do not seem to make comparable provision to try to reduce suicides.

If we have difficulty recalling such information how much more difficult is it likely to be for lay people, such as judges and tribunal inquiry members? It is critically important that professional risk-takers do not assume that others have more knowledge than they do. As a risk-taking professional you, or rather your managers and employers, should be providing them with regularly updated and improved data on comparative likelihoods relevant to your work. One of the authors of this books has encountered mental health professionals who had limited knowledge of the relative difference between the likelihood of homicide and suicide by mentally disordered people and had suggested that their ignorance did not matter because the public concern is with homicide and not with suicide. Many relatives will demand justice and a public inquiry when a homicide occurs; fewer voices are raised about the much more serious problem of suicides. Although this response is understandable, having comparative figures available would help professionals to put things into perspective for lay people. The issue before the court may be whether the mental health professionals breached the standard of care when deciding on the care of one patient who killed another. No suicide is involved. But it could only be valuable to ensure that the court understands that suicide is a much more likely event. Rare events (such as homicides by mentally disordered people) are – strangely – rare. Consequently, they are more difficult to predict.

It is important that professional groups and managers identify and make available, both to those who make risk decisions on their behalf and the lay public, relevant information about the likelihood of different outcomes that can arise in their service. The key quality of this information should be its reliability, that is, its scientific credentials, and it certainly should not just comprise information that is regularly repeated. Unfortunately, it will often be the case that the current science is relatively weak, but it will always be better than rumour and guesswork. This should include both *absolute* information, say, how likely certain outcomes are within a particular timeframe and area, and *relative* information, in order to encourage decision-makers to think about the degree of difference between the likelihood of alternative outcomes. However, care should be taken to ensure that they are fair comparisons. Clearly, it would be wrong to compare likelihood in a week with chance in ten years. But unfair comparisons can arise in other ways. When you think about it, for example – and contrary to the frequency of media reports – we 'know' that deaths on roads (in particular as passengers) exceed those on railways and in the air. That is especially true if the measure is the distance travelled. But is that the most appropriate comparator? What if the measure was the number of trips made?

Adjusting our estimates

One finding in decision research has been called the 'anchoring and adjustment bias' (Greene and Ellis 2007; Rachlin 1989; Slovic, Fischoff and Lichtenstein 2000). This states that when you make estimates, and are uncertain, you tend to adopt a starting point and make relatively small adjustments from it. You may estimate the likelihood of X_1 as being 0.5 but, on further analysis, decide you should be estimating the likelihood of X_2. The suggestion is that, whilst you know you need to change your estimate of 0.5, you will not make a sufficiently big change. You will be conservative. The original estimate has provided an anchor which restricts your thinking. If managers develop a 'bank' of likelihood information, as suggested above, that would help risk assessors who have to adjust estimates to particular cases. For instance, in the earlier example, the comparative likelihood of suicide and homicide could be a valuable anchor to help courts appreciate just how unlikely homicides are, despite media representations.

When risk-takers come to make their assessments they could consider the data available and perform a check on their estimates by considering comparative differences. For example, have they assessed a mentally disordered patient, contrary to the research, as more likely to injure another as to injure him- or herself? Particular outcomes may be identified as rare, but is that 'rarity' only ten times more unlikely than something considered 'likely'? We tend to overestimate rare events. Which of the following, if any, gives you or your friends the most, if any, anxiety: flying, going by train, going by car? Which, being rational, should give you the most, if any, concern? Rarity is often exciting, because it so unusual, so it is somehow worthy of notice. But it remains rare. Just because a one in a million chance occurs – most weeks someone wins the lottery – it does not become any more likely.

Hindsight

Risk-takers take decisions about, and for, the future without complete information. They would love to know what is going to happen before it happens. They would love to have the benefits of hindsight – in advance of making their decisions. But, of course, that is not possible. However, there is one occupation which is especially fortunate because it can wallow in hindsight – lawyers. A court or tribunal reviewing a risk decision – whether in the form of a claim for compensation or an inquiry to ascribe any appropriate blame – already knows the outcome. It knows that the medicine had side-effects, knows that the prisoner re-offended, that the parents injured their child. Indeed, that is why the trial or inquiry is taking place. But hindsight is a regular source of error. It biases expectations. (See

Wexler and Schopp (1989) for an attempt to avoid its effects in court and, for a discussion of hindsight problems, see Heilbrun and Erickson (2007).)

A court or inquiry might be told by risk assessors that they thought there was only a 1 in 1000 chance of serious harm. But it happened. We know it did; that is why we are here in court. So how could there have only been such a small chance? The assessment must have been wrong. Obviously, it must have been negligent. Everyone involved with such an erroneous prediction clearly deserves blame and censure. No. It is reactions and reasoning of this sort which deserve the clearest condemnation. The assessment may have been wrong, may have been negligent, but there must be a much more detailed examination of how the decision was made before you can fairly come to those conclusions. Quite simply, if there is a 1 in 1000 risk of death from a particular risk activity, you are recognising that once in every 1000 instances the predicted event 'should', in a statistical rather than moral sense, occur. Further, because this is an estimate there has to be an acceptable range. So, in one set of 1000 examples there might be three fatalities but in three other sets of 1000 examples there could be none. The degree of variation from the prediction will vary depending upon the quality of the science upon which the prediction is made. But if there are 100 fatalities in a set of 1000, and no proper explanation can be provided, you must question the quality of the data and the wisdom of relying upon it.

It is tempting to conclude that these points are too basic; that everyone knows about hindsight and how important it is to take it into account. Then try an experiment. Put the same risk-taking question to a large group of people. For example, should a client of residential services for adults with learning disabilities, who also has epilepsy, be allowed to take a bath unsupervised? He or she has no speech and last experienced a fit three years ago and, as a consequence, is no longer prescribed anticonvulsant medication. You could ask your audience, at this stage, for their best estimate of the likelihood of the client being seriously injured whilst unsupervised and in the bath. You can continue by providing more information. For example, in this case you could add that he or she has been taking unsupervised baths for the past two years, without experiencing harm. The proposal is not to take a 'new' risk but rather to undertake a review of whether the same decision, to allow the unsupervised bathing, should be allowed to continue for a further specified risk period. Ask your audience to put themselves 'into the shoes' of the decision-maker and to consider the likelihood of serious harm. However, let half of your audience know that the client actually did have a fit, slipped and drowned in the bath. Do not give this information to the other half. Ensure everyone is making the same assessment, which is what the risk assessor should think is the likelihood of serious injury by continuing the practice of unsupervised bathing.

Just before you collate and study the responses, tell the rest of your audience what actually happened, that the client drowned. Now ask them to write down, without conferring, what was the 'real' likelihood of that happening. This time you are asking them to write down the 'actual' likelihood, not what the risk-taker should have thought before he or she decided to continue with the unsupervised bathing.

It is hoped that many in your audience will 'see through' all or part of the exercise. Just because the feared harm occurred it does not follow that the prediction was wrong. If the best estimate, before the event, was 1 in 100, then that estimate remains 'the best' until it can be demonstrated that it was wrongly reached. The adverse outcome, on its own, cannot demonstrate error. To demonstrate negligence or other forms of error in reaching that 'best estimate' you would have to examine the processes by which it was concluded, not just the outcome. You must not slip into the sloppy thinking or lapse into the practices of many journalists, managers and politicians who have ulterior motives for making points about the outcome, without going through the more difficult steps of thinking about the processes for which they may bear some responsibility.

If some of your audience did accede to your request, and gave a different estimate for 'the real likelihood', use that to make a point. Hindsight often leads us into error. There is no 'real likelihood', although there are better and worse estimates. Now, go back to the original exercise where half your audience knew, and the other half did not, about the client's death. You will almost certainly (undertaking the exercise involves a risk) discover that those who knew about the death will have predicted the likelihood of serious harm as being more likely than their ignorant (it is a polite expression here) colleagues. If so point out that everyone was supposed to be making the same prediction; those who knew that the death occurred should not have taken it into account as part of the assessment which had to be made before that happened. The exercise demonstrates the potency of hindsight. Give special praise to anyone who complained that they were not told the period for which they were making the risk prediction.

Judges know about hindsight. They know they have the benefit of it in court. They accept that it is inappropriate to use that advantage when judging others. So they make allowances. But, and here is the rub, do they know how much allowance they ought to make, and do they do that? Does anyone? Recall the exercise above. Those who knew about the drowning were biased by that knowledge in comparison with those who did not know. But both groups were asked to predict the risk shortly before the event occurred. Being asked to undertake that task could have biased their assessment. It could have put them 'on guard' about the event. Members of the group are likely to have wondered, or felt self-conscious, about why they were being asked to undertake that exercise. Would anyone ask them that sort of question unless it was significant, unless a point was to be made? Perhaps those who did not know of the death suspected that something 'was up'. What if you had asked them to put themselves in the position of the assessors who had to predict the likelihood of serious loss from unsupervised bathing the very first time it was proposed? Then you could have added in 'the hindsight' that, as was provided in the initial story, the individual had not had a seizure for three years and had successfully been having unsupervised baths for two years. That ought to make a considerable difference to the assessments. And, critically, the 'hindsight' of two and three years of success is relevant and should be taken into account. The original risk assessor had a continuing responsibility to manage and review this risk, or pass it on to someone else. He or she should have learnt from what happened. In this case he or she would be entitled to use the experience of not having fits and years of bathing with no adverse effects both to adjust his or her estimate of the likelihood of harm downwards and to have greater confidence in its accuracy. If one of your risk assessments is being judged you should insist that full allowance is made for the benefits of hindsight.

You are likely to have been given quite high estimates of likelihood in this example. Consider that this unsupervised bathing has been taking place for two years. So, if the individual took only two baths a week that means 104 risks were taken. Do any of the estimates you have been given reflect this? How many are at the 1 in 100 level? It is not suggested that the likelihood *is* one in 100, but that that is an appropriate anchor to consider.

The actual problem was the propensity to fit, and the client had not had a fit for over three years, which is why medication was stopped. What was the likelihood of having a fit, let alone within the relatively narrow time range of being in the bath? There were five years, at least, of no fits. None in over 1800 days. This example is based on a real case, where the coroner commended the authority caring for the victim, particularly because it was able to explain the positive – client-related – reasons why it had taken the risk.

As Mr Justice Cresswell said in *Burt* v. *Plymouth and Torbay Health Authority* (19 December 1997, unreported):

> Knowledge of an event which happened later should not be applied when judging alleged acts or omissions which took place before that event. In those situations which call for the exercise of judgement, the fact that in retrospect the choice actually made can be shown to have turned out badly is not in itself proof of negligence. The duty of care is not a warranty of a perfect result.

In that particular case a clinician decided to ignore, in reaching his diagnosis and treatment plan, a symptom which he considered out of line with other findings. After surgery for a spinal tumour, which the patient argued had been delayed because of a negligent diagnosis, the patient was rendered tetraplegic.

Confidence

Risk-taking requires working on imperfect knowledge. If it were otherwise it would not be a risk. And assessing the quality of the information available is a critical part of a risk decision. Sometimes there will be reliable, high-quality, information. Sometimes you will be confident in your assessment, or part of it. That will be fortunate. But that can also be the source of another kind of error. Confidence, sureness in your decision, is in a different category from likelihood. Doctor A may assess the likelihood of a side-effect from treatment as being 10 per cent. Doctor B may assess the likelihood of a side-effect from a different treatment as 20 per cent. Doctor A may, with good cause, because of the quantity and quality of the research which informs the prediction, be very confident. Doctor B may be very unsure and anxious, because of the absence of such research. What are the *real* likelihoods, in these cases? They remain 10 and 20 per cent. Confidence does not affect the likelihood. It would be erroneous reasoning to think that something was more, or less, likely to occur just because you had better data.

It is, of course, appropriate to take confidence into account, but at the risk-taking, not risk assessment, stage. When deciding whether to take the risk, the decision-maker must consider how reliable is the information that he or she is proposing to act upon. If the information is all of high quality then he or she can be confident in it and rely upon it when making the decision. But if confidence is impossible or inappropriate then the decision-maker is going to have to take that into account. It is at the decision-making stage that the decision-maker should take into account any 'margin for error'. He or she should explicitly allow for the assessments of each outcome considered varying from that stated. It may still be the case that, even after allowing for considerable variation, the anticipated benefits are very valuable and highly likely, whilst the harms are relatively unimportant and unlikely. So, in such a case, it would still be clear, and easy, to make the risk decision. However, there will be other cases where, before taking the quality of the information – and confidence in it – into account, the balance was against taking the risk. Now, allowing for the quality of the information, there could be a case for taking it (or the converse in other examples). In such cases, if it is at all possible (e.g. it is not an emergency where action must be taken), the decision-makers should investigate opportunities for more risk management. They should consider what could be done, what could be invested to make it more likely that the potential benefits will be achieved and the feared harms avoided.

Experience
Professional risk-takers will, over time, gain experience. It will be tempting, and intuitive, for them to utilise this experience. But should they? They may discover that a particular harm, frequently cited in risk assessments as being rare, is 1 in 100. But it occurred in only the second relevant risk they were involved in taking. Should they, in future, take advantage of their experience and rate the likelihood as one in two? No, that sort of experience is irrelevant unless it provides reasons for believing that the best estimate of likelihood is wrong. That person does not know whether the incident which he or she experienced is the fabled 1 in 100 or evidence that the likelihood assessment was wrong. He or she needs more information in order to decide which of those provides the correct interpretation. The professional could let colleagues know about his or her

experience, thereby generating a learning opportunity where the likelihood assessment could be reviewed. But he or she should not revise the original assessment of 1 in 100 without good reason to believe that it was wrong. That he or she has experienced a case which could be regarded as one of those 1 in 100 does not – on its own – provide those reasons. It would be wrong simply to rely upon an individual experience, particularly as it may be very idiosyncratic, and depart from what were – and still are until a proper analysis has been undertaken – best estimates according to a responsible body of co-professionals.

Indeed, individual experience should not be relied upon when making risk assessments unless there is no better source of knowledge. Relying upon individual experience rather than research studies is an invitation to be sued. Recall the discussion about the cognitive continuum in Chapter 4. It is, at the very least, much wiser to rely upon a collective opinion of relevant experts – better still on quality research – than upon a single opinion. However, it would be appropriate to utilise experience when considering a risk management plan. Experience of, for example, local resources and their competence and capacity for making a difference would be highly relevant information. Experience is relevant, at the risk management and risk decision-making stages, for making judgements about the extent to which people, services and arrangements may be relied upon.

Voluntariness and presentation

On most occasions the final decision to risk or not to risk will be made by the patient, client or other. This, as emphasised in Chapter 3, presupposes competence and voluntariness. These are estimable qualities but they can hide common errors. The fact that a choice is voluntary does not make a particular outcome any more, or less, likely. That you make a voluntary decision not to wear your seat-belt, for example, does not make it any more or less likely that you will have an accident, although it will affect the degree of injury if it does happen. Yet a lot of the people who opposed the legal requirement to wear seat-belts in cars seemed to think so. Side-effects from drugs are no more or less likely just because they are imposed upon us. It seems that we respond to the right to make a decision for ourselves with an understanding that adverse risks are, therefore, less likely. That is not the case. Certainly, taking away an individual's right to make a voluntary decision is very serious and affects the significance, or degree of harmfulness of the outcomes. But it does not relate to their likelihood.

The way in which the information is presented can affect how it is understood. There could be a 10 per cent chance of something occurring. It should follow that there is also a 90 per cent chance of it not occurring. Take an example of the risk of a treatment failing. That information can be presented as either: 'There is a 90 per cent chance of success' or 'There is a 10 per cent chance of failure'. You are much more likely to consent to a 90 per cent chance of success than a 10 per cent chance of failure, even thought they refer to the same thing. You can influence people's choices by describing the success or benefits side of the equation, rather than the failure or harms. It would be time-consuming, and could be confusing and possibly patronising, to insist on putting the information to clients or patients in both ways. It would be understandable for professionals to put the information in the most positive form, which is likely to be the format that is most likely to produce their clients' consent. But it would, surely, be unprofessional knowingly to encourage or to allow someone to consent to, or to oppose, a risk just because of the manner in which the information was presented. It could be difficult to say the individual had fully understood the issues. It could be appropriate to check why a client is consenting to, or opposing, a risk when his or her responses appear uncertain or inconsistent.

Quality of data

Chapters 2 and 4 commented on the debate over actuarial or 'clinical' risk factors. 'Actuarial' data is 'objective' information about the person concerned. Key examples include a client's gender, age, occupation, number of previous offences and so forth. This actuarial information exists, and is relatively concrete rather than interpretative. We all fit into these categories. 'Clinical' data are much more individual and interpretative. The label 'clinical' gives a lot away. It includes the sort of information which clinicians generate about us (although they also use and collect actuarial data) when we are patients. It, very much, involves their interpretations and professional judgements about us. In actuarial terms a person could be adjudged 'dangerous' because young, male, unemployed and possessed of a long string of convictions for previous violent acts. In clinical terms someone could be adjudged 'dangerous' because of the manner of his or her behaviour, statements and apparent lack of sense of guilt or ability to learn from experience. Of course, these are not mutually exclusive categories. Some interpretation is involved with actuarial data, not least in the choice of which items are to be considered significant. And extensive efforts can be made to make clinical assessments consistent and reliable between practitioners. Perhaps it would be best to think of them as ends of a spectrum, rather than as separate categories. But there are major differences between them, and their adherents can be passionate about which is the more appropriate source of data to rely upon. (For an example of the contrasting beliefs compare Maden (2002) and Hare (2002), in the same book.)

It is a fascinating dispute; it is good to see academics getting passionate about something. But, with all due respect to the protagonists, it can be rather artificial. For example, there can only be such a dispute when and where both forms of data exist. Otherwise there is no contest, although there may be an urgent case for someone to collect the data. With regard to many of the types of risks that readers of this book are confronted with, the key problem is the absence of data rather than its form as actuarial or clinical. The first, or prior question, should be the existence of data to inform the risk-taking. The second should be quality – for purpose.

Let us take a risk. Let us suggest that there is actually a means of turning this actuarial versus clinical dispute into a resolution for maximum benefit. Actuarial data are particularly appropriate for use when assessing a risk. 'Clinical' data are particularly appropriate for use when managing a risk. Both have their role. Actuarial data are most appropriate for risk assessment because they focus on the occurrence of concern, for example the side-effect, the violence, the re-offending. Here, the fact that the focus is on the event rather than the idiosyncrasies of the individuals involved is a strength. The focus is on what it is common to this person or risk and other directly comparable people or incidents. The 'clinical' approach tends to focus on differences, on what distinguished this person from others in similar positions. It is very easy, and regularly appropriate, to be influenced by the individual and his or her unique circumstances. But research has regularly shown, and insurance and other actuarial business are premised upon the fact, that it is the non-unique that is the most predictive. This is clearly demonstrated by the very high quality research of the MacArthur Research Network on Mental Health and the Law (Monahan *et al.* 2001), which examined the risk of violence posed by people with certain mental disorders.

Clinical data are more appropriate for risk management (see Chapter 5) because the focus is on the individual and thereby the particular, most appropriate, arrangements that could be made to help him or her negotiate the risk. So, for example, clinical understandings of an individual's attitudes, preparedness for or motivation to change and incentives and disincentives for that unique person, will be powerful information. It will invariably be invaluable in tailoring a risk management programme for the individual involved (Heilbrun 1997, 2003). When assessing the risk, that is, the likelihood and seriousness of a child being damaged by his or her parents versus the likelihood and seriousness of intervening in the family in the manner proposed (plus the benefits of intervening or not intervening), the best actuarial data available should be used. But, when deciding how to control the risks, given the decision to intervene or not, it is the 'clinical' or 'professional' information about the particular child and family that is most important.

But a caveat, a warning, is needed. Some 'clinical' or individual information is extremely important to risk assessment. James (a male) has ten convictions for serious violence, is unemployed, divorced and so on. In actuarial terms James is a prime candidate for a prediction of further serious violence. So you should not take the risk. But, actually, James is currently imprisoned. It is this sort of 'little' individual detail that is critical for any risk assessment. The risk of James committing another violent act – outside of prison – whilst imprisoned is, by definition, reduced to zero. It relates to causation. And James could not cause the risk in question (it would remain appropriate to assess James's risk to others within the prison). To guard against this potential mistake, which is unlikely to arise in such obvious circumstances, risk assessors should adopt a checklist question: 'Is there anything about this particular person, or proposed risk, which would alter its likelihood of occurring, the severity of consequence or the degree of benefit, in comparison with the types of person or event upon which our assessments are based?'

The clinical versus actuarial debate can arise in court. Judges and other tribunals deal with particular individuals and particular circumstances. They want to know whether Sam, the particular man or woman, will re-offend, or whatever the particular risk concerns. The law particularises.

It does not want to know about what happened to a group of men with certain similarities to Sam. They are not before the court. But Sam is. Other people might share certain features in common with Sam but they are also different in many ways, for example in the colour of their eyes and inside leg measurements. Lawyers are skilled in identifying and emphasising differences, in distinguishing cases from each other. Put another way, courts have a natural appetite for clinical, rather than actuarial, data. But the message is always the same. They, like everyone else, ought to be using the best and most appropriate data.

Risk assessors who have to appear before a court or tribunal should prepare themselves for pointing out that it would be unprofessional and incorrect for them to use clinical data when there is more appropriate actuarial information available. They should be prepared to explain how it is correct practice to utilise base-rate or actuarial information because the individual before the court is comparable to the group studied. This may be counterintuitive for the lawyers involved. (Blame their legal education for – still – not being interdisciplinary.) They may insist on the witness providing information and predictions about the particular client. They may protest that the court is not interested in other people who were studied, but on the unique individual before the court. You will have to explain that you *are* giving them information about the client, in the most appropriate manner. Nobody actually knows for certain; that is a core feature of risk-taking. We all, and that includes the judge, lawyer, jury and so on, have to make inferences and, when doing so, should use the most powerful information and be careful to avoid errors (Schum 1994).

If court proceedings are involved, where the rules of evidence should apply, you could point out that, as an expert witness, you are not entitled to give evidence on the 'ultimate issue' (Dennis 2007). An expert, that is someone with special knowledge, skill or experience, is allowed to state opinions and is not just limited to facts, as are other witnesses. However, expert witnesses should not infringe on the role of the finder of fact, which is the judge or jury. Experts should not, directly, express opinions on the ultimate issue that the court has to decide, for example whether the defendant is dangerous, lacks capacity and so on. Expert witnesses should not be asked to express an opinion on whether the person before the court is dangerous, for example, if that is the issue which the courts should decide. Of course it is understood that courts regularly allow such questions because the information will help them. But an expert witness would be behaving perfectly properly if he or she were to explain, for example, that 87 per cent of a group of people sharing five characteristics did X, and to refuse to say whether he or she thinks the client is in the 87 or 13 per cent group. Providing such actuarial information for the court, being able to explain why the characteristics are important, able to comment how exact that 87 per cent figure should be taken, and leaving it to the court to draw its own conclusions, would be very appropriate.

Conclusion

This chapter has identified a number of things which can go wrong during risk assessment, management and judgement. Employers and managers are recommended to facilitate their staff in developing procedures and processes that will minimise the likelihood of these problems occurring. The next chapter explores the need for employers to support their staff in developing 'risk policies' or 'protocols' which will inform courts and help risk-takers to justify their decisions (in particular, the value base for them).

CHAPTER 8

Risk Policies

Chapter 3 was concerned with the law relating to risk-taking and it recommendeded that risk policies were developed and regularly reviewed to ensure that professional standards are explicit. This chapter will focus primarily on the role and recommended contents of these 'policies'. Many 'policies' already exist; they are given other names, such as 'protocols'. The name is unimportant in comparison with their content.

Risk policy

A risk policy is a document, or documents, which has been agreed by a substantial group of professionals as articulating principles, values and standards (and possibly other information) relevant to the risks that they take because of their work. The requirement for endorsment by a substantial group of professionals is so that it may be argued that a risk policy satisfies the requirement of the standard of care, in the law of negligence. It would be helpful if the document covered a service (e.g. child protection services in Nessex County) or services (e.g. health, housing, policing, social services and probation in relation to sex offenders in Greater Budlington) encompassing several different professions. Where necessary, for example where only one particular profession makes certain decisions, perhaps because required by law (e.g. approved social workers in relation to mental health decisions), only some sections of the policy might apply to them.

Note that the standard of care, for the law of negligence, has to be adopted by a 'responsible' body of co-professionals. This is a vague expression whose legal meaning depends upon its context. There may only be a handful of professionals working in a specialist area. If so, a small number of them, even just one in a very small group, could constitute the 'responsible body'. It may be more helpful to think in terms of proportions, emphasising that it does *not* have to be a majority of professionals. The policy should be written for a service rather than for an office, a ward or a team. However, if a ward, team or other group has a distinctive role, for example it deals with a distinctive type of risk-taking about which their colleagues in other teams or wards are not knowledgeable or experienced, then it should have a section of the document, on that type of risk-taking, to itself. The goal is to have a substantial number of people signed up to the document so that the courts can quickly appreciate that the standards are adopted by a 'responsible' body or number of people from the relevant professions. It is not simply a question of numbers but the courts need to be able to see that it is a realistic, important, reflective document.

The risk policy which has been referred to so far would be a multidisciplinary document. That could create problems. If a risk decision is to be reviewed in the courts one of the first tasks will be to identify the particular decision to be criticised, although there could be more than one. Was the apparently poor decision attributed to the paediatrician, the social worker, the health visitor or the teacher? Once the person is identified then the relevant standard of care is that of the profession concerned. So, if it is thought to be the fault of the health visitor then it is the standards of that profession which count. But, consider a different approach. The reality is that a great deal of service delivery in contemporary professional services for clients and patients is dependent upon good interdisciplinary relations. There is considerable reliance on other disciplines and learning from their insights. That is how it is anticipated that most of the types of risk-taking covered by this book will be understood and taken. Certainly, there will be occasions when only one discipline has the necessary information to make the risk decision (e.g. a doctor prescribing medication), but those people will still rely on others (e.g. pathology tests to help them diagnose and test success, or researchers to identify any contraindications). It is important that the different professionals in a service, say police officers and social workers, have confronted potential issues arising from their different orientations and working practices in order, for example, to ensure effective collaboration in child protection services.

Only a few members of a particular discipline may have been involved in drawing up part of a risk policy. There may only have been one community psychiatric nurse on the team that drew up the section of the risk policy relating to suicides by mentally ill people residing in the community. That could not constitute a 'responsible body' of community psychiatric nurses' opinions. It may be impractical to involve every community psychiatric nurse in drafting the document, but they ought to be given an opportunity to consider whether to adopt it. A document that is written by one individual or a few people, which others are then instructed or expected to adopt, is not going to succeed. The professionals have to support the standard of care voluntarily, which requires consideration and choice. Instruction in what to think and do is inimical to the development of professional standards. It is not the employer's standards that matter; rather it is those of the profession. That one community psychiatric nurse ought to consult with his or her community psychiatric nurse colleagues on the relevant parts of the policy, and seek their agreement. The role is as a representative, not as a leader or boss. What is critical is that those colleagues (or a responsible body of them) endorse the standards articulated. Where the service only has one, or very few, specialists it remains desirable to articulate the standards. Those specialists should consult their peers in other services in order to ensure that they would approve the standards.

The risk policy should be 'owned' by the professionals it covers, in the sense of being something they are happy to sign their names to, although actual, formal signatures are not required. It is quite likely that a risk policy, say for a mental health service, in one county will be similar to one in another. They may borrow ideas and ways of articulating the standards. Some will argue that the policies should be identical, but not only do issues and problems differ around the country but so does the nature, quality and quantity of resources. People have different ideas and service philosophies. Considerable commonality between some risk policies should be expected, but the risk policy also provides an opportunity to identify, justify and proclaim differences. The courts have always been happy to accept that jobs can be done in different ways, provided that professional standards are met. Indeed, the policy should be capable of being read as a response to any particular problems the service experiences, and to its organising and motivating philosophy. Indeed, the risk policy could be a tool for attracting staff to a particular service. Whilst the risk policies of a particular service could be distinctive because of features of the population served, its resources or philosophy ought, in the main, to interlock with those produced by other services. There should be similarities and continuities, with differences of detail, rather than incompatible ways of responding to the same types of issues.

It is critical that the risk policy is reviewed regularly. It would be inappropriate to prescribe the frequency of review, as it might be very important to learn from experience and to review particular parts of the policy on topics where standards are changing quickly or there was uncertainty when it was drafted. A less than annual review might be difficult to justify. However, if that is the local practice case then arguments should be prepared to demonstrate how, in that particular context, things do not change, and therefore risk policies do not need to change frequently. Opportunities might be seized to involve a different range of staff, from different levels in the service, during each review. This could be a useful way of demonstrating that staff have different experiences within, not just between, disciplines. It should encourage interest and commitment.

It is *highly desirable* that the employers of the staff covered, whether public or private, adopt the risk policy. It is not *essential* because the relevant standards are those of the professions concerned and not the employers, but it is in everyone's interests. It will enable staff to see that their employers have also 'signed up' to the standards agreed. That should produce greater understanding and appreciation of different perspectives. The risk policy is a wonderful medium for communication between employees and employers as well as between levels and parts of an organisation. It ought to have a major effect, even as a side-effect, in promoting communication throughout the organisation.

Risk policies are, very much, in employers' interests. If standards are clearly articulated then staff members are more likely to know what is expected of them. It will be easier to identify whether problems are, for example, caused by a lack of resources or due to a lack of professional competence. And it should be much more difficult for employers to be sued. As was explained in Chapter 3, if complainants see that what happened to them was consistent with the standard of care articulated in the organisation's risk policy, then they will know that their chances of successfully suing will be limited. It will always be possible that, as Chapter 3 explained, a court might reject the standard articulated, but the risk of that happening will have been reduced, substantially.

What could and should be in a risk policy?

It is not possible to write statements of the standards that would apply in every contingency imaginable. We would not recommend that you attempt this: it would become a rather sterile exercise. A major goal is to provide a statement that will guide the courts when they seek to discover the professional standards that are applied, and whether they were followed. But that can be achieved in a number of different ways. The following suggestions seek to identify information which would help a court understand the content of, and rationale for, the standards as declared by the witnesses involved in any particular case. The importance of providing a rationale is emphasised. Indeed, it is recommended that the risk policy be written as if it is to be read by a consumer of the particular service. Consumers, like judges, need to know *why* certain things are done in a particular way, as well as *what* doing that involves. It is only too easy to assume – wrongly – that everyone understands things from your standpoint. So it is important that all counterintuitive points are covered. Take the case of *Burne* v. *A* [2006] EWCA Civ 24. A mother telephoned her doctor about her child's symptoms. The doctor decided, on the basis of the information provided by the mother, not to visit the child. If he had visited the child would have been taken to hospital for an emergency operation which, unlike the one necessary a day later, would have prevented major life-long disabilities. When the doctor was sued the trial judge could not understand why the doctor, let alone the expert witnesses for both the doctor and the family, agreed that, in such circumstances, doctors should only ask patients 'open' questions. They should not, even to clarify matters, suggest any symptoms which the patient might adopt. For the trial judge that was counterintuitive; it did not make sense, and he found the doctor negligent. On appeal, however, when it was emphasised that both expert witnesses agreed that a responsible body of doctors would not have asked the mother questions which suggested possible symptoms, that decision was reversed.

Service objectives and goals

This may appear foolish. Everyone knows what a mental health service is for; why we have child protection services. Why waste time restating the obvious? But, it is stressed, it is not obvious, in particular to people – like judges – who do not work in those services. This can become very apparent when harm results from professional risk-taking: 'They knew she was mentally ill. She'd been in hospital several times after injuring herself. They visited her occasionally. But they let her kill herself. It was just waiting to happen.' Such a response, which is not too uncommon from members of the public or media, assumes that a simple and core goal of a mental health service is to stop patients killing themselves. And judges and coroners can think the same. If only it was that easy. Service goals and objectives are often much more complex, and qualifications are regularly needed: 'Child protection services are there to stop children being injured. That is obvious. This child, whom they knew about, was injured. It simply follows they were negligent.' Again, it is so much more difficult in practice. But after the event it is so difficult to convince people that child protection teams must also consider the harm to children caused by intervening in their families. Arguments after the fact have a horrible quality of appearing to be desperate attempts to make excuses.

Thus it is recommended that the service articulates what it is trying to do. Particular attention should be paid to opportunities for misunderstanding. This would be a good opportunity to indicate how a particular service differs from others, perhaps because it is more rural than others, perhaps because it has more community homes and fewer foster parent placements than another.

Service limits

The risk policy should include an indication of what the service *cannot* do. This should include legal limits. Again, a valuable approach is to consider what lay people assume you are entitled to do. For example, lay people regularly assume that police powers of arrest are greater than they are; that psychiatrists can detain people just because their behaviour is unusual or distasteful. What does the law not permit you to do? In particular, which forms of control are you not entitled to exercise? Include things you are *not* resourced to do. This is not an invitation to use the risk policy as a means of complaining about employers or the government, but, rather, to recognise the simple fact that risk-taking costs. This could be a difficult section to write as it concerns negatives – what you cannot do – rather than being positive. But if the intelligent lay reader audience is kept in mind it should be relatively easy to think of the things he or she might anticipate. That would include the number of inpatient beds available, the number of clients that different community staff can realistically be expected to supervise, the drugs that are mentioned in the media but which are not licensed for use. This could also be a useful place to mention the limits of science and current practice. It might be the case that, even in the best-resourced and best-run unit, there is a survival rate of only six months for half the patients. Unrealistic expectations might be kept in check by providing some of this information.

This section should also identify some of the things that, even if the service were allowed to provide them, it would be counterproductive to attempt to do so. For example, it is often thought appropriate that professionals should take decisions for vulnerable people, should not require them to make decisions for themselves. Whilst this is unlawful since the Mental Capacity Act 2005 came into force, it has long been unprofessional not least because it increases, rather than reduces, dependence. The importance of motivation might also be stressed. It might appear appropriate to discount a client's views or values – where that is legally permissible – but doing so could be counterproductive in terms of the consequences for his or her motivation and willingness to co-operate. Examples of particularly difficult – or at least apparently so – risk decisions could be highlighted. For example, it is sometimes suggested that professionals working with people with serious sexually transmissible diseases should breach their confidentiality in order to warn current or future partners. The policy could explain how that would be counterproductive, not just because it would simply mean that that person went beyond any possible persuasion by professionals.

The service's 'philosophy' or value system

It is recommended that the risk policy contains a section with a coherent statement about how its clients, patients, consumers, howsoever described, are regarded, valued. This will provide a valuable framework for understanding how evaluations of outcomes were reached in individual cases. For example, are people with learning disabilities regarded as needing to be protected from themselves? How important are clients' dignity and privacy? Is the primary goal quantity, or quality, of life? Whilst these are important issues it ought not to take too long to write this part of the policy; these issues ought to have been sorted out some time ago and it should only be a matter of incorporating the statements, directly or by reference, into the risk policy. Remember the real case, described in Chapter 3, about Mrs Partington, who was knocked down by a young woman with learning disabilities. The problem there was that the service had not – at least so it appeared when the case reached court – identified an explicit value system. It allowed the court to imply that the young woman was not entitled to full rights of citizenship, to go where and when she wished. All members of an organisation may have been imbued with its value system during training or induction programmes, but it is still worth articulating those principles in a risk policy in order to convince other people that those were, indeed, the values which the risk-takers relied upon.

It would be useful if this section confronted apparently competing values. For example, letting children take certain risks could lead to them experiencing harm. But discouraging, let alone preventing them from doing so, could produce other harms. In terms of their experience of this type of decision-making, judges and other lay people may assume that the more conservative approach was more appropriate, particularly as they are reviewing the circumstances of someone who has been harmed. This may be a good place to address the importance of making 'mistakes' and taking risk. The very word 'mistake' implies that it is a bad thing. But a lot of learning is experiential and much of it involves learning from errors. It is not automatically inappropriate to advocate letting people make some mistakes; the critical issue is identifying those that could have major consequences. Risk-taking is frequently assumed to be a bad thing; the risk policy should emphasise not only that risk-taking is inevitable but that it is often a creative tool.

The service's position on controversial issues

Many of the services envisaged as the audience for this book have to confront some controversial issues. It is suggested that these issues should be identified and explained in the risk policy. It will always be wiser to have articulated a position in advance of having to make the risk decision. It is recommended that the risk policy is circulated, in advance, to opinion-formers who are liable to comment upon or criticise, or both, future risk decisions. Doing so may lead some, for example journalists, to write a story about parts of the risk policy. If they do so it will be in much less explicit terms, and likely much less length, than if they were able to tie it to a specific case that has just occurred. Those who prepared the new policy will also be in a good position to comment upon it at that stage, when it is fresh in their minds. Then, if a risk decision does lead to media attention and public comment, it will be much easier for the service to point to the risk policy. The service will be able to point out that it is a public document in which its approach was described, in advance, in some detail and to demonstrate that the service responded as it said it would – if it did. It will be so much easier to demonstrate that there was a thought-through system to valuing different potential outcomes.

You are entitled to kill yourself, provided you put nobody else at risk of personal injury. Nobody is legally entitled to stop you from doing so, unless they can show you are both mentally disordered and incapable of making that decision properly. (Of course, there would be defences for people who did stop you wrongly thinking you were disordered and incapable.) People do commit suicide. Is it a responsibility of a mental disorder service to stop its patients and clients from exercising this right? Even where the individual concerned has made several previous attempts, which would have been successful but for others' interventions, and continues to express, after a detailed, open, informed and rational discussion of alternatives, over a prolonged period, a settled desire to die? This is difficult. Public responses, which are largely likely to be made with little information, knowledge of the issues or thought, are almost certainly going to be against allowing death. It is not an issue we wish to face. But services should confront them and, it is recommended, should declare their position.

Many such issues surround services for people with learning disabilities, perhaps because service philosophies have been changing rapidly. But there continues to be a reluctance to tackle certain issues. For example, what is the attitude of the service towards their clients' sexuality? As it is embarrassing for us we often just wish the issues would go away. But that is inappropriate. What if a person's inappropriate, perhaps frustrated, behaviour is rooted in an inability to express his or her sexuality in appropriate ways? Ignoring likely causes of future, if not already current, problems will not help anyone. There may be a risk of public disapproval if a particular case is highlighted but, again, if the values and principles have been agreed by the appropriate professions and articulated in a public document this may be considerably reduced.

Should criminal behaviour be prosecuted? 'Of course!' those assuming a criminal justice clientele or context are likely to answer. But what if the reference is to patients or clients regularly regarded as not 'really criminal'? It is regularly considered inappropriate to prosecute patients and people with learning disabilities – unless the harm caused (which can be accidental rather than intentional) is considered serious. Public attitudes can be 'charitable', but in a demeaning sense because the offences are not considered to be serious. But it is very inappropriate, in practice, to teach people that prohibited behaviour will be ignored. Services should consider issues such as these where public attitudes often differ from professional knowledge and objectives. Explaining professional values and goals in a risk policy is recommended.

The views of the service on systemic problems

We all have to work within organisational frameworks and according to rules. These are, among many other objectives, designed to ensure that the way you interact with colleagues and other parts of the service is productive and efficient. Unfortunately, however, these arrangements can not only break down but may be the cause of many problems. The system, not the people working within it, can be the reason why things go wrong. It is easier, and more customary, to look for and identify individuals to blame; but it is inappropriate to ignore 'the system'. Individuals may be able to prevent problems with 'the system' leading to harm, but that cannot be guaranteed.

But the 'system' is exceptionally vague and broad. Failure within the system can range from the failure of individuals, or departments, to consult each other, to an inappropriate corporate culture. Individual risk-takers should be on the look-out for working arrangements that make risk-taking more difficult. They should not only seek to avoid the problem but take steps to have it remedied. Negligence need not be in the decision taken but in the failure to act where responsible professionals would.

Arrangements which are, in a sense, 'bigger' than the organisation are a concern. Take, for example, risk-taking around the detention and discharge of people with mental disorders, whether because they constitute a danger to themselves or to others. Detaining someone is an extreme interference with their civil liberties. Thus it is governed by detailed legislation. That legislation accentuates the distinction between being detained and not being detained. It is a dichotomy, an either/or, with which the law is replete. It appears, certainly at first consideration, entirely appropriate; it just has to be one thing or the other. But should it be? Could there not be a sequence of degrees of being detained? If a patient satisfies a tribunal that detention is no longer justified then the legal answer is that the former patient is entitled to be discharged. But, in terms of managing the transition from living in hospital to living in the community, and making a success of it, that is a considerable 'jump'. The difference in degree is so significant that it is liable to make the transition more difficult. Thus the patient obtains his or her rights but the system of implementing them is far from the best.

Does your service have problems of this sort, such as where the law makes quality risk-taking more difficult to achieve? If so, presuming that the problem cannot be tackled – because it is 'the law' (which is not the same as an employer's or boss's instruction) – this should be highlighted in the risk policy. Professional risk-takers should not be blamed for following the law where it is the source of problems. It could be problems in obtaining necessary information because of confidentiality laws. It could be periods of time. Legislation, for example the Mental Health Act 1983, allows certain patients to be detained for specified periods of time. These include 6- and 12-month periods, even though risk prediction research does not support skilful prediction over such long periods.

An outline framework of values
This section should be the core of the risk policy. Here, it is suggested that the service identifies, as best as it can, how it values a number of the possible outcomes which regularly appear in the risk assessments involved with that service. It should draw upon ideas suggested by the paragraphs above. Which examples are included, and how many, will vary between services and according to their experience and type of risk. The goal is not to cover every type of risk, let alone outcome, which could occur. This is to be an aid, not a solution. This is to be a source which risk-takers in the relevant organisation could turn to and read a statement that indicates how, relatively, important they should consider different outcomes. It is a starting place. It cannot predict the circumstances of every future case but it can provide an indication that the risk assessor can use to increase or decrease depending upon the circumstances of the case. For example, the document might provide a statement, in relation to childcare issues, about how important it is that a home provides no, or very little, intellectual stimulation for young children. The absence may be particularly dire in one case and less so in another but at least social workers, who could be very new to such work, will have a basis for developing an individualised assessment.

Because this statement will have been discussed with other relevant professionals, for example educational psychologists, health visitors and teachers, it will contain considerable authority. Because it will have been written before a risk decision is associated with harm or failure, those who relied upon it will have at least one less problem. Any allegation that the value system has been invented after the fact to make it easier to justify the decision will be easy to disprove. If the service, for example, values increased motivation, privacy, self-determination and so on, as more important than a judge or lay people would, in particular after someone has experienced harm, then the proof that this is a genuine assessment will exist in the pre-existing risk policy. It is only too easy for a lawyer, or other critic, to respond to a claim by saying 'Well you would say that, wouldn't you?' It suggests that claims are being made up. If the value statement is there in the risk policy, or can be inferred from comparable issues, then that cannot be claimed.

A risk procedure

A risk policy helps at a particular stage in the decision-making process. it informs, in particular, the valuation of the outcomes. A risk procedure concerns processes; it informs the manner and order in which decisions are made. So it can be argued that a risk procedure has no place in a risk policy. But there could be some advantage from including the procedure: important documents would be kept together. Just as opinion-formers would get to read how the service and its professionals approach the difficult task of assessing risks and valuing comparative outcomes, they could also read about how decisions are made. This would provide an opportunity to emphasise such critical issues, regularly forgotten by the media and public, as are the relationships between risk assessment and risk management, and the difference between risk-taking and dealing with dilemmas. It would also be a useful place to summarise the problems that can arise with decision-making. For example, it would be useful to emphasise the significance of hindsight, an advantage those who judge risk-taking have, which is unavailable to the decision-makers – knowing what the outcome was.

An outline statement of indicative likelihoods

It is recommended that a document – it could be the risk policy or risk procedure – contains a section in which information about likelihood is brought together. This would, of course, be relevant to the particular type of risks that the service is concerned with. If this is published in the risk policy it will inform opinion-formers, such as the local and national media, enabling them to read and think before casting blame too readily.

More importantly, such a section will inform decision-makers. It should be possible using existing statistics, for example, to discover the local suicide rate, and even further details such as the difference in rates between those who were, or were not, receiving treatment for a mental disorder at the time. Just as with the list of statements about the values of different outcomes, such a list would provide a starting point. The risk-taker may have to start with one figure, perhaps national suicide rates, and then adjust that for the fact that the individual has a mental disorder, more so if he or she has a history of self-harming. The document would not remove any individual's ability or duty to think of the most appropriate likelihood for that case in those circumstances (i.e. taking account of the risk management plan). But it would help to 'anchor' the decision by reference to a source of quality knowledge. It will also encourage the use of actuarial over 'clinical' estimates.

Endorsement

Finally, the risk policy should be explicitly endorsed by the professional associations involved. They should indicate that the standards described are supported by substantial numbers of the relevant professions. Perhaps there is a local branch of a national professional body which is prepared to say it endorses the statements. Perhaps the statements copy or reflect similar statements by national bodies. It would be appropriate also to describe the nature and extent to which people were consulted. The goal is to make it as clear a fact as possible that, in case there is litigation, the standards comply with the relevant standard of care (i.e. what a responsible body of co-professionals would agree with). If the stated standards are likely to be perceived as deviating from lay opinion then more care will be required. Trial judges may have to decide whether other co-professionals would agree with those stated standards, and they might wish to use the case of *Bolitho* v. *City & Hackney Health Authority* ([1988] AC 232) (see Chapter 3) to decide they are too low. Where that might happen the risk policy should seek to forestall the conclusion by emphasising the degree of professional agreement and rationale for the standards.

Ideally, the policy should also be endorsed by the employers involved. The courts are not concerned with whether it approves of the standards or not – it is the professionals who count – but their endorsement will help in other ways. It will encourage employees to believe that they are supported in their difficult role of risk-taking. And it will go a considerable way to improving the organisation of risk-taking within the service or services concerned. Regular consultation about desirable changes should produce useful suggestions for improvements in working relationships. It is a primary means whereby employers can develop their overall risk-taking strategy, to which we turn in Chapter 9.

Risk Strategies

Introduction

To this point the focus has been on individual risk decisions and decision-makers. It is hoped that, although that may be valuable for explanatory purposes, it has been conveyed that this is artificial because all decisions are made within a larger systemic context. It has been recognised that professional risks are regularly taken by groups of people. Even where the decision needs to be taken by one person, for example by an approved social worker under the Mental Health Act 1983 (or approved mental health professional under that Act when amended by the Mental Health Act 2007), he or she should be seeking information and considering advice from others, especially those in different disciplines with alternative perspectives and knowledge to offer. This chapter will eschew the individual and, instead, focus on 'the system'. Although only one chapter has been devoted to this, the balance of this book reflects the current reality of approaches to professional risk-taking.

Professional risk-taking rightfully involves contributions from many people and it takes place within an organisational context. There is a growing tendency to identify 'the system' as a, or even the main, cause of risk-taking failures (e.g. the inquiry into to the death of Victoria Climbié (Johnson and Petrie 2004; Laming 2003). This is both appropriate and unfortunate. It is unfortunate because 'the system' is so vague and amorphous that it can become an easy excuse for not identifying who or what needs to be changed. But it is appropriate because factors external to us, for example expectations, values, customs, working practices, ways of doing things and so on, do influence how we behave. We may not like to admit it but a great deal of our behaviour is socially influenced, if not determined. What is needed are better ways of identifying and analysing the contributions that 'the system' makes, and developing procedures which ensure that we act on system, as well as individual, negligence.

The law

It is much easier for 'the law' to focus on individuals' contributions to risk-taking. Chapter 3 explained the law of negligence. It emphasises – almost takes for granted – that risk decisions are made by individuals. We must expect that law to continue to be the most important legal regulator of professional risk-taking for a long time. But it is possible to discern, and we should encourage, some changes. For example, important changes are taking place in our criminal law. For very many years it has been very difficult to obtain convictions for corporate manslaughter. Large numbers of people are killed each year by activities for which organisations, such as railway companies and construction firms, are responsible. But, for corporate – rather than individual – criminal responsibility it is currently necessary to prove that a 'directing mind' of the organisation or firm, for example the Board of Directors, knew of the unsafe practices which led to death (Ormerod 2005). Where the organisation is small the directors have had that knowledge. But the bigger the organisation the less likely it is that the bosses will know about practice at service-delivery or production level. They will not have the *mens rea* necessary for criminal liability. (Also, it is not possible to imprison a company – only people – and it is too easy for fines to be passed on to customers or taxpayers.) But things have changed with new, albeit still weak, corporate manslaughter laws being introduced in the UK, at the time of writing (Peck and Brevitt 2006).

The Government's long-delayed proposals for England and Wales were stated in a Home Office paper (Home Office 2005). These were considered by, among others, a Select Committee of the House of Commons, to which the Government responded (Secretary of State for the Home Department 2006). The Scottish Executive, concerned about possible differences in the law between parts of Great Britain, established a committee of experts. Its recommendations were more radical than the proposals for England and Wales (Scottish Executive 2005). A majority proposed adopting the approach of federal Australian law, where a poor safety culture could lead to criminal responsibility (Criminal Code Act 1995 (Australia)). The Government decided that this was a topic which the Westminster Parliament could legislate for the whole of the UK (Peck and Brevitt 2006).

The Corporate Manslaughter and Corporate Homicide Act creates an offence of corporate manslaughter for England and Wales and corporate homicide for Scotland. It will be an offence if an organisation owed a duty of care to the victim, but the manner in which the organisation's activities were managed or organised by its senior managers amounted to a gross breach of that duty, causing the victim's death. The test for the existence of duty of care will be the same as that in the law of negligence.

But it remains easiest to explain the relevance and impact of the law on 'system negligence' by starting with the ordinary, civil law of negligence. If a professional risk-taker's decision was made negligently, and led to loss, then he or she can be sued. But if he or she was employed to make those sorts of decisions then the person suing, known as the claimant, is also entitled to, and in practice will prefer to, sue the decision-maker's employers. Not only are the employers likely to have more money with which to pay any compensation awarded, but they are also vicariously liable (Rogers 2006). The reasoning is sound. If that risk-taker had not been employed to take that decision, or one like it, then it would not have been made and the loss would not have occurred. So employers are a, albeit a background, cause of the loss. However, whilst the employers will have to pay the compensation award, and they will be named in case title, it is the individual decision-maker(s) who will have their conduct forensically investigated and raked over for blame. Vicarious liability applies even if the employers cannot control the risk-taker's decision; for example, a hospital director would not – it is hoped – tell a consultant surgeon how to perform a triple heart bypass. But the risk decision has to be related to the employment context. Employers are not responsible for the risk decisions which their employees take during their private time. So, for example, if an off-duty nurse came upon someone injured in a road accident and took the risk of tending to them, she or he might be sued if the help – taking into account the circumstances – was negligently given. And her or his employers would not be vicariously liable because the help was not provided because the nurse was employed by them.

Vicarious liability is a reassuring rule for professional risk-takers. But the law is still focused on individual, rather than upon organisational or systemic errors. Notice the 'dynamics'. If the claimant can find an individual employee negligent for a professional risk decision, then that is enough; the employers are vicariously liable. Perhaps several employees were negligent. It does not matter; their employer must pay. Perhaps employees of different employers were negligent. It does not matter; it is up to the employer of any negligent employee who is sued to join the other employers in the case so that they can spread the cost of paying any compensation that the court awards. In the vast majority of cases where there actually has been negligence, it will be possible to identify an individual to blame. From that fact all else flows; the employers are vicariously liable. So there will be no need to identify any organisational or systemic negligence. It might be useful, in order to reduce the likelihood of recurrence, but that is for the employers to act upon. It is of no relevance to the compensation issue.

There is, unfortunately, little legal incentive to identify systemic negligence. Take the unusual case of *Bull* v. *Devon Area Health Authority* ([1989] 22 BMLR 79). Mrs Bull entered an Exeter hospital as she was expecting a child. The first baby, for she had twins, was born spontaneously. A registrar, or more senior obstetrician, was required to deliver the second twin. However, there was a delay in calling and/or getting such a doctor to attend, which was particularly worrying as bleeding had begun. (The case was brought 17 years after the event so witnesses' memories were stretched and some were unavailable.) Part of the problem was that in Exeter, at that time, gynaecology services were provided at one hospital and obstetrics at another, requiring doctors to travel between them when needed in emergencies. The court, being careful to apply standards appropriate to 17 years earlier, decided that there were sufficient doctors available to be called. Those standards included that the second child should be delivered by a registrar, or more senior obstetrician, and not by a midwife or less experienced doctor. But, because of the passage of years, it was not known why the registrar who had examined Mrs Bull when she arrived in hospital before the first birth either was not contacted or did not respond. It was readily accepted that the duty consultant who was then called attended within an appropriate time and delivered the second child properly. However, the delayed delivery, it was decided, caused the second twin's disabilities.

Mrs Bull's lawyers had problems in finding anyone negligent, largely because the delay made it difficult to find witnesses and evidence. Certainly all the doctors and nurses owed a duty of care to her and her twins. But had any broken the then-relevant standard of care? In the end the trial judge and Court of Appeal blamed the system:

> In cases where multiple births were involved, the system in operation at the hospital in 1970 was obviously operating on a knife-edge. It had to be operated with maximum efficiency. Otherwise, mother and child would be at obvious risk. In the present case I think that the delay of 28 minutes which elapsed between...birth and the first calling of...[the consultant who delivered the second twin] was substantially too long. (Slade, L.J.)

The two courts initially looked to see if they could find an individual who satisfied all five requirements of the law of negligence. Because of the special features of this case, they could not. But the judges' analysis identified a defective system, even though they made allowances for emergencies and competing calls on doctors' attention. For this the health authority was directly, not vicariously, responsible as it designed and/or managed that system.

The law reports do not indicate what, if anything, was done at the time to discover why the registrar had not attended. This appears to have been an incident from which the organisation could, and should, have learnt. It is still not known whether any individual was at fault. The Authority complained bitterly in court about having to defend a case that had happened so many years ago. How could it, and its witnesses, be expected to remember? The Authority received considerable judicial sympathy, but it was, substantially, the author of its own misfortune because it did not hold an internal inquiry, and did not seem to have tried to learn from the incident. Perhaps an organisation (or key managers if the focus is on individual responsibility) could be found to have broken the standard of care for failing to have a safe system of working, in the sense of one that learns from experience (Chief Medical Officer 2000).

So it may seem that there is little or no point in discussing or investigating system negligence, particularly if traditional approaches, focusing on individuals' fault, can cover most if not all cases. But that does not follow. You do traditional things because they are traditional, or involve easy thinking. You would only investigate whether someone had been negligent if you, or your client, believed you had been a victim. You tend only to think about suing when you realise you have experienced something adverse, when something has changed, or a legitimately expected change has not occurred. You do not usually notice when you have missed some-thing that you could have had. For example, the doctor gives you some medication. You experience an adverse reaction. That would be enough to make you wonder whether he or she made a mistake (possibly negli-gently). But what if the doctor could have provided a treatment, say, for back pain, but did not. How likely are you, who goes to a professional because you do not have their knowledge, to know what you are missing? But that omission might have been negligent. You could sue for the omis-sion to treat. And, although that example referred to individuals being negligent, the same thing could occur with systemic or organisational neg-ligence. What could, and should, the organisation have done, which led to harm when it was not provided or performed? What services, consultation, interactions should there have been, which it was negligent to fail to undertake, from which you have suffered?

Examples may be found in newspapers on a regular basis. An example arises from the newspaper of the day this paragraph was (first) written (*Guardian*, 12 May 2006). The news report is titled: 'Doctors urged to be more vigilant over drugs' side-effects'. It states that 250,000 people are hospitalised, and 5000 die, as a consequence of the side-effects of the drugs they are taking. The source is the British Medical Association, which ought to know. It complains that the 'yellow card' scheme for reporting side-effects is not used enough:

> 'Doctors have a professional duty to report all adverse drug reactions, especially if children or the elderly are involved,' said Vivienne Nathanson, head of ethics and science at the BMA.
>
> 'Unfortunately too many health professionals are confused about reporting procedures. Doctors must make sure they report any suspected [adverse drug reactions] and at the same time increase awareness among their patients about the reporting process.'

Clearly, 'the system' for learning from adverse reactions is not working very well, and many are injured. It is likely, in very many of those cases, that the clinician who prescribed the drug from which the patient suffers (or dies) was not negligent. On the information available to him or her, he or she made a decision which a responsible body of colleagues would also have made. But the clinician could have known more, could have been better informed, and could have been part of a system which involved a much better learning loop. The patient is a victim, likely not of the clinician's negligence, but of 'the system'.

Lawyers might have to think more imaginatively to identify the causes of individuals' losses caused both by commission and omission. Their academic education certainly needs to be greatly improved to give them both better thinking skills and knowledge of other disciplines' contributions. But it is perfectly proper to identify system causes. Indeed, doing so should help us to identify and begin to put right so many problems which have been sidelined because perceived as just part of the amorphous 'system'. Equally, it should provide the initiative to tackle human-made problems. Another recent newspaper story (*International Herald Tribune*, 25 September 2006) reported that British Airways was to be fined £14,000, by US aviation authorities because pilots decided it was more appropriate to fly from Los Angeles to the UK with only three of the aircraft's four engines working, than to have to meet £100,000 costs of compensation to passengers for delay. Using only three engines, and having to fly at a lower altitude, it consumed more fuel than usual. The aircraft had to make an emergency landing at Manchester Airport. Nobody was killed or injured in the making of this example – but should that stop us from learning from the episode? In particular, should the financial disincentives against safer practice be so dramatic?

Precepts about risk

As a step to counteract the 'blame culture', where there is such extensive fear of being blamed for risk-taking that it can discourage professionally appropriate action, it is recommended that professional risk-takers press their employers to adopt a statement of principles, or 'precepts', about risk-taking. This statement would identify key understandings about risk-taking, which are accepted and shared with the staff. It should be formally adopted and become a public document. By adopting these precepts the employers would be communicating with the public, with clients or patients and with their staff. The key role for such a statement would be to begin to tackle the 'blame culture'. The precepts should make it clear that the employers agree with their staff on the key features of risk-taking and accept the consequences. It would also indicate to the public that freedom from risk is neither possible nor desirable. The following precepts are offered as a starting point. It might be useful to add some, or all, of the elaboration of each point.

By definition, it is inevitable that harm will sometimes occur from risk-taking, even with the highest-quality decisions

Professional risk-taking involves trying to achieve benefits but with awareness that harms may occur where there is incomplete knowledge to determine the decision and imperfect control over its implementation. Even the best risk decisions can lead to harm. Complete risk of harm avoidance is not only unrealistic, indeed impossible, but it involves a contradiction in terms. The principal goal of a risk-taking strategy should be, by harnessing better knowledge, skills, experience and so on, to produce a year-on-year reduction in the likelihood of and/or the degree of harm possible, and to increase the likelihood and/or degree of benefits possible.

Appropriate risk-taking involves considering both the likelihood and the consequences of action

It is improper to assess a risk in terms only of its outcomes or its likelihood. The risk of causing serious harm can be justified by its low likelihood. Equally, the risk of a very probable event can be justified by its low level of seriousness. Risk assessment that does not take account of both the outcomes and their likelihood is unprofessional and, if harm results, could cause liability for negligence.

Appropriate risk-taking involves considering both the likely benefits and the likely harms of action

Judging a risk involves balancing the likelihood of achieving beneficial outcomes against the chance of harmful consequences. Even if current usage, or understanding, of 'risk' suggests that it is only concerned with potential harms, the act of risk-taking properly requires consideration of both the possible benefits and harms. Risk assessment, either to advise on or to take a decision affecting another person who is a client, patient or similar, will be unprofessional if it ignores the potential benefits as well as the possible harms. Risks can, and in our daily lives are, justified because the perceived likely benefits are sufficiently more valuable than the likely harms.

When judging a risk decision both the assessment of the risk and the management of its implementation should be considered

Risk assessment involves collecting and assessing information in order to make a decision. Even if taking the risk is justified it remains important to intervene, where and when possible and appropriate, to reduce the likelihood of harms occurring and increase the likelihood and degree of benefit. Risk management can, and should, influence the outcome of the decision. Good risk management can prevent the adverse consequences of a poor risk assessment. A risk which is perceived as serious because of highly rated serious outcomes and/or likelihood can justifiably be taken, even without considering the balancing benefits, if its implementation is susceptible to close monitoring and control.

The quality of a risk decision cannot be determined just because harm resulted
Because risk is involved harm will sometimes occur, even with the best-taken and managed risk decisions. That is in the nature, and implicit in the definition, of risk. To judge a risk it is necessary to examine the quality of its assessment, its management and the actual decision-making process.

It is inappropriate to assume that a risk decision, its assessment and management, was good just because no harm results
Given that it is a risk, so that the outcomes are neither perfectly predictable nor controllable, a successful – or non-harmful – outcome may have more to do with good luck than good decision-making. Just as risk decision-makers should not automatically be blamed when harm results, so they should not automatically receive praise where harm does not arise:

> If an organisation cannot distinguish between good luck and good management, bad luck and bad management, individuals will manage risk accordingly (Chapman and Ward 1997, p.36)

Managers, and others responsible for supervising, learning from and supporting professional risk-taking, should be concerned about poor risk-taking, whether harm does or does not result
Whilst the occurrence of harm, for example injury to a client, provides good reason for an investigation into how and why it occurred, the absence of harm does not justify inaction just because no harm results. It is inappropriate, and liable to induce poor working relations, to auto-matically investigate occurrences of harm but ignore non-occurrences:

> Blaming individuals is emotionally more satisfying than targeting institutions. (Reason 2000, p.768)

Valuable lessons and information can be gained from investigating instances where no harm resulted from risk-taking, as when it does

More lessons may be learnt from a high-quality risk decision than from a poor decision. A poor decision may identify what should not be done, what should be avoided. But a good decision will demonstrate good practice and successful techniques.

The harm – or benefit – that follows upon a risk decision may not be a consequence of it

It might have had independent causes. The harm, or benefit, may occur such a time (which varies according to the nature of the risk involved rather than absolute duration) after the risk decision that it would be inappropriate to link it, in terms of cause or responsibility, with that decision. If the harm (or benefit) was not caused by the risk-taking then no criticism (or praise) should be associated with the risk-taking.

By definition, risk assessment involves imperfect knowledge

It is inappropriate to criticise a risk decision for being based on incomplete or imperfect knowledge. Different risks will involve different kinds and qualities of information. Risk-taking requires trade-offs between different quantities and qualities of information, and the time and cost of obtaining, if possible, more and better information. It is appropriate to consider whether those trade-offs, which were a form of risk-taking, were appropriate – but at that time and in the appropriate context.

Professional risk assessment inevitably involves difficult, and sometimes controversial and contradictory, issues of value judgements

If the risk decision is being taken for or on behalf of someone who is, legally, unable to make the decision for him- or herself, the decision-maker must act in accordance with the law. That may, for example where danger to the public (including children) is concerned, require adoption of public safety values. Otherwise the professional must act in the best interests of the individual affected. When the Mental Capacity Act 2005 becomes law its requirements must also be satisfied.

If the risk decision is one which the patient, client or other is entitled to make then the professional must permit this. However, the professional cannot avoid his or her duty of care by failing to offer advice. That advice should take account of the client's interests and values and not involve an attempt to impose the professional's. That advice can, and sometimes should, include challenges to the client's approach where, for example, error has been noticed. For example, inappropriate assessment of likelihood or degree of outcome should be challenged and corrected where possible.

As differences in values are liable to be a source of disagreement within, as well as without, professions and occupational groups, employers should, after consultation, provide frameworks to assist and to support their staff when making these difficult judgements.

The standard of care, in the law of negligence, requires that individual professionals take decisions that a responsible body of co-professionals would endorse, provided that those decisions are not irrational

Employers and professional associations should articulate, and regularly review, statements of current professional standards so that there will be guidance for the courts to rely upon. These statements should be made widely available so as to discourage litigation, and thereby expense and frustration, where standards of care have not been breached.

However, negligence may lie in the manner in which risk decisions are taken, not just in their content. Extensive research has identified ways in which people regularly make decision errors. Employers and managers should encourage the development and adoption of risk-taking procedures which minimise the likelihood of decision error and maximise achieving planned benefits.

An organisation, its procedures and processes, the 'system', can be a potent cause of poor risk-taking; it is inappropriate to focus exclusively on the contribution of individual decision-makers and to ignore that of managers and others with power to control 'the system'

It is suggested that the five-level model of risk, described in Chapter 2, should be considered. Inquiries into risk-taking should consider: (1) the risk decision (the risk assessment); (2) the context within which it is implemented (risk management); (3) the quality of decision-making processes; (4) the support provided for risk-takers; and (5) the systems within which decision-makers have to work.

Without a systematic approach, and the adoption of a learning paradigm, risk-taking will not improve as much or as fast as it can and should

Risk-taking is the rule, not the exception. We all do it several times a day. It involves core skills for professionals. It is inappropriate to conceive of risk-taking as only a sequence of individual decisions. Both the individuals and organisations involved have interests in learning from others' experiences. Actual experience is a valuable source of data, particularly where other likelihood data is difficult to obtain.

Learning

There is no question that individuals can suffer greatly as a consequence of others' risk decisions or advice. But more people will suffer, over time, if we do not learn from those and the many other risk decisions which are invariably successful, in the sense of not resulting in loss. Investment in discovering, disseminating and adopting good practice provides better value for money than inquiries into relatively rare cases of dramatic harm. Table 9.1 is an elaboration of the five-level model of risk-taking described Chapter 2. It identifies possibilities, and responsibilities, for preventive action – based on learning.

System perspectives and analyses need to be developed. Supervisors should ensure that they are providing the tools, information and support that their staff require to take good-quality risk decisions. Managers should ensure that the different parts of a service integrate appropriately and efficiently. Employers should ensure that there are no impediments to policy or practice (e.g. non-disclosure of information because of different confidentiality policies) which deter good risk-taking practice. Learning is the most appropriate paradigm for the future of services where risk-taking is a professional requirement.

This requires a rigorous approach. We need to stand up against the simplistic and ill-considered responses we often read about in the press or hear in the media. For example, note that we actually 'need' risk 'failures'. Imagine a service where many risks are taken with patients or clients but harm or loss is never experienced. Would that be a good, or a bad, service? It may be a politician's fantasy but not only is it unrealistic, it is undesirable. One means of producing a service which never, or rarely, experiences losses from risk-taking would be to ensure that it never takes risks. No prisoners should be released, no patients discharged, no aircraft allowed to fly. But it should quickly be clear that that would have to be a poor service, causing harm by wrongly detaining or missing opportunities to achieve benefits. Risk-taking is difficult enough without sloppy thinking.

Table 9.1 Overview of levels of risk-taking and responsibilities for improving its quality

Shorthand label	Focus on	Highlights	Drawing on	Liability focus on	Prevention possibilities
Individual	A person, likely a client (including a family) or patient, and his, her or their potential contribution to the occurrence of the risk (its benefits and/or harms), and/or the extent to which they would be affected by its occurrence	Risk assessment Determining as best can, the subjective evaluations, of the person entitled to decide, of the potential outcomes and marrying with best objective assessment of likelihoods, both benefits and harms	Controlled research into risk factors Scientific credentials important Development of professional consensus statement about appropriate values and practices to inform a legal standard of care	Quality of the actual decision made Conformity of predicted likelihood and evaluation of outcomes, used or advised, with current professional practice Use of client's values where apt Value of likely outcomes sufficiently exceeding seriousness of possible harms	Improved range (i.e. types of risk) and quality of actuarial data to inform decision-assessment, particularly for the longer risk periods involved in practice
Situational	The setting, geographical, social, technological and so on (imprisoned, near school, locked ward) and its potential effects on the outcome experienced by people	Risk management Taking advantage of situational factors (e.g. services and facilities, skills and other resources) available to influence outcomes towards benefits and away from harms	The quality, quantity and flexibility of resources available (human and otherwise) to maximise control of implementation of risk decisions Reliance on qualitative research	Sufficient quantity and quality of resources (human and physical) allocated to manage implementation of risk decisions Were resources rationally applied?	Improved appreciation of the roles of resources (including reflective (clinical) experience) to influence risk-taking outcomes

continued on next page

Table 9.1 *cont.*

Decision-maker	The risk-taker(s) and the extent to which they (e.g. by their knowledge, skills, experience, power to affect outcomes, practices) and procedures, may affect the occurrence, and degree, of outcome	Decision-making The competence of the decision-maker (or advisor) both on issues of professional practice (e.g. the standard of care) and risk-taking science	Behavioural science research into factors influencing error-prone decisions Analytical work on how decisions should be made Recognition of human limitations	Quality of decision-making process, (e.g. action taken to avoid common errors, provision of decision-making aids, involvement of apt people and so on)	Breaking down detailed decisions into more manageable parts Training in decision-making, not just professional knowledge
Decision-supporter	A supervisor or manager of, or provider of services (e.g. of information or decision aids) to, a decision-maker or advisor	Appropriate support The quantity and quality of the support provided (including information, aids and feedback) to risk decision-makers	Information and support services Provision of actuarial and 'clinical' information about risk factors and outcomes of risk-taking, successful and otherwise	Quality, quantity, timely and apt format of information provided to decision-makers to support good, as well as avoid poor, decisions	Collection of information about successful, as well as unsuccessful, outcomes, to inform better decision-making
System controller	An employer, director or manager sufficiently powerful to effect organisational changes, such as in operating procedures, goals, principles, within or between related services (e.g. prison and probation, policing and child protection)	Reflective management The use, misuse or failure to use managerial information to continually review working relationships, principles, policies and procedures	Audits of processes and procedures Reviews of extent to which organisational structures and arrangements facilitate or inhibit quality decision-making	Quality of managerial oversight committed to pro-active review of risk-taking practices and procedures The 'rationality' of managerial responses (e.g. support for good practice v. blame for inevitable harms)	Sufficiency and quality of resources to allocate to discover and respond to improvements needed in decision-making and risk management

CHAPTER 10

Conclusion

In writing this book the principal objective was to support those who, as part of their job, must take risks – or advise about them – affecting other people, principally their clients, patients, pupils and so on. Whilst analysing this professional risk-taking, a number of practical suggestions have been provided, designed to make it less likely that these professionals will be unfairly criticised for their decisions or advice. People cannot be stopped from exercising their right to criticise, but it is hoped that this book has demonstrated ways in which those professionals will be able to show quickly and correctly that even if their decision or advice led to harm they were not to blame. Criticism for identifying a range of issues is anticipated, for example the problems that can arise from poor communication about risk assessments or the misuse of risk factors, to which too few people have paid attention in current practice. But these problems already exist and constitute poor practice, and it is only a matter of time before they feature more prominently in litigation and inquiries. It is hoped that the guidance given in this book will help to prevent future problems and, in the process, risk decision-making will improve.

The book began by analysing the nature of 'risk'. A range of definitions is in use, even though some of them do professional risk-takers no favours. Definitions which emphasise that professional risk-taking is a purposive activity where possible benefits should be compared with likely harms have been provided and justified. The elements of risk (the outcomes and their likelihood) were compared with the dimensions (the quantity and quality of the resources available to implement the decision). And key definitions for a shared vocabulary of risk-taking were offered.

Chapter 2 offered a 'map' of risk-taking. This demonstrated the inter-relationships between the parts of risk-taking and the whole. For example, it was emphasised that since risk-taking is one type of decision-making it is possible to learn from the extensive research that has been undertaken on the common errors that are made when taking other decisions. It showed how the law affects risk-taking in both direct and indirect ways. Subsequent chapters developed these ideas, for example showing how risks factors can be misused. But the second major role of the 'map' was to demonstrate how important it is, if risk decision-making is to improve, to act on all the components. A similar point was made by the five-level model of risk developed in the second half of that chapter, which emphasised that, if risk decision-making is to improve, action is needed on all five levels. The model identified and stressed the role of managers and employers to ensure appropriate support and structures exist to enable professional risk decision-makers, or advisors, to do their jobs well. By emphasising the potential contribution of, and thereby the responsibilities of other people, often with more power and resources to change things, it is hoped that this model will contribute to a reduction in the 'blame culture' because it is focused on actual decision-makers even though their role and contribution is limited.

Chapter 3 focused on the law and its implications for risk-taking. Although emphasising that the civil law was much more relevant in practice, the key provisions of the criminal law concerning recklessness were outlined. This area of law has been complicated by the Government enacting the Corporate Manslaughter and Corporate Homicide Act 2007. We must wait to see how it is enforced and interpreted. But we have pointed out how it might seriously affect professional risk-taking. With regard to the civil law, the distinction between the duty and the standard of care, which is often confused, was emphasised. The existence of a duty of care does not determine the issue, as some practitioners seem to think. There must also be, among other things, a breach of the applicable standard of care. It was emphasised that this is articulated by the relevant professions with the courts only interfering when the standards become indefensible. The potential for the prevention of litigation and other disputes by the professions concerned articulating their principles and current practices was stressed, whilst also emphasising the importance of considering *whose* risk decision it actually is. In practice most patient, clients, pupils and so on, will be legally competent and entitled to make the final decision. The professionals who provide them with services, however, will still have to give quality advice and guidance. The importance of the Mental Capacity Act 2005 was stressed, for both the tests for determining legal competence and the principles to be adopted when making those decisions, although the Act was criticised for not taking sufficient account of the psychology of complex decision-making.

Chapter 4 developed the analysis of risk assessment and provided ideas and suggestions to support professional risk-takers. It stressed, for example, that both the outcomes and their likelihood must be taken into account; that it is not just bad practice to refuse to contemplate a risk because of the seriousness of the outcomes without also considering their likelihood. Suggestions were provided to help risk assessors think about potential benefits. It was emphasised that inaction, that not taking a risk, can be problematic and that that needs to be included in the assessment. It was acknowledged that these ideas would give risk assessors more things to think about, but it was argued they should be thinking about these issues already, for example the length of period for which they would be taking a risk. However, it was stressed that the legal, and equally the moral and professional, requirement was only to act reasonably. Professionals have special knowledge and experience which they ought to use, provided only that they regularly review and update it.

Risk management was examined in Chapter 5. It was suggested that greater attention should be paid to the potential for controlling the implementation of risk decisions, that is, risk management. In many areas, for example the prediction of dangerous behaviour, it is unlikely that further research will do more than hone current practice, particularly for low likelihood events. A much greater impact may be achieved through developments in risk management. That, however, depends upon the quantity and quality of the resources, human and otherwise, that are available. This will often depend upon the contributions of people other than the risk-takers, for example managers and employers.

The types of risk that you are particularly concerned with will often involve contributions from several people, often from different disciplines and perhaps service providers. That makes communication critical. And in Chapter 6 it was demonstrated how easy it is, in risk-taking, for one person to mean one thing but for another to understand something very different when information is communicated. Poor communication has regularly been identified as a problem in official inquiries (Laming 2003), and it was anticipated that it will increasingly be a focus for lawyers wishing to demonstrate negligent decision-making. The benefits of using numbers to communicate clearly were noted, but the problems both with the unrealistic impression of knowledge and accuracy which that can give and the relative absence of such a knowledge base were also noted. The potential of services adopting a restricted range of expressions where everyone would know the ascribed meaning of each term was also considered.

Chapter 7 was concerned with the procedures adopted when undertaking a risk assessment, in particular the potential for the misuse of risk factors. Although it is good practice to use them, they must be used fairly; for example, the potential for 'double-counting' and not relating risk factors to appropriate 'risk periods' was noted. In Chapter 8 the idea of a 'risk policy' was developed, which was raised earlier in Chapter 3. There it was shown how the courts, invariably, adopt contemporary professional standards but that these are often inexplicit and difficult to identify. If professional standards are clear then those contemplating litigation may be dissuaded when they can see, in advance, the criteria which a court is likely to apply. But it was also argued in favour of risk policies on several other grounds and some of the topics which could be covered in such statements were identified.

Although, in Chapter 2, the roles and contributions of supervisors, managers and employers were identified, the analysis in this book has, predominantly, been concerned with the position of individual risk-takers. In Chapter 9 the position of managers and employers was considered. The extent to which employers are vicariously liable, in civil law, for the negligence of their employees was examined and it was suggested that it would often be appropriate to sue managers and employers directly because of their negligent design, implementation, review and management of risk-taking systems. Whilst this may be unnecessary in legal practice because compensation is payable upon proof of negligence by an individual it was argued that systemic causes need to be identified if preventive action is to be taken and the 'blame culture', which can lead to individuals becoming even more negligent in their practices (e.g. avoiding taking risks in the mistaken belief that that will prevent them being negligent), is to be tackled. The potential for organisations to be prosecuted for corporate manslaughter, because of the serious negligence of their senior managers, must now also be considered when the Corporate Manslaughter and Corporate Homicide Act 2007 comes into force.

To help tackle the 'blame culture' a number of 'precepts' about risk-taking were offered. It was recommended that professional risk-takers, managers and employers agree to adopt these. These implicitly adopt a learning paradigm which echoes our core 'message'. For too long, and too frequently, risk assessment has been treated as something which is simply done. People are sent off to *do* 'risk assessments'. Changes cannot be adopted without a 'risk assessment'. Yet another study discovers that another set of issues can be analysed in terms of risk. In one sense we are feeding off these attitudes and reactions, and yet we want to scream. Risk assessment should not be treated as a substitute for clear and rigorous thinking. The more we depart from improving our thinking skills, being critical, imaginative, reflective and open to learning, and rely upon pro forma procedures such as risk assessments, the poorer will be the risk decisions taken. Power's (2004) concern that we are beginning to risk-manage everything is endorsed in this book, in particular, his concern about the effects this is already having on professional risk-takers:

> [T]he risk management of everything poses a different agenda of concern, namely that the experts who are being made increasingly accountable for what they do are now becoming more preoccupied with managing their own risks. Specifically, secondary risks to their reputation are becoming as significant as the primary risks for which experts have knowledge and training. This trend is resulting in a dangerous flight from judgement and a culture of defensiveness that create their own risks for organisations in preparing for, and responding to, a future they cannot know. (Power 2004, pp.14–15)

It is hoped that this book has provided a way into analyses and discussions of risk – tools for thinking about risk – which will empower, rather than disempower as bureaucratic calls which, in ignorance of the law, emphasise procedure over substantive quality of decisions. We cannot, and should not seek to avoid risk-taking. The focus needs to be on the quality of decision-making, not on risk.

But to help us achieve that we need appropriately structured and responsive organisations. Westrum (2004) has distinguished three types of organisation. They can be distinguished by their response to harm arising from risk-taking:

> When things go wrong, pathological climates encourage finding a scapegoat, bureaucratic organisations seek justice, and the generative organisation tries to discover the basic problems with the system. (Westrum 2004, p.23)

Readers will quickly identify which type of organisation they work for. If the quality of risk-taking is to improve over time, we need to recognise the centrality of a learning paradigm and generative organisations.

Appendix: Shared Vocabulary of Risk and Risk-taking

These definitions are offered as aids to understanding and communicating about risk and risk-taking.

Dilemma: A situation where every option available bodes ill, although there may be less harmful options and some potential benefits. Further action needs to be taken because even delay is harmful.

Likelihood: To avoid misunderstanding when communicating with colleagues about risk likelihood it is suggested that services ask their staff to only use these expressions and always to use them according to the meanings given here.

- *Foreseeable*: by which mean in the range of 0–10% likelihood.
- *Chance*: by which mean in the range of 10–20% likelihood.
- *Possible*: by which mean in the range of 20–30% likelihood.
- *Real possibility*: by which mean in the range of 30–40% likelihood.
- *Good possibility*: by which mean in the range of 40–50% likelihood.
- *Evens*: by which mean in the range of 45–55% likelihood.
- *Likely*: by which mean in the range of 50–60% likelihood.
- *Very likely*: by which mean in the range of 60–70% likelihood.
- *Probable*: by which mean in the range of 70–80% likelihood.
- *Real probability*: by which mean in the range of 80–90% likelihood.
- *Highly probable*: by which mean in the range of over 90% likelihood.

Risk: An occasion when one or more consequences (events, outcomes and so on) could occur. Critically (a) those consequences may be harmful and/or beneficial and (b) either the number and/or the extent of those consequences, and/or their likelihood, is uncertain and/or unknown.

Risk assessment: Collecting information (a) about a risk, both the possible consequences and the likelihood, and (b) about the sufficiency and reliability of that information.

Risk judgement: Comparing the value and likelihood of the possible benefits with the seriousness, and the likelihood, of the possible harms, but always in the light of the plans for managing the implementation of that risk decision.

Risk management: Identifying, in advance of a decision to risk, and thereafter utilising the resources available to make it more likely that a risk decision will succeed, in the sense that the benefits and/or the likelihoods of taking it will be maximised, and that the harmful consequences, and/or their likelihood, will be reduced.

Risk policy: A document, or set of documents, which has been agreed by a substantial number of professionals as articulating the principles, values and standards relevant to the risks that they take in, and because of, their work. It is designed to be cited to courts as constituting what a responsible body of co-professionals would do, with a view to being adopted as the standard of care. It must be regularly reviewed as standards and values change. Where it relates to interprofessional or multi-agency work or practices it should be supported by all the relevant professions. It is a document reflecting professional, not employer, standards if the two are different. It could contain further information which supports risk decision-makers, for example information about local resources to utilise in risk management, or likelihood ratios (e.g. suicide rates).

References

Adams, A.M. and Smith, A.F. (2001) 'Risk perception and communication: recent developments and implications for anaesthesia.' *Anaesthesia 56*, 745–755.

Anderson, T., Schum, D. and Twining, W. (2005) *Analysis of Evidence.* Cambridge: Cambridge University Press.

Bain, A. (2004) 'From redemption to rehabilitation to resettlement.' *Criminal Justice Matters 56*, 8–10.

Bernstein, P.L. (1999) *Against the Gods: The Remarkable Story of Risk.* New York, NY: Wiley.

Blackburn, R. (2000) 'Risk Assessment and Prediction.' In J. McGuire, T. Mason and A. O'Kane (eds) *Behaviour, Crime and Legal Processes: A Guide for Forensic Practitioners.* Chichester: Wiley.

Boseley, S. (2006) 'Doctors urged to be more vigilant over drugs' side-effects.' *The Guardian,* 12 May. Accessed on 01/12/07 at www.guardian.co.uk/society/2006/may/12/health.medicineandhealth

Brearley, C.P. (1982) *Risk in Social Work.* London: Routledge and Kegan Paul.

British Medical Association (BMA) (1990) *The BMA Guide to Living with Risk.* Harmondsworth: Penguin.

Calman, K.C. (Sir) (1996) 'Cancer: science and society and the communication of risk.' *British Medical Journal 313*, 799–802.

Campbell, J.C. (1995) 'Prediction of Homicide of and by Battered Women.' In J.C. Campbell (ed.) *Assessing Dangerousness: Violence by Sexual Offenders, Batterers, and Child Abusers.* Thousand Oaks, CA: Sage.

Carson, D. (1989) 'The sexuality of people with learning difficulties.' *Journal of Social Welfare Law* 355–372.

Chapman, C. and Ward, S. (1997) *Project Risk Management: Processes, Techniques and Insights.* Chichester: Wiley.

Chief Medical Officer (2000) *An Organisation with a Memory: Report of an Expert Group on Learning from Adverse Events in the NHS Chaired by the Chief Medical Officer.* London: The Stationery Office.

Dennis, I.H. (2007) *The Law of Evidence.* London: Sweet & Maxwell.

Department for Constitutional Affairs (DCA) (not dated) *Mental Capacity Act 2005 – summary.* Accessed on 03/05/07 at www.dca.gov.uk/menincap/bill-summary.htm

Department for Constitutional Affairs (DCA) (2007) *Mental Capacity Act 2005: Code of Practice.* London: The Stationery Office. Accessed on 02/05/07 at www.dca.gov.uk/legal-policy/mental-capacity/mca-cp.pdf

Department of Health (DoH) (2000) *An Organisation with a Memory: Report of an Expert Group on Learning from Adverse Events in the NHS Chaired by the Chief Medical Officer.* London: Department of Health.

Department of Transport (DoT) (2004) *Tomorrow's Roads – Safer for Everyone.* London: Department of Transport. Accessed on 9/10/07 at www.dft.gov.uk/pgr/roadsafety/strategytargetsperformance/tomorrowsroadssaferforeveryone

Dillon, L., Chivite-Matthews, N., Grewal, I., Brown, R. *et al.* (2007) *Risk, Protective Factors and Resilience to Drug Use: Identifying Resilient Young People and Learning from their Experiences.* London: Home Office. Online Report 04/07. Accessed on 11/06/07 at www.homeoffice.gov.uk/rds/pdfs07/rdsolr0407.pdf

Ferner, R.E. and McDowell, S.E. (2006) 'Doctors charged with manslaughter in the course of medical practice, 1795–2005: A literature review.' *Journal of the Royal Society of Medicine 99*, 309–314.

Fischoff, B. (1975) 'Hindsight ≠ foresight: The effect of outcome knowledge on judgment under uncertainty.' *Journal of Experimental Psychology: Human Perception and Performance 1*, 288–299.

Gigerenzer, G. and Goldstein, D. (1996) 'Reasoning the fast and frugal way: Models of bounded rationality.' *Psychological Review 103*, 650–669.

Greene, E. and Ellis, L. (2007) 'Decision Making in Criminal Justice.' In D. Carson, B. Milne, F. Pakes, K. Shalev and A. Shawyer (eds) *Applying Psychology to Criminal Justice.* Chichester: Wiley.

Hamm, R.M. (1988) 'Clinical Intuition and Clinical Analysis: Expertise and the Cognitive Continuum.' In J. Dowie and A. Elstein (eds) *Professional Judgment: A Reader in Clinical Decision-making.* Cambridge: Cambridge University Press.

Hammond, K.R. (1978) 'Toward Increasing Competence of Thought in Public Policy Formation.' In K.R. Hammond (ed.) *Judgment and Decision in Public Policy Formation.* Boulder, CO: Westview Press.

Hare, R.D. (2002) 'Psychopathy and Risk for Recidivism and Violence.' In N. Gray, J. Laing and L Noaks (eds) *Criminal Justice, Mental Health and the Politics of Risk.* London: Cavendish Publishing.

Health and Safety Executive (HSE) (2006) *Five Steps to Risk Assessment.* Sudbury: Health and Safety Executive. Accessed on 28/02/07 at www.hse.gov.uk/pubns/indg163.pdf

Heilbrun, K. (1997) 'Prediction vs management models relevant to risk assessment: the importance of legal decision-making context.' *Law and Human Behavior 21*, 91–106.

Heilbrun, K. (2003) 'Violence Risk: From Prediction to Management.' In D. Carson and R. Bull (eds) *Handbook of Psychology in Legal Contexts.* Chichester: Wiley.

Heilbrun, K. and Erickson, J. (2007) 'A Behavioural Science Perspective on Identifying and Managing Hindsight Bias and Unstructured Judgement: Implications for Legal Decision Making.' In D. Carson, B. Milne, F. Pakes, K. Shalev and A. Shawyer (eds) *Applying Psychology to Criminal Justice.* Chichester: Wiley.

H.M. Government (2006) *Explanatory Notes to the Compensation Act 2006.* London: HMSO. Accessed on 2/5/07 at www.opsi.gov.uk/acts/en2006/2006en29.htm

Home Office (2005) *Corporate Manslaughter: The Government's Draft Bill for Reform.* London: Home Office.

Hoyano, L.C.H. (1999) 'Policing flawed police investigations: Unravelling the blanket.' *Modern Law Review 62*, 912–936.

Janis, I.L. and Mann, L. (1977) *Decision Making: A Psychological Study of Conflict, Choice and Commitment.* New York, NY: Free Press.

Jeyarajah Dent, R. (ed.) (1998) *Dangerous Care: Working to Protect Children.* London: Bridge Child Care Consultancy Service.

Johnson, S. and Petrie, S. (2004) 'Child protection and risk-management: The death of Victoria Climbié.' *Journal of Social Policy* 33, 2, 179–202.

Kahneman, D., Slovic, P. and Tversky, A. (eds) (1982) *Judgment under Uncertainty: Heuristics and Biases.* New York, NY: Cambridge University Press.

Kassin, S. (2004) *Psychology* (4th ed.). Upper Saddle River, NJ: Prentice Hall.

Kemshall, H. and Pritchard, J. (1995) *Good Practice in Risk Assessment and Risk Management.* London: Jessica Kingsley Publishers.

Kemshall, H. and Pritchard, J. (1997) *Good Practice in Risk Assessment and Risk Management 2.* London: Jessica Kingsley Publishers.

Kindler, H.S. (1990) *Risk Taking: A Guide for Decision Makers.* London: Kogan Page.

Laming, Lord (2003) *The Victoria Climbié Inquiry.* London: HMSO (CM 5730).

Law Commission (2005) *A New Homicide Act for England and Wales? An Overview.* London: Law Commission (Consultation Paper No 177).

Law Commission (2006) *Murder, Manslaughter and Infanticide* (Law Com No. 304). London: Law Commission. Accessed on 8/10/07 at www.lawcom.gov.uk/docs/LC304.pdf

MacCrimmon, K.R. and Wehrung, D.A. (1988) *Taking Risks: The Management of Uncertainty.* New York, NY: Free Press.

Macpherson of Cluny, W. Sir (1999) *The Stephen Lawrence Inquiry: Report of an Inquiry.* London: HMSO (CM 4262-I).

Maden, A. (2002) 'Risk Management in the Real World.' In N. Gray, J. Laing and L Noaks (eds) *Criminal Justice, Mental Health and the Politics of Risk.* London: Cavendish Publishing.

Monahan, J., Steadman, H.J., Appelbaum, P.S. *et al.* (2005) *Classification of Violence Risk™ (COVR™).* Lutz, FL: Psychological Assessment Resources, Inc. Accessed on 8/10/07 at www3.parinc.com/products/product.aspx?Productid=COVR

Monahan, J., Steadman, H.J., Silver, E., Appelbaum, P.S. *et al.* (2001) *Rethinking Risk Assessment: The MacArthur Study of Mental Disorder and Violence.* New York, NY: Oxford University Press. (An extensive number of references to the study and its data are available at the research network's website: http://macarthur.virginia.edu/risk.html)

Montgomery, J. (2003) *Health Care Law.* Oxford: Oxford University Press.

Moore, B. (1996) *Risk Assessment: A Practitioner's Guide to Predicting Harmful Behaviour.* London: Whiting & Birch.

Nash, M. (2006) *Public Protection and the Criminal Justice Process.* Oxford: University Press.

National Confidential Inquiry into Suicide and Homicide by People with a Mental Illness (2001) *Safety First: Five-Year Report of the National Confidential Inquiry into Suicide and Homicide by People with Mental Illness.* London: Department of Health. Accessed on 14/02/06 at: www.dh.gov.uk/assetRoot/04/05/82/43/04058243.pdf

Norman, A.J. (1980). *Rights & Risk*. London: National Corporation for the Care of Old People.

Ormerod, D. (2005) *Smith & Hogan Criminal Law*. Oxford: Oxford University Press.

Parsloe, P (ed.) (1999) *Risk Assessment in Social Care and Social Work*. London: Jessica Kingsley Publishers.

Peck, M. and Brevitt, B. (2006) *The Corporate Manslaughter and Corporate Homicide Bill*. London: House of Commons Library (Research paper 06/46). Accessed on 14/05/07 at: www.parliament.uk/commons/lib/research/rp2006/rp06-046.pdf

Power, M. (2004) *The Risk Management of Everything*. London: Demos.

Rachlin, H. (1989) *Judgment, Decision, and Choice: A Cognitive/Behavioural Synthesis*. New York, NY: W.H. Freeman and Company.

Reason, J. (2000) 'Human error: models and management.' *British Medical Journal 320*, 768–770.

Ritchie, J.H, Dick, D. and Lingham, R. (1994) *The Report of the Inquiry into the Care and Treatment of Christopher Clunis*. London: HMSO.

Rogers, W.V.H. (2006) *Winfield and Jolowicz on Tort*. London: Sweet & Maxwell.

Royal Society (1992) *Risk: Analysis, Perception, Management*. London: The Royal Society.

Ryan, T. (2000) 'Exploring the risk management strategies of mental health service users.' *Health Risk and Society 2*, 3, 267–282.

Samaritans (2007) *Information Resource Pack 2004*. Accessed on 11/06/07 at www.samaritans.org/pdf/Samaritans-InfoResPack2007.pdf

Schum, D.A. (1994) *Evidential Foundations of Probabilistic Reasoning*. New York, NY: Wiley.

Schwartz, W.B. and Aaron, H.J. (1988) 'Rationing Hospital Care: Lessons from Britain.' In J. Dowie and A. Elstein (eds) *Professional Judgment: A Reader in Clinical Decision Making*. Cambridge: Cambridge University Press.

Scottish Executive (2005) *Corporate Homicide: Expert Group Report*. Edinburgh: Scottish Executive.

Secretary of State for the Home Department (2006) *Draft Corporate Manslaughter Bill: The Government Reply to the First Joint Report from the Home Affairs and Work and Pensions Committees Session 2005–06*. London: HMSO.

Simmons, J. (2002) *Crime in England and Wales 2001/2*. London: Home Office. Accessed on 14/02/06 at www.homeoffice.gov.uk/rds/pdfs2/hosb702.pdf

Simon, H.A. (1956) 'Rational choice and the structure of the environment.' *Psychological Review 63*, 129–138.

Slovic, P. (ed.) (2000) *The Perception of Risk*. London: Earthscan Publications.

Slovic, P., Fischoff, B. and Lichtenstein, S. (2000) 'Cognitive processes and societal risk taking.' In P. Slovic (ed) *The Perception of Risk*. London: Earthscan Publications.

Slovic, P., Kunreuther, H. and White, G.F. (2000) 'Decision Processes, Rationality and Adjustment to Natural Hazards.' In P. Slovic (ed.) *The Perception of Risk*. London: Earthscan.

Steadman, H.J., Monahan, J., Robbins, P.C., Appelbaum, P.S., *et al.* (1993) 'From Dangerousness to Risk Assessment: Implications for Appropriate Risk Strategies.'

In S. Hodgins (ed.) *Crime and Mental Disorder.* Newbury Park, CA: Sage Publications, pp.39–62.

Steele, J. (2004) *Risks and Legal Theory.* Oxford and Portland, OR: Hart.

Titterton, M. (2005) *Risk and Risk Taking in Health and Social Welfare.* London: Jessica Kingsley Publishers.

Tversky, A. and Kahneman, D. (1974) 'Judgment under uncertainty: Heuristics and biases.' *Science 27,* 1124–1131.

Twining, W. and Miers, D. (1999) *How to Do Things with Rules: A Primer of Interpretation.* Cambridge: Cambridge University Press.

Walker, N. (1996) 'Ethical and Other Problems.' In N. Walker (ed.) *Dangerous People.* London: Blackstone Press.

Webster, C.D., Douglas, K.S., Eaves, D. and Hart, S.D. (1997) *HCR-20: Assessing Risk for Violence* (Version 2) Burnaby, BC: Mental Health Law and Policy Institute, Simon Fraser University.

Webster, C.D., Harris, G.T., Rice, M.E., Cormier, C. and Quinsey, V. (1994) *The Violence Prediction Scheme: Assessing Dangerousness in High Risk Men.* Toronto: University of Toronto, Centre of Criminology.

Westrum, R. (2004) 'A typology of organisational cultures.' *Quality, Health and Safety Care 13* (Supplement ii), 22–27.

Wexler, D.B. and Schopp, R.F. (1989) 'How and when to correct for juror hindsight bias in mental health malpractice litigation: some preliminary observations.' *Behavioural Science and the Law 7,* 4, 485–504.

Wolfensberger, W. (1972) *Normalization: The Principle of Normalization in Human Services.* Toronto: National Institute on Mental Retardation.

Woodley, L., Dixon, K., Lindlow, V., Oyebode, O., Sandford, T. and Simblet, S. (1995) *The Woodley Team Report: Report of the Independent Review Panel to the East London and the City Health Authority and Newham Council, Following a Homicide in July 1994 by a Person Suffering from a Severe Mental Illness.* London: East London and the City Health Authority.

Yates, J.F. (ed.) (1992) *Risk-taking Behaviour.* Chichester: Wiley.

Statutes

Adults with Incapacity (Scotland) Act 2000

Children Act 1989

Compensation Act 2006

Criminal Code Act 1995 (Australia). Accessed on 17/10/06 at: www.comlaw.gov.au/ComLaw/Legislation/ActCompilation1.nsf/0/F50A71634 790BDB3CA257116001525A3/$file/CriminalCode1995_WD02_Version3.pd

Human Rights Act 1998

Mental Capacity Act 2005

Mental Health Act 1983

Mental Health Act 2007

Offences Against the Person Act 1861

Theft Act 1968

Case law

Adomako [1994] 3 All ER 79

Bogle v. *McDonald's Restaurants Ltd* [2002] EWHC 490

Bolam v. *Friern HMC* [1957] 2 All ER 118

Bolitho v. *City & Hackney Health Authority* [1988] AC 232

Brooks v. *Commissioner of Police for the Metropolis and Others* [2005] 2 All ER 489

Bull v. *Devon Area Health Authority* [1989] 22 BMLR 79

Burne v. *A* [2006] EWCA Civ 24

Burt v. *Plymouth and Torbay Health Authority* (19 December 1997, unreported)

F v. *W Berkshire HA* [1989] 2 All ER 545

Gauntlett v. *Northampton AHA*, 12 December 1985. (The decision is not formally reported but is available via the LexisNexis database.)

Gillick v. *West Norfolk & Wisbech AHA* [1985] 3 All ER 402

Hill v. *Chief Constable of West Yorkshire* [1989] 1 AC 53

JD v. *East Berkshire Community Health NHS Trust and Others* [2005] 2 FLR 284

Kirkham v. *Chief Constable of Greater Manchester Police* [1990] 2 QB 283

Lawrence v. *Pembrokeshire CC* [2007] EWCA Civ 446

Maynard v. *W Midlands RHA* [1985] 1 All ER 635

Meadow v. *General Medical Council* [2006] EWHC 146 (Admin)

Osman v. *UK* (2000) 29 EHRR 245

Osman and another v. *Ferguson and another* [1993] 4 All ER 344

Paris v. *Stepney Borough Council* [1951] AC 367

Partington v. *London Borough of Wandsworth* [1990] Fam Law 468

Porterfield v. *Home Office* (1988). *The Times*, 8 March

R v. *Bowman* [2006] EWCA Crim 417

Re C [1994] 1 All ER 819

Sidaway v. *Bethlem RHG* [1985] 1 All ER 643

Stanton v. *Callaghan* [2000] 1 QB 75

Tomlinson v. *Congleton BC* [2003] UKHL 47

Van Colle v. *Chief Constable of Hertfordshire* [2007] EWCA Civ 325

Vellino v. *Chief Constable of Greater Manchester* [2002] 1 WLR 218

Wilsher v. *Essex Area Health Authority* [1987] QB 730

Subject Index

Author Index

Index of Legislation

Index of Case Law